For Bernie Loomis
with warm regards
of the author
Charles P. Taft

Cincinnati, May 17, 1973

CITY MANAGEMENT

CITY MANAGEMENT

THE CINCINNATI EXPERIMENT

BY

CHARLES P. TAFT

With A New Introduction
To The 1971 Edition
By The Author

KENNIKAT PRESS
Port Washington, N. Y./London

CITY MANAGEMENT

Copyright 1933, (c) 1961 by Charles P. Taft
Reissued in 1971 by Kennikat Press by arrangement
with Holt, Rinehart and Winston, Inc.
Library of Congress Catalog Card No: 73-93074
ISBN 0-8046-0687-0

Manufactured by Taylor Publishing Company   Dallas, Texas

PREFACE

My friends tell me that I should wait till I die before I publish this. Well, they probably are right, as they have been in suggesting many changes for the better in my manuscript. For that I thank them, and for their solicitude over what they call my future I love them. But I can see a lurking twinkle in their respective eyes that indicates they really want to see this in print.

My information comes from sources that I believe to be reliable, but I don't guarantee it.

I couldn't mention by name every person who deserves it for his services to the Charter, for this would be like the Book of Numbers—and about as widely read. The condition of the city we love is the true reward of all of us anyway, not the publicity we get.

And finally, oh, reader, take warning from the dear Old Mandarin:

> All round the margin
> Of any consignment of print
> Is a continuous flicker of readers
> Leaping to Conclusions—
> Excellent conclusions for them, no doubt,
> But not necessarily the author's.

C. P. T.

INTRODUCTION TO THE 1970 EDITION

by

CHARLES P. TAFT

I appreciate greatly the initiative of the publisher in making this book available to a new generation of people interested in good city government. I am very glad to add this brief updating.

I add first what were felt in 1933 to be necessary omissions. In the Hamilton County Democratic Party were two groups, one represented by William J. "Bill" Leonard, and one by James H. "Jimmy" Sullivan. The Leonard group supported the Charter fusion; the other was annoyed at the association and somewhat hostile, but for over a decade lay low, seeing no alternative.

The other omission was the fact that in the switch from the Birdless Ballot League in 1924, to the City Charter Committee, a decisive element was the anonymous contribution of the Reverend Herbert S. Bigelow, who was elected to City Council later in 1935. Bigelow's legal advisor - Ed F. Alexander - was responsible for the inclusion of Proportional Representation in the Charter. Bigelow was also planning the organization of the 1924 LaFollette campaign in Hamilton County. He considered the collection of the necessary signatures for the Charter Amendment a useful exercise for his organization.

The reason for not publicizing his participation was that he was a very controversial character in Cincinnati. He served as chairman of the great Ohio Constitutional Convention of 1912. He was a single-taxer, a pacifist in the First World War, and a utility-baiter. His motives in helping initiate the 1924 Charter may have involved some personal ambition to get back in public life. Proportional Representation did in fact help in that direction.

The principal sponsors of the Charter, therefore, including Alexander as Bigelow's representative, agreed that the major issue of a new Charter should not be complicated by encumbering it with a fight over Bigelow. I always have been somewhat conscience-stricken that I did not tell the full story in 1933 and give due credit to a very unusual man, admirable in many ways.

A brief sketch of events after 1933 - the point where the book ends - may also be helpful.

In 1933, the Charter Committee again elected five of the nine Councilmen, and Russell Wilson became Mayor again.

In 1935, Herbert Bigelow ran for City Council as the representative of the Coughlinites of Cincinnati. Although he was a graduate of Lane Seminary (Presbyterian) and pastor of the Vine Street Congregational Church, to the beliefs mentioned above, he thus added some unorthodox views on money.

His supporters were personally extraordinarily loyal and Bigelow produced the largest P.R. vote ever accorded an independent candidate. But he could not carry any of his ticket with him and the race ended as four Charter, four Republicans, and Bigelow.

Bigelow bargained to the top of his bent, and finally agreed to vote for Russell Wilson for Mayor if he were made chairman of the Public Utility Committee of City Council. In fact, it was not much of a concession because two Charterites controlled the committee of three. But the Times Star ran an eight column headline "Charter Sells Out to Bigelow." The headline hurt, and for more than one election.

INTRODUCTION

On the strength of this victory, Bigelow organized to take over the 1936 Democratic primary. He nominated himself and an associate for Congress, and won in November in the Roosevelt landslide. He nominated 9 out of 12 in the Democratic primary for the Legislature. All were defeated in 1938, the "off year."

Bigelow's going to Congress left a tied Council. Clarence Dykstra, City Manager, resigned at this moment, to become President of the University of Wisconsin. After several months' deadlock, C.O. Sherrill was elected City Manager again.

In November, 1937, Bigelow's man, Craig, was elected to City Council, but he turned out to be a Republican stooge, and cast the deciding vote for James Garfield Stewart as Mayor on January 1, 1938, to establish the first Republican control of Council since adoption of the Council-Manager Charter. Albert D. Cash, Edward N. Waldvogel, and I, in the same race, had been elected to Council for the first time.

In 1939, Bigelow ran and beat Craig handily. This time he got no chance to bargain. After one vote in which Bigelow voted for himself and we Charterites voted for Russell Wilson, I voted - on the second ballot - for Jim Stewart and broke the tie.

With the 1941 election the Republicans won their first clear majority, and repeated it in 1943 and 1945.

In this period the Charter minority pushed through, under Al Cash's leadership, the appropriation for a new Master Plan. It was finally completed and published in 1948.

In 1947, the Charter elected five again, Rollin H. Everett, an able newspaperman and Guild representative, making the majority. Cash as Mayor, and I as chairman of the Finance Committee, set out to make the new Master Plan come alive. Our majority continued with a substitution of the able Negro lawyer, Theodore M. Berry, for Everett. I retired on December 1, 1951, to run for Governor. The Republicans got my seat to regain a majority, but in 1953 the Charter won again. However, a few months later (1954) one of the Charter Councilmen, Albert Jordan, a business agent of the United Steelworkers, refused to go along with an income tax supported by seven councilmen from both parties, and he resigned from his Charter Committee connection. Shortly afterwards, the new Mayor, Eddie Waldvogel, died, and a deadlock developed over his successor. Charterite Dorothy Dolbey, the Vice Mayor, served as acting Mayor until after the County election. Jordan then voted for a Republican, Carl Rich, for Mayor, though Rich was hardly a labor supporter.

In 1955, Jordan ran as an independent, finished 112 votes behind John J. Gilligan, and demanded a recount. The accuracy of P.R. in a total vote of 153,886 was clearly shown. Gilligan won and the Charter majority organized Council with myself as Mayor and Ted Berry as Vice Mayor.

Delays in the urban renewal program and in the public off-street parking program were now completely resolved, and both went forward rapidly.

The Republicans had attacked P.R. no less than five times unsuccessfully, and finally in September, 1957, in a special election 60 days after Little Rock, knocked it out in an underground racist campaign. In November, Ted Berry, the only Black councilman, did not make it, on a 9X ballot at large, with no elimination primary.

The loss of P.R. produced exactly the result Charterites had predicted. In early 1959, the Democrats and Charterites split. Each then elected two, and Berry again was defeated.

With the election of Republican Eugene P. Ruehlmann

INTRODUCTION

as Mayor, after 1965, when Mayor Clancy and Mayor Bachrach had retired, the Republicans took over the Charter policy of making the Mayor's office one of real political leadership. Republican Mayors, as distinguished from Charterites, were pretty much gladhanders.

In 1961, I was the only Charterite left, while the Democrats put in three members.

In 1963, the Charter Party changed its policy and endorsed some Republicans and some Democrats. We put on a special TV program for Ted Barry and elected him. In 1964, Berry, because of his leadership in organizing our Cincinnati poverty program, became one of three principal assistants to Sargent Shriver in the Office of Economic Opportunity. Myron Bush was our selection to succeed him.

In 1967, ex-Congressman John J. Gilligan led an effort of big name Democrats, but failed when he was the only one elected. We put on the same kind of push for Bush and elected him as the only elected Negro member of Council.

Our first racial difficulties developed in 1967. Our police-National Guard cooperation was the best in the country in the June riots. We had a good set of remedial programs and strengthened them, especially in building code enforcement, and in recreation. The police-National Guard coordination was improved, and the really accidental outbreak following the Martin Luther King memorial service in Cincinnati was very effectively dealt with.

The urban renewal program, vigorously revived in 1956, has been extremely well handled, especially in the core area where seven blocks, in whole or in part, are being cleared and rebuilt, plus a new skyscraper, and the new Provident Bank and Procter & Gamble office building outside the renewal area.

This program is supplemented by a new stadium to

be occupied by the Cincinnati Reds for baseball, and the new Cincinnati Bengals for football under Paul Brown.

The University of Cincinnati has gone through extraordinary growth. It has become a partner at least with The State, getting a sizable subsidy and operating a University College, and one or more Junior State Colleges. The total enrollment, including night college, is 30,983. The City still provides a contribution of $3,800,000 a year.

Cincinnati, Ohio
August, 1969

CONTENTS

PREFACE v

INTRODUCTION TO THE 1970 EDITION . . vii

CHAPTER
I. INTRODUCTION 1
II. THE GOOD OLD DAYS 8
III. CINCINNATI UNDER THE ORGANIZATION—1921 22
IV. THE CINCINNATUS ASSOCIATION, MURRAY SEASONGOOD, AND THE EXTRA LEVY OF 1923 31
V. HENRY BENTLEY AND THE NEW CITY CHARTER—1924 46
VI. THE GREAT DECISION AND THE FIRST CHARTER VICTORY—1925 . . . 71
VII. PROPORTIONAL REPRESENTATION . . 94
VIII. THE CHARTER VICTORS IN ACTION . . 106
IX. NOW THE COUNTY—1926 121
X. THE GREAT TEST FOR THE CITY CHARTER COMMITTEE—1927 145
XI. NATIONAL POLITICS FOR THE FIRST TIME—AND THE SECOND COUNTY BATTLE—1928 160
XII. THE THIRD CAMPAIGN FOR COUNCIL IN THE CITY—AND THE RESIGNATION OF SHERRILL—1929 AND 1930 . . . 175
XIII. PUBLIC UTILITIES 187

CONTENTS

CHAPTER		PAGE
XIV.	Fusion in the County and Its Results for the Charter—1930-31	195
XV.	The Plot Thickens—1932 and 1933	215
XVI.	By Way of Conclusion	234

APPENDIX

A.	History of Recommendations of the Upson Report	238
B.	Cincinnati Bureau of Governmental Research	246
C.	Bibliography on the Government of Cincinnati and the City Charter Movement	249
D.	Results of Elections	251
E.	General Fund—Income by Years	258
F.	General Fund—Expenditures as Contracted by Years	262
	Index	269

CITY MANAGEMENT

CHAPTER ONE

INTRODUCTION

THIS is the story of a distinctive movement in municipal politics. To those not residents of Cincinnati I find I must use the word "reform," although neither friends nor enemies have called the movement by that name at home, for it differs in many respects from any previous effort of the kind anywhere.

There have been many reform movements in American cities in the past. I recall as the occasion for my first interest in that direction an address twenty-five years ago at the school I attended as a boy. The speaker told the story of a victory, in a Chicago ward fight, over that terrible monster, the corrupt political machine. I don't know to this day whether it was the Republicans or the Democrats he defeated, but it was a glorious victory of righteousness over the forces of evil, and it thrilled the whole school. Later I read the novels of Holman Day and Winston Churchill, painting the same scene on a broader canvas.

Now that I am a man I find many people indifferent to or suspicious of reform as such. For some with wet sympathies it is because they identify the term with prohibition. For many the extremes of partisanship of the "lunatic fringe," who are so often in the forefront of reform, discourage their moderate support. Only too often the leaders of reform, as the popular interest wanes and a favorable opportunity offers, desert their cause for their own personal profit. Hypocrisy of that kind leads the ordinary citizen to echo with feeling Senator

Conkling's words, "When Samuel Johnson said that patriotism was the last refuge of a scoundrel, he ignored the enormous possibilities of the word reform." [1]

One important element, consciously or unconsciously, in the citizen's suspicion of the reformer is due to the fact that these municipal reform movements in the end have generally been unsuccessful. The Chicago ward was probably lost to the gang the next time, and the conquering hero of the novels was permanently victorious only in print. No reform movement, at least in the larger cities, has ever won twice in succession. It has often welded for a white-hot moment on election day many inconsistent elements of opposition to the "ins," but then, cooling gradually, it has disintegrated. It has never won in enough cities at the same time to have any appreciable effect on state or national politics, except, of course, where publicity for a leader has proved it a stepping-stone in his career. The great cities today are governed as if municipal reform had never been.

The editor of the *Yale Daily News* last spring advised his readers against going into politics because it was too dirty, but I cannot conceive that his pessimism was due as much to the dirt as to the apparent impossibility of overcoming it. We are not fond of lost causes, we modern Americans, and we don't like reform so long as it is a lost cause. When it succeeds we are apt to give it a different name.

The reason generally given for this eventual want of success is that the citizen, after a spurt of activity, goes back to his business, while the machine makes politics its business 365 days in the year. That is perhaps an accu-

[1] Republican State Convention, Rochester, New York, September 26, 1877. If they remembered his motive they would be less approving. He was attacking President Hayes for the President's courageous attempt to reform the New York Customs House, previously the Senator's personal perquisite.

INTRODUCTION

rate description of what often happens, but it is not an excuse for letting it happen.

Besides, the explanation is too simple. We assume that all the politician does, politically speaking, is bad and must be ignored. It is no part of the science of government, says the university professor; it is not in our textbooks; the idealism expressed by the metropolitan daily in its editorial column is the true guide. But people vote as if the editorials had never been printed and we find that the political boss has a certain verbal or emotional magic and a penetrating knowledge of human nature, which wins elections. Is his technique any less the science of government because it is prostituted to the personal profit of individuals not accepted in the best society?[1]

You still have the time element, says the cynic. The reformer quits when his business calls him back. True, but is not that a part of the politician's magic? Aren't the cards stacked against the amateur by the primary system, by the method of voting, by the form of government, that often could not be better designed to prevent the ordinary citizen from sharing in its responsibilities? It is no wonder that when means are devised to make it easier for the citizen to take part in politics on an amateur basis, the politician tries to damn it by calling it "un-American."

This explanation that the politician wins because that is his business assumes that all good citizens are on one side and only wicked politicians on the other. Of course, there are some business men hand in glove with the political boss, principally those who sell important goods or

---

[1] For a stimulating development of this theme see T. W. Arnold, "Law Enforcement" (1932), 42 *Yale Law Jour.* 1. A complete description of the technique of the municipal politician will be found in Frank Kent's two books, *The Great Game of Politics* and *Political Behaviour*. Every American boy and girl should be compelled to read them in school, and his indignation should be cultivated.

services to the city. But there is a group of business and professional men who back the machine against reform because of a sincere conviction that the evils are necessary incidents of the promotion of the national welfare. The conviction that the machine is necessary lives because of a belief that we must have two national parties and that a national party cannot exist except by means of strong local organizations. The minor peccadilloes of the machine are necessary evils to be mitigated by the presence in party councils of these honest men, and the more serious charges are laid to the mistaken fervor of enthusiastic partisans or the slanderous efforts of the minority party to reach power by way of the reform.

I hesitate to criticize these men, whether Republicans in Chicago or Democrats in Cleveland, because they are honest and sometimes acquire a position of influence in the organization that enables them truly to eliminate many of its corrupt practices. But they cannot make the politicians swing their votes for the best candidates and there is always hidden from them a residue, most often in the courts and especially the police courts, of the viciousness that jobs and spoils inevitably permit to exist.

There is a far larger group for whom I have no such sympathy. They support the machine for motives that are a combination of fear and self-interest. They have none of the genial rascality of the blatant buccaneer and none of the high purpose of the honest party leader. They may indeed have in mind that the boss can influence a tariff schedule or grant a privilege that means livelihood to their employees and their families, but they lack the strength of character to see that the blackmailer succeeds only with cowards. These men shut their eyes to the most brazen graft and permit themselves to be made the respectable front for the machine. In the old days the politician and the profiteer could often run the show

INTRODUCTION 5

against all comers, but today the badge of respectability is generally needed, especially in the face of a reform movement, and these men furnish it. In such a situation they may be the determining influence that defeats reform, for they add strength to the mass inertia of less prominent citizens whose active indignation is essential to the first victory.

To the young editor of the *Yale News* I trust this book may carry a word of good cheer. He turns to pessimism because he distrusts as much as I do the theory that by "boring from within" you can overcome graft, corruption or what-have-you in the party. But I oppose to that theory not pessimism, but a faith which I submit is proven worthy by ten years' experience in a normal American city. I believe that a citizen organization can establish good local government and maintain it permanently on a business basis without patronage, without yielding to either national party and without injuring either. I believe that whatever we have of corruption and stupidity in state and national government is largely due to the local patronage machine and the conditions which permit it to exist. England, with two national parties far more compact and disciplined than ours, has no local machines of jobholders, corrupt or otherwise.

Of course, I recognize that cynics are plentiful in this field of politics, whether ancient, battle-scarred and now philosophical or youthful and distended with facts. I suppose childlike statements of faith like those above expose me to such names as "kid-glove goo-goo." [1] Nevertheless, I set forth in this book the ground of my faith and here it is in brief.

At the beginning, ten years ago, some practical idealists molded existing techniques into a new political method

[1] See Chamberlain, *Farewell to Reform,* passim. I assume he gets "goo-goo" from "good government" or "goody-goody."

adapted to the seasonal activity of the ordinary citizen. It was a method that gave full opportunity for the expression of enthusiastic loyalty of women, who will not take part in party politics and are used by ordinary party chieftains as scenery at headquarters only, if there.

The method was successful enough to win four successive elections in eight years, after procuring the adoption of a complete and well-conceived new form of government. It stimulated the use of similar methods in the county containing Cincinnati, which won the two elections in the last three years. Certain difficulties in the county have emphasized how well the form of city government is adapted to citizen activity.

The public officials elected by this movement and these methods were as a matter of principle left to conduct their offices without interference. With patience and persistence they have studied their problems and gradually have installed methods that are in many cases models for the United States. There are many bureaus of governmental research attempting to improve the efficiency of their various local governments, but the Cincinnati bureau has seen more of its reports and recommendations for the city and county carried out in full than have all the rest of them put together. With all that it seems safe to predict that Cincinnati will be the rare city of over fifty thousand in the United States on December 31 of this year without a deficit; its bonded indebtedness has decreased in the last seven years while it was being rebuilt physically; it has seen that none of its citizens starved, and none of its essential services to its citizens has been seriously curtailed.

Last but not least, the leaders of this movement in office or out have neither sought nor secured financial profit, and they have succeeded to an amazing degree in destroying the invariable tradition in city politics, "To the victors belong the spoils." It is this fact and the confidence it gave the voters in their good faith that has prevented most of the usual opposition to a reform movement from appearing in Cincinnati.

We are going into our fifth city election and we may be beaten, but the movement will not die. It has a vitality that will make it of equal value as a minority group, and if we lose, this story may be of even greater usefulness. These are the reasons for writing it. Besides, it was great fun in prospect and in execution.

CHAPTER TWO

THE GOOD OLD DAYS

THE old days were the good old days in Cincinnati politics. It is a tradition that during the Civil War the Republicans were quite convinced that the necessities of the Union justified any informalities in electoral methods. Unfortunately, this tradition of informality lasted long after 1865 and was turned to good advantage by the Democrats in the next two decades.

In each precinct at six in the morning of election day the persons then present, by viva-voce vote, selected the judges and clerks of election. There was no registration list and a challenge was decided (if persisted in) by having a Democratic and a Republican official visit the place the voter claimed to live. Those interested in elections went armed and the gangs of repeaters were not often challenged.

The functions of city government were at that time performed by many boards, the Fire Board, the Police Board, and so on, all of them corrupt and maintained in power by open and notorious election frauds of the Democratic organization. It began to turn the stomachs and the votes of our honest and thrifty German citizens, who, strangely enough, had voted Democratic. An outrageous sample of jury-fixing acquitted some murderers, produced a riot, and destroyed our courthouse in March of 1884; and with that the tide turned.

The election frauds, which may still be reviewed in some of the Ohio Supreme Court decisions in the eighties, did not go on without an effort on the part of the better element to prevent them. I have heard my father tell how, as a member of the Honest Elections Committee, he helped to secure a force of United States deputy marshals to supervise the election of 1884. The Democrats promptly appointed an equal number of deputy sheriffs, and feeling ran high. My father was judge of elections at a polling place on Central Avenue, and about the only man in the place without a revolver. One little Irishman would eventually have shot it out with a political enemy on the inside, if fortunately he had not been shot in another precinct during an interval. But a deputy sheriff drew on a deputy marshal in the street just outside the door and was shot and killed by his quicker opponent.

In that same election, Mike Mullen, then a Democratic lieutenant of police, loaded every colored voter he could find on the streets into a patrolwagon and locked them up for the day in the basement of the Hammond Street police station.

William G. Caldwell, the respected proprietor of a store on Fourth Street, had allowed his porter, Wm. McAllister, to leave during the morning to vote, and he failed to return. As he had Mr. Caldwell's keys, his employer was a little worried, and after lunch went to look for him, seeking him first at the Hammond Street police station. The first person he saw as he came in was McAllister, not in a cell, but behind the barred gate. He asked Mullen at the desk if Wm. McAllister was there and Mullen promptly denied it. Caldwell saw his own bunch of keys in the open drawer of the desk at which Mullen sat and reached for them. Mullen grabbed them back. Caldwell headed straight for the Federal Building and the Republican United States Attorney, for the city government was hardly likely to be sympathetic. And he was angry enough to press the prosecution to a conviction and a year's sentence. But by then Cleveland was president and Mullen was represented to him by the leading Cincinnati Democrats as just an honest but overzealous partisan made into a political martyr. He was pardoned.

Is it any wonder that Bryce, writing his *American Commonwealth* at about this time, called the government of cities the one conspicuous failure of the United States?

It was not long after that John McLean, then head of the Democratic organization, ran for public office and spent money like water to be elected. In one precinct he was recorded with more Democratic votes than there were men, women and children in the precinct. The Democrats claimed that William January, John February, Alfred March, James April, William May and many others like them must have moved since the election, but the votes were thrown out and McLean did not win.

In 1886 Foraker, who was then Governor of Ohio, secured control of the Board of Public Affairs, which had under its jurisdiction some two thousand jobs. Foraker gave George B. Cox, then only a ward leader, but already prominent, the power of appointment to those jobs, and Cox distributed them carefully throughout the various wards of the city. The result was the beginning of Cox's citywide power, and the beginning of Republican control in Cincinnati politics. The inauguration of McKinley and the victory of Mark Hanna gave to Cox federal patronage in addition, and later many politicians shifted from the Democratic to the conquering Republican ranks. The Democrats seemed to find difficulty in retaining power after old-time ballot-box stuffing was made so difficult by the new Australian, or secret, ballot and registration.

In 1887 a most interesting local election occurred. That was the heyday of the Knights of Labor, and the United Labor party failed to win the spring election for mayor by only 700 votes in a three-cornered fight. Their cam-

THE GOOD OLD DAYS

paign was based on bettering labor conditions. They had a complete volunteer organization. They found little difficulty in securing in all the wards and precincts men who would work for them among the voters and at the polls, enthusiastic in the hope of improving their own situations with shorter hours and higher pay. The enthusiasm rapidly slowed down, however, and no such vote was recorded in the fall of the same year.

It was not until 1897 that an organization of independents was able to prevail over Cox and the Republican gang. Gustav Tafel was elected mayor on a fusion ticket by a combination of independent Republicans and Democrats. But, under that kindly, ineffective old gentleman, the politically-minded Democrats ended up in occupation of nearly all the offices, while the real independents proved only to have voted. More amazing still, after election many of these Democrats, including Mike Mullen, found it desirable to enter the Cox alliance, and Cox at the same time secured control of the county offices. The result was that, before Tafel's term was over, the power of the Republican organization was actually approaching its height.

An analysis of the members of council in 1905, showing that twelve of the twenty-four were saloonkeepers and that Mullen was one of the leaders, gives perhaps as good a picture as any of the general character of the machine. An analysis of the ward organization is equally significant. There were at that time in the city of Cincinnati twenty-four wards. Only one member of the group of twenty-four ward captains was not a jobholder. That was Lou Kraft, who was at that time the leading gambler of the city, and was said to have the "gambling privileges." The other twenty-three occupied positions of importance throughout the city and county government. Four of them were members of council. The machine was dominated by the saloon and sporting elements, although it must always be remembered that a number of the saloons in Cincinnati had much of the atmosphere of the old-time German beer garden.

By 1905 the constant pounding of newspapers and other reforming elements in the community had produced a considerable volume of publicity, helping to establish in the minds of the people the real character of the government by machine. One of the most important leaders of reform through all these years was E. H. Pendleton, a man to whom little enough praise came for the thankless task of fighting the evil and corrupt powers that were.

He came of a distinguished political family and inherited high ideals of public service. He fought George B. Cox in a day when it cost something to do it, and there were times when even some of his friends crossed the street when they saw him coming, because they feared to be seen speaking to him; it might be reported back to the Big Boss up over the Mecca saloon. With a lovely voice famous from college days, always in demand at joyous reunions, he went through a bitter experience almost single-handed in pursuit of political idealism, and bitterness darkened his latter days. He did not live to see the realization of his dreams.

In that city election of 1905 a distinguished lawyer, Edward J. Dempsey, was the Democratic candidate for mayor and was making a splendid race on a reform platform. A combination of circumstances resulted in his election and that of a largely independent legislative ticket.

Under Dempsey as mayor the waterworks, begun in 1898 under Tafel, one of the finest and most successful of any large city, was completed. Even in that project, with an incorruptible engineer and able and honest men in the majority on the board, there were rumors, probably with foundation, that the machine had succeeded in shaking down the contractors for at least their profits and perhaps more. The method was obscure, but the result well authenticated. It is beyond question that when the city secured a judgment against Lane & Bodley for $238,000, Cox sent for the three judges of the Circuit Court, and asked them to reverse the case. Judge Ferdinand Jelke, Jr., replied that he would try it on the record like every other case before him, and the court split one to one, the third having gone south for his health. The case was settled by the city for $65,000 and Jelke was not renominated in spite of an excellent judicial record and unbroken precedent.

During Dempsey's term the plan of Cincinnati's parks was laid out by Kessler, and formed the basis of the City Plan of 1925. But Dempsey could not battle the gang successfully again, and in 1907 he was defeated. The Australian ballot and registration did not solve everything and it took a rather substantial majority to appear as such on the official count. On election day one of Pendleton's aides came to Dempsey's office to report that he had personally seen Mullen handing out the dollar bills to those who had voted right in the old Silver Moon district by the waterfront. "Get the chief," he said, "and don't let him out of your sight until we get down there, even to get his hat." But Dempsey, perhaps rightly, refused to be so suspicious. When they arrived, the payoff had stopped, tipped off from some of the many sources of the machine's information. So ended the second reform administration, a great improvement on the first, Tafel's, but stifled without many accomplishments other than the one mentioned; unless I should add that the Dempsey administration helped to lay the basis for the election in 1908 of Henry T. Hunt as Democratic prosecuting attorney of the county.

In the meantime, through the efforts of the new group

in the legislature and with the assistance of similarly-minded legislators from other parts of the state, the Drake Legislative Investigating Committee was instructed to make an investigation of city and county government in Hamilton County.[1] This committee succeeded in bringing out, among other things, the fact that the county treasurer, or his deputy, had been receiving back from the various banks in which public funds were deposited the entire interest earned by such deposits, and that a clerk had in turn delivered it directly to George B. Cox.[2]

It is perhaps typical of the attitude of business interests in those days that some of the bankers involved made every effort, including departure from the jurisdiction, to prevent the disclosure of the facts so far as they knew them. But past treasurers, including R. K. Hynicka, settled suits against them for ten years' back interest for $214,000, a substantial sum even if it was only a fraction of what had been taken. George B. Cox was called to the grand jury room and asked what had become of the interest. He denied ever having received it. When the other testimony was presented showing that it had gone directly to him, Henry T. Hunt, as prosecuting attorney, made every effort to have him indicted for perjury. The control of the machine over the selection of grand and petit jurors, as well as their general domination of the state bench at that time, prevented the indictment of Cox. Judge Frank Gorman, a Democrat just elected, and absolutely incorruptible, was given the assignment to the criminal court only after Hunt's first term as prosecutor. But Hunt was reëlected and Gorman called a special grand jury, which he named personally, in January, 1911. The

[1] See Espy, *Legislative Investigations in Cincinnati*.
[2] For this same carelessness as State Treasurer, Len Small was forced to disgorge in Illinois, and a similar charge was made against the sheriff of New York County in 1931, but was not the basis of his removal by Roosevelt, then Governor.

indictment followed and then strenuous efforts to bring Cox before a jury, against every technical defense. The indictment was quashed, and the reversal in the Supreme Court of Ohio did not come until February of 1913. Hunt, before finishing this second term as prosecutor, ran for mayor of the city and was elected to that office for the years 1912 and 1913. His organization successor as prosecutor, of course, sought no new indictment and the case of State vs. Cox was dead.

Hunt was a Democrat, but he avoided at least to a degree the mistake which had cost previous Democratic reform administrations their success at the end of their first term. The able men placed at the heads of the various departments of city government, under his administration, succeeded in laying the groundwork of many reforms which later were carried into effect. Yet he was sometimes no diplomat, and was unable, when he ran for reëlection, to build up a big enough majority to overcome what his friends have always believed was a corrupt count. Even so, he nearly won and would have except for the street car strike in 1913. The origins of this were obscure, and the strike dragged on. Finally, Alfred Bettman, the city solicitor, threatened to ask a receiver for the Traction Company, who could furnish the necessary transportation to the public. That settled the strike, but it was a most unpopular move, nevertheless, and lost Hunt many votes. That ended the third reform movement, by far the most successful up to that time. Hunt's own disappointment was keen, and not long afterward he moved his home to New York.

At about the same time those who were interested in the schools and education had been carrying on a steady fight, with the assistance of those opposed to the machine, in the state legislature and had finally succeeded in securing the passage of a bill which provided for an optional small School Board elected at large, with a nonpartisan ballot, and serving without pay, instead of the old School Boards elected by wards. It is true that the teachers themselves had never been really subject to politics, but the jobs of all the business employees of the board in connection with the maintenance of buildings and so forth had been a portion of the spoils, and a place on the large ward board was a petty distinction. Again it included many saloonkeepers and a number of complete illiterates. The outstanding figure of this battle was John M. Withrow, a prominent physician of the city, short and stocky, soft-spoken, with a pleasant, quizzical smile, and a supreme determination that the children of his community should be properly educated without the interference of politics.

This movement was supported by the better element in the organization from the start and when the small board was once installed, John Holmes and even Hynicka were consulted on the personnel for the board and helped elect the tickets of the Citizens School Committee. Opposition continued from the saloon elements but was ineffective. In more recent years there has been some criticism of the beauty of the new school buildings as causing too great expense. While I feel personally that this charge is not justified, occasionally there has been evidence of irritation of the members of the board at criticism of any sort, that has assisted a few independent candidates of ability to break through the slate in less prosperous times.

One of the elements of Cincinnati's good fortune that assisted its citizens to free themselves from political bondage was the presence in the Constitution of Ohio of the provision that permitted a municipality to adopt its own charter quite free from any restraint by the legislature. One cannot realize the importance of this until he hears the story of Indianapolis, which finally pushed a city manager bill through the legislature, with difficulty secured a favorable vote of its citizens, and was at the point of preparing for the first election four years later, only to have the Supreme Court of Indiana hold the whole act unconstitutional.

The home rule amendment was adopted during Hunt's administration, in 1912, when submitted by the state constitutional convention along with a number of other provisions, including the direct primary and the initiative and referendum.

A charter commission was chosen during the Hunt administration in 1913 and a charter was submitted in 1914, but it was voted down by the influence of the organization in the absence of any real citizen interest. Later more interest developed, but again the organization kept the whip hand and put its own charter commission in, and the new charter of 1917 simply adopted the same form as the existing statutory one. This interesting and important section adopted as part of the charter all the municipal laws of Ohio then in force, apparently without reference to any changes the legislature might make in the future.

The Hunt administration did more than demonstrate good government in action and laid some basic plans that were gradually carried out even by hostile administrations. Those very accomplishments had deep-seated effects on the organization itself.

One great change was obvious. George B. Cox was in retirement,[1] a sick man, and Rudolph K. Hynicka had succeeded him. For the solitary dictatorial autocrat, in effect the owner of the machine, was substituted the suave politician of a more familiar kind. Cox did continue to

[1] For some of his life story see Wright, *Bossism in Cincinnati* (1905), and a paper by Herbert Koch before the Cincinnati Literary Club, "An Ohio Warwick" (in the Cincinnati Public Library).

wield power where he chose, as for instance a few years later when he forced the choice and election of A. E. B. ("Buzz") Stephens as clerk of courts. Hynicka had been related to Cox in some of his business enterprises also. As head of the Columbia Burlesque Wheel he was forced to spend more and more of his time in New York. But that did not prevent him from taking hold of his new political task with energy and new ideas. The most important of these was directed at the overcoming of the old cry, so effective with Hunt, "Down with the Boss!" He created the Republican Executive and Advisory Committee to be the governing body of the party, at least nominally. The legal and statutory control was vested in the Central Committee, made up of the captains of the wards and townships elected at the August primary in 1914 and in even-numbered years after that by vote of declared Republicans. The new ruling body was made up of the more important members of the legal Central Committee and a group of leading Republicans not so active in politics, but prominent in business and professional life.[1]

The most important new member was John R. Holmes, an experienced lawyer associated with every reform movement as far back as the eighties and with a growing interest in politics. Under Spiegel he was named as safety director in charge of fire and police, with the declared object of preventing the connection between certain ward bosses, the police court, and vice, gambling and other forms of crime. With the inauguration of Puchta as

[1] There may be some interest in giving names. After those who were ward captains is inserted the number of the ward. Albert Bode, 14; Robert Z. Buchwalter, 13; John J. Burchenal, E. W. Edwards, Frank R. Gusweiler, 9; Henry G. Hauck, 20; James J. Heekin, John R. Holmes, Rudolph K. Hynicka, chairman, 6; August Kirbert, 17; Albert H. Morrill, George T. Poor, secretary; William Cooper Procter, Louis L. Rauh, treasurer; Murray Seasongood, Leonard S. Smith, George W. Tibbles, 4.

mayor in 1916, Holmes was replaced, but when John Galvin came in in 1918 [1] he returned.

The later history of the Republican Executive and Advisory Committee after John Holmes's death has obscured for most of us what happened under his dynamic leadership. The Republican organization has always been made up of two very different kinds of men: one the mean and vicious individual seeking protection as he preys on the weak and unfortunate (or rich and foolish); the other the respectable man of family, known and liked in his neighborhood and consulted as oracle on political matters. The ethical standards of the first unfortunately sometimes affect the second group.

Both groups eyed John Holmes askance at first. But gradually he inspired respect and fear in the vicious part of the organization and respect and enthusiasm in the others. He was that rare combination, a man of fine and attractive personality and character and an extraordinarily able politician. The combination of Holmes and Galvin became the dominating influence in the organization, backed up as they were by the leading Republicans on the Executive Committee and off it. I do not mean to say that they had eliminated graft, for Hynicka and Hermann were always associated with contracting interests, and the specifications of brick, granite, wood block and patented pavements was more than a fad, just as the recurrence of the same names in the award of city and county contracts was more than an accident. Nevertheless, Holmes and Galvin were aiming to get rid of just that, and Holmes was definitely headed for the chairmanship of the party when, unfortunately, he died.

Hynicka would have been quite willing to retire in favor

[1] It was the case of John Galvin, incidentally, that created the term "Galvinized"; he had secured the nomination for judge over the opposition of the gang some years before, and was punished for his presumption by the election of his opponent, a Democrat.

of Holmes, but there was no one else of that caliber in sight and he continued to carry the responsibility as best he could. The partially reformed organization with the Cox tradition still alive, but the bullying, fear-inspiring methods of the Big Boss largely eliminated, was a far different machine in fact from what it was at its height in 1905, whatever the public might continue to think about it.

Hynicka was none too popular in various quarters. In 1920 the candidates for delegates to the Republican National Convention agreed to abide by the preferential vote between Wood and Harding. Harding won, but after the first votes the delegates, except John Galvin, switched from what amounted to a mandate for Harding to Wood, at Hynicka's orders. Galvin characteristically stayed put. Republican feeling in many quarters can best be described in the language of the *Times-Star,* the principal Republican newspaper, after that event:

HYNICKA MUST GO

The Republican organization in Hamilton County is facing one of the major crises of its history.

It was made odious in the eyes of the Republicans of the nation by Hynicka's treachery to Harding at Chicago. No one had anything but respect for the nine Ohio delegates who were openly for Wood at the beginning and held to him practically to the end. But the performance of the Cincinnati district delegates, who wrote the last chapter of an unexampled story of political perfidy by leaving Harding at the most critical period of his candidacy, was universally appraised at its true value!

Cincinnati Republicans are growing tired of absentee control. They are bored to death at a situation which keeps important decisions waiting upon the very occasional appearances of a visitor from New York. As things have been going since the death of John R. Holmes, it will not be long before the organization rattles itself to pieces. Hynicka is a political executive of unusual ability—but no man can live in New York and efficiently direct the course of a party organization in Cincinnati.

When to the everyday disadvantages of absentee control, Mr. Hynicka adds the handicap of such double-faced leadership as he displayed at Chicago, the situation becomes unbearable. At last week's convention the influence and the votes of the Republicans of Hamilton County were traded and delivered as they used to be in the days of George B. Cox. The methods and results were the same. But this much could be said for Cox: he was a resident of Cincinnati.

The *Times-Star* is not hostile to the local Republican organization. In a general way we believe in that organization and its possibilities for service to the people. But we believe also that Hynicka should get out, or be put out, at the earliest practical moment. His place should be taken by some Republican who lives here, who is in touch with the feelings of our people and who will not attempt to pull off such stuff as Hynicka pulled off last week in Chicago.

It may be that the present is not the best time to work for this change in leadership. Our first object must be the success of the Republican ticket in November. Also the county ticket has been named and candidates for the Central Committee determined upon. But whether the fight on Hynicka comes this month, or next month, or next year, the *Times-Star* desires to register its indignation at the present situation and its determination to assist, as opportunity arises, in bringing about that change in leadership which is necessary if the Republican Party in Cincinnati is to remain abreast, or a little ahead, of the times.

CHAPTER THREE

CINCINNATI UNDER THE ORGANIZATION—
1921

I CAME to Cincinnati in the fall of 1921 after I finished law school and a football coaching job at Yale. It was not long after the November election, and I have been greatly interested to look over the campaign booklet of the Republican organization for that year. It presents a most impressive front for the political battle, although there are a few places where irritability seems to burst the restraints of print, and others where little is said though much more would seem to be called for.

"The sole purpose of the Republican party of Cincinnati is to create and maintain good government."

"Good government is best secured through party responsibility."

"Cincinnati's experiments with Fusion governments have proven that Fusion spells CONFUSION."

"Party responsibility is but another name for 'teamplay.'"

"Three municipal tickets are presented to the electors of Cincinnati for their suffrage in November:

    The Republican—named at the primary polls through the votes of 27,078 Republican voters.

    The Democratic—named at the primary polls through the votes of 7,291 Democratic voters.

    The Independent—named in secret conclave, after deals with Democratic leaders by a small self-selected coterie of disgruntled office-holders and ex-office-holders, who had refused to submit their pretensions to a vote by the Republicans of the city."

CINCINNATI UNDER THE ORGANIZATION 23

"For many years prominent men worked to secure the enactment of a primary election law whereby any member of a political party could submit his claim for a place on the ticket of his party to a legally-conducted primary of the voters of his party."

"Cincinnati Republicanism is a political column builded on a foundation of elected representatives and that foundation is the enduring principle of Republicanism and of Americanism."

"What is meant by the phrase 'Party Responsibility'? It means that the Republican Party of Cincinnati has a definite plan for the government of the city, and a fixed set of principles, which it sets forth in its platform, and to the fulfillment of which it pledges its candidates and for whose conduct in office it accepts the fullest responsibility."

The booklet asked for an additional tax levy for the city of 2½ mills, or $2.50 per $1,000 valuation, which was to make the total tax rate only 24.84 mills. It was cheerfully pointed out that fourteen years before, in 1907, the rate was 29.16 mills and that twenty-four years before, in 1897, it was 26.18 mills. It gave as one evidence of our wonderful progress the building of our Rapid Transit System (now an unoccupied tunnel and a melting road-bed, graced by occasional empty stations).

It was predicted that the election of the Democratic party or the so-called Independent party would mean the dismissal from office of the "municipal experts" who had been developed by the Republicans and who had given their years of experience to the public.

Reference was made to the likelihood that during the next administration (Carrel's) the railroads would take up the question of a great central passenger station with appropriate freight terminals for the city.

Much was made of the recent reduction in the rate of fare of the Cincinnati Traction Company, but the ordinance enacted on September 20, 1921, prepared by City Solicitor Zielonka at the request of council, and continuing for an indefinite period the existing gas rate, was dismissed with seven lines in a book of 134 pages. It was stated that the rate was continued until litigation between gas companies and municipal corporations in other parts of the state was disposed of in the courts.

That makes a good place to begin my story, for in the very week following my arrival in Cincinnati there was published in the Cincinnati *Post* and then in the *Times-Star* a telegram, whose source and date were not disclosed, but which could nevertheless be placed with the greatest accuracy. For the gas ordinance passed September 20 was temporary and a new one was introduced after election. It represented the proposal of the Union Gas & Electric Company, a wholly-owned subsidiary of the Columbia Gas & Electric Corporation, and many were the loud announcements by councilmen that they would not vote for its "outrageous" provisions. But when the ordinance was submitted, many voices were stilled and it was passed, without further explanation. The telegram published on November 28, 1921, solved the mystery.

It came from New York and was addressed to August Kirbert, then clerk of the municipal court, Froome Morris, then chairman of the City Central Committee, and Cliff Martin, then floor leader of council. It read as follows:

Understand Council committee with help of our friends working out most equitable gas contract ordinance. Very essential that Republican Councilmen agree and that organization get behind Council and share responsibility. I assure measure will represent concessions and compromises. While we should aim for best obtainable, we must not permit unfriendly influences stampede. They will pick anything to pieces. You are authorized to discreetly make any use of this you see fit.

HYNICKA.

I have no recollection of reading that telegram in the papers. My attention to local politics was negligible, but gradually I discovered a scene that differed from what it was assumed to be. The organization was in operation with all the prestige of many years of success behind it. The few revolts against its power were matters of history and were not recorded in any such way as to give inspiration to those who were looking for any improvement in their government. At that time the city was divided into twenty-six wards, and in addition to the twenty-six members of council from those areas, six were elected at large. A mayor was elected by the people as the chief executive of the city, and appointed his department heads except the city auditor, who was also elected. But this was the scenery only.

The real government of the city was exercised by the machine through the ward and precinct organization. In the twenty-six wards there were approximately five hundred precincts. The precinct is fixed shortly after the time of the decennial United States census on the basis of the area holding approximately four hundred votes in a presidential election. Of course, in primaries, which displaced conventions in 1912, the vote is far smaller and the same is true even in the city election, or in an election for state or congressional offices.

Such a voting precinct was in charge of a precinct committeeman who was almost invariably a public employee. He was expected to see to it that all the voters necessary to control a primary went to the polls on the day of such an election. In his precinct, curiously enough, there would generally be found approximately nine or ten more public employees. It was a condition of holding a job that each of these should produce his own vote and three or four more on the day of the primary. It was the duty of the precinct committeeman to see to this accomplishment, and that, too, was a condition of his continuing to hold his job: 500 precincts × 10 jobholders × 5 votes = 25,000 votes. And twenty-five thousand votes controlled every primary from 1912 to 1926.

The precinct executive, as he was called, was expected to know the names of all the voters in his precinct, their business, their prejudices, their faults; in fact, everything that was to be known about them. It was the way and policy of George B. Cox to know those things which would most effectively influence votes. If the individual was a business man without anything about him that he would prefer to keep hidden from his family or other individuals, then it was always true that there were some privileges to be given by the city which meant value to his business, such, for instance, as the right to store goods on the sidewalk. Always there was the question of the valuation of his house or business premises for tax purposes. He might have an elevator in his building, and the elevator inspector, if friendly, might avoid the necessity of requiring a new cable. There were certain individuals, such as Viv Fagin, holding no public position, but through whose intervention as "tax counsel," shall we say—on a fifty per cent contingent basis—it was found possible within a brief period to secure a substantial reduction in the valuation of property. Young lawyers who came to the city, who were beginning practice and needed business, were always readily assisted by appointments as appraisers, by appointments in small receiverships, by appointments to defend indigent prisoners. They, too, found it most advisable to be on the right side of those who were politically powerful. If this was the picture for one precinct, you only need multiply it by five hundred in order to find springing to arms overnight an army of five thousand men controlling twenty-five thousand votes and more in a pinch, having one object only, and that the

CINCINNATI UNDER THE ORGANIZATION

successful nomination of those suggested to them by the controlling committee which distributed their jobs. How could you expect them to have any minds of their own, when they knew that any sort of insurgency, or a vote against the desires of those more politically powerful, meant the loss of the means of support for their families?

These five thousand employees were divided between the city hall and the courthouse. The courthouse, which included the county offices, was far more desirable because in a number of offices there were fees and other perquisites which were not so readily obtainable at the city hall, and the general salary scale was far higher.

Many of the public employees occupying positions as precinct executives and even ward captains had been there for many years, and their activity and brain capacity had substantially decreased. That, however, was a development under the surface which was not realized by most of the citizens of Cincinnati, and the fear complex, the idea of the bogey man who would get you, to say nothing of the tremendous inertia, the feeling that it was impossible ever to overthrow such powers, made the organization apparently impregnable.

Was there graft at this particular moment in 1921? It has never been proven. There were certainly petty privileges like the dollar or so received by precinct executives for investigating a claim to the $100 given by the county commissioners toward the funeral of an indigent veteran of any past war (or that of any dependent of his). Certain families had places on the street markets for which they paid the city little or nothing, but which they sublet for good money. Was there a gambling privilege or a slot-machine privilege? Was there a group of contractors who apportioned the business, and for whose benefit the city inspectors saw to it that no contractor outside the ring who dared bid low on a city job ever wanted to get another? What connection was there between vice and the police court? None of this can we prove in court, and it is typical of modern Cincinnati politics that the newcomers, when they got in, were willing to let bygones be bygones, if only the bygones were thoroughly put out of office and of power.

I shall never forget one experience brought about by the death of one of the county commissioners in a grade-crossing accident. He had been almost a nonentity, and a group of young business and professional men gathered together in a supper club felt that there was great necessity for the improvement of the general caliber of the county commissioners. Accordingly the spokesman of this group, C. Lawson Reed, stirred up sufficient interest to secure the support of the leading bankers, manufacturers, retailers and real estate men, who together visited Mr. Hynicka. I happened to be a new member of the club and a member of their committee interested in this particular enterprise. So I was present shortly after noon in the Strand Building on Walnut Street, when this group made their visit. I had never seen him before. He was at that time the Republican National Committeeman from Ohio. He looked the typical politician, a suave, pleasant and agreeable gentleman to meet. "I am very glad to see you here, gentlemen; what can I do for you?" he said. Mr. Reed explained to him that the group was very much interested in the caliber of the new county commissioner, who, they assumed, would be appointed largely upon his recommendation. Mr. Hynicka disclaimed any such complete influence with the public officials charged with making the appointment, but indicated that he would be glad to transmit to them any recommendations that these distinguished gentlemen chose to give him. Mr. Reed then suggested the name of George Warrington, at that time a prominent attorney of the city, and now president of the

Board of Trustees of the University of Cincinnati. The suggestion had been endorsed by two of our newspapers and commented on favorably by the others. "We feel," said Mr. Reed, "that the county commissioners should have among their number a lawyer. There are so many matters," he went on, "on which the county commissioners are required to have some basic knowledge of legal affairs that it would be highly desirable to have a person so qualified as a member of the board, in spite of the fact that the county prosecutor is, of course, their legal adviser." "That is an excellent suggestion," said Mr. Hynicka. "I think it is one which should be called to the attention of the Executive Committee. The committee will decide on the basis of integrity and ability only. I appreciate very much the thoughtfulness and public service of this group coming to me with such an idea." After a few more courteous words, the entire group was ushered out. The next day it was announced that the Executive Committee had met and had decided upon the appointment of Clifford Brown, a lawyer, but better known for his political activity in the northern part of the county than through his profession.

Thus were the political affairs of the city controlled by the organization and the boss, suavely, imperturbably and apparently permanently.

Very differently were the social welfare enterprises of Cincinnati handled. That might at first blush seem irrelevant to my story, but in fact it is fundamental. I do not mean that our Community Chest is in politics, for nothing could be farther from the truth. But through its influence the altruistic people of the city of every creed and color learned to work together with goodwill for objectives which they were told were impossible—but they reached them.

We have one of the oldest Councils of Social Agencies and our first campaign was led by Fred. A. Geier in 1915, but the first great effort came in 1919 with the War Chest. The great majority of social welfare enterprises, Catholic, Jewish and Protestant, were brought together for that campaign, and have continued together without a break in their ranks. Since then the executive direction and social vision of C. M. Bookman and the spiritual leadership of Reverend Frank H. Nelson have given to the campaign and year-round organizations of volunteers a most distinctive quality. It is not that we raise each year an amount greater per capita than most other cities, although we do that; but it seems to one attending our gatherings that all the men and women of goodwill in our community have come together and that their spirits are welded together in a great cause, the education of the whole city to the highest standards of health, character and welfare.

CHAPTER FOUR

THE CINCINNATUS ASSOCIATION, MURRAY SEASONGOOD, AND THE EXTRA LEVY OF 1923

UPON this political and social background appeared the Cincinnatus Association. It was formed in 1920 by Captain Victor Heintz. Captain Heintz, in 1917, having been elected to Congress the fall before, entered the service of the United States when he had barely taken his seat and emerged from the war with an outstanding record of heroism and bravery in the infantry of the 37th Division. While he was away in 1918 he was not renominated. Mr. Heintz, in calling a group of twenty-five young business and professional men, mostly ex-service men, together in 1920, proposed to them the formation of an organization resembling the Sunday Evening Club in Chicago. He had in mind something in the nature of a forum, and on a number of occasions in the last ten years he has again revived his idea. The outcome, however, was far different. When the original group, in answer to his letter, arrived at the Business Men's Club (now the Cincinnati Club) they found no Mr. Heintz. After waiting for some time they called his residence and found he was not there. After waiting still longer, they decided that there must have been some mistake and they separated. It turned out that his own memory had been at fault. However, he persevered and was able to bring the group together. They liked each other, enjoyed each other's company, and the dinner club they started, meeting every two weeks, had for its aim and principal interest the advancement of their own city.

The incident I have described in reference to the county commissioner vacancy is perhaps typical of those matters in which they interested themselves. In December, 1922, Henry Bentley, a member, read a paper pointing out the anomalous condition of the county finances. One newspaper printed a little of it and a little later another reprinted it all. The vacancy in the commissioners occurred, to be filled by the Probate Judge, the Auditor, and the Recorder (of course, on the recommendation of the Republican Executive Committee, i.e., R. K. Hynicka). The matter was brought before the Cincinnatus executive committee by the president of the association, and, after some discussion, a committee was appointed from the membership to promote the candidacy of George Warrington. Editorial support was secured, the call on Hynicka arranged, and the whole affair reported to the association for discussion at its next meeting.

Such a committee might be appointed at any Cincinnatus meeting for the investigation, for example, of the garbage contract; or perhaps for an investigation of the specifications for the repaving of some prominent highway, known to all the members. This committee was then empowered to make any study it desired, and in particular it always took as part of that assignment the consultation with the public officials who were supposed to know something about the facts. The association started with no prejudice against the powers that were, but with a desire to know the truth. When a committee, at the next biweekly meeting of the association, presented its report, sometimes in the form of a debate, the statements were apt to be phrased in a straightforward way which took into account everything except the old fear concept that had prevented anyone from uttering a word that might be construed as criticism of the public officials. The fear complex had applied even to most Democrats, and the voices of the few exceptions in that party carried little weight, for in Cincinnati the domination of George B. Cox had established a Republican majority of twenty to twenty-five thousand, which could be expected in any year, even a Democratic year. The members of the Cincinnatus Association were, generally speaking, Republicans, and for that reason their comments acquired greater importance than if they had been primarily interested in ordinary political opposition.

Under such circumstances what they said was news. It was not long before the newspaper reporters were regular attendants at their meetings, and publicity no longer had to be sought.

The stream that brought the political renovation of Cincinnati began to run faster October 9, 1923, with the debate of a committee of the association appointed to investigate the proposal of the city for an extra levy of taxes. And with that I must explain briefly the tax situation in the state of Ohio as it affected the cities.

The Ohio Constitution contained, until 1929, what was called the uniform rule, that is, the requirement that all property, real and personal, should be taxed by uniform rule at its true value in money. Personal property, of course, included stocks and bonds, but a tax rate sometimes as high as 31 mills, or 3 per cent, was confiscatory and led to a universal omission to return intangibles, and for those more conscientious or fearful of discovery or death (the same thing in this case) trusts were created in other states which apparently avoided the tax. In either case large amounts of property of Ohioans escaped taxation entirely.

In 1910 Judson Harmon was elected Governor and he conceived the idea that if the tax rate were limited to 10 mills, or 1 per cent, the tax would be low enough to bring the intangibles out of hiding. This was more than a pious hope in days when tax avoidance was less a specialized branch of the law than it is today. But the plan never had a chance in the legislature, and while the act passed was called the Smith 1 per cent law, from the first it was really a 1½ per cent law with exceptions that were constantly widened.

The general limitation included sinking fund and interest on new bond issues, while, of course, bond issues were not included, so that the natural effort of tax-spending public officials was to place as much of their normal expenditure in the class of permanent improvements as they found it possible to do, even at the risk of destroying the meaning of the English language. It will readily be seen that as more money was spent through the issue of bonds the amount of interest paid on these bonds would be added to the total that must come within the tax limitation. As sinking fund and interest had to be paid first, it simply meant that the portion within the limitation available for current operating expense went steadily down.

In an urban Ohio county there are three main taxing subdivisions: the county, the city and the schools. Each of them is for most purposes quite independent of the others in its own administration.

The schools have always been politically powerful in this state. The result was that they were able to go to the legislature and procure the passage of laws which fixed *minimum* limitations for the amount or portion of the tax rate allocated to their purposes. Now the official body which brought about the division of the total tax rate between the three subdivisions was a county body, the County Budget Commission, made up of county officers. What could be more natural than for the budget commission, after allotting to the schools the amount which the legislature said they must give them, to take what they needed for their own purposes and to turn over what was left to the city?

The results of such a policy over a fifteen-year period were not surprising. Ohio cities were nearly bankrupt and their bonded indebtedness many times increased; the counties, with salary scales far higher, were in quite satisfactory condition; and the schools, generally speaking, were getting along well enough in between.

Some of the cities, Cincinnati among them, had gone to the desperate device, with the approval of all its leading citizens, of issuing deficiency bonds to close the gap between income and outgo. On December 31, 1925, there were outstanding $7,426,820 of such Cincinnati bonds. They had been issued: $340,000 in 1917, $1,000,000 in 1918, $2,980,000 in 1920, $2,873,000 in 1921, $259,800 in 1923.[1] It was this situation that made necessary the request of the city of Cincinnati, in the fall of 1923, for an extra levy of taxes beyond the 15-mill limitation.

The committee of the Cincinnatus Association appointed to investigate arranged the debate, with Leonard Smith, Jr., for the levy and Murray Seasongood opposed. The latter was a lawyer, and formerly interested in politics as I have mentioned, but not active in any way at this time. The stage was set.

Seasongood had been graduated from Harvard a number of years before and inherited from that experience an effective literary background which he found it possible to utilize in a most effective way in speaking.

I cannot better present the atmosphere of the Cincinnatus Association and the flavor of Seasongood's rhetoric

[1] On December 31, 1932, there were still outstanding from these same bonds $1,391,960, about $850,000 a year having been paid off under the Charter administration.

than by quoting from the story published the next morning.

CINCINNATUS ASSOCIATION HEARS CITY ADMINISTRATION CRITICIZED BY SEASONGOOD, OPPOSING TAX LEVY

Before the Cincinnatus Association at the Literary Club last night, Murray Seasongood, Republican and well-known attorney, severely criticized the city administration in an address opposing the extra tax levy. He spoke at the request of Douglas Allen, President of the Association, and when he had finished a motion already before the meeting to indorse the levy was rescinded.

"They tell you at the City Hall," said Mr. Seasongood, in his address, "that they have no money for this, no money for that. What I want to know is what becomes of the money?

"Another excuse is that the county receives more than its just share of the taxes. There is no excuse in that. The city and county are run by the same gang.

"It is not so much the extra taxes that we pay that I object to; it is the moral and psychological effect which this machine is working upon the citizens of Cincinnati.

"In what other city in the country does the administration place the payment of dividends to a public service corporation before the just payment of a franchise tax? You cannot find one. But here in Cincinnati we charitably postpone and then eventually wipe out what the Traction Company owes the city because it must pay dividends to the stockholders, not only of its own company, but of holding companies as well.

The Rapid Transit Plan

"What is to come of the Rapid Transit plan? Ask anyone on the streets and he will shrug his shoulders. Ask the officials of the city. They do not know.

"We have the fourth largest per capita expenditure of any city in the country. What do we get for it? Nothing, absolutely nothing! We have the only occupational tax system of any city in Ohio. What becomes of that money, and how much is collected under that system? Nobody seems to know.

"In what city in the country would the people tolerate the passage of a gas rate ordinance on the orders of a political boss six hundred miles away, after members of the City Council had refused to enact it? We do in Cincinnati even after the affair is given wide publicity by the press.

"Why are our streets in such bad condition? Read the specifications on which the contracts are let. They are perfect. If they were followed, the streets would be good for years. On the street I live, Washington Avenue, we formed a committee to see that all the conditions in the specifications were carried out. The street is as good as it was twenty years ago.

"Another point. If the county gets more than its just share of the taxes, what does it do with it? Recently the County Commissioners attempted to spend something like a quarter of a million dollars to purchase unauthentic records of deeds. The records are not good as evidence in court, and every attorney knows that. Why did the County Commissioners find it so important to have the records?

"Another thing I object to as a citizen of this community is the fact that the Common Pleas Judges of this county, in whom are vested the power to appoint trustees of the Southern Railroad [1] and who are supposed to exercise all their judicial knowledge in determining the fitness of any applicant for the position, wait for the Hamilton County Executive Committee, which is only another name for the leader who lives in New York, to make its recommendation, and the Judges immediately concur in the appointment.

[1] The City between 1876 and 1890 built the Cincinnati Southern R. R. from Cincinnati to Chattanooga, and leased it to the C., N. O., & T. P. It is now the road underlying the main line of the Southern Ry. from Cincinnati south. The lessee railroad pays $500,000 per year more than the debt service on the bonds.

Income from the Railroad

"In addition to the taxes, there is a cold half million derived yearly from the Cincinnati Southern Railroad. In figuring taxes this amount is somehow left out in the computation.

"When a person calls at the City Hall to ask for an improvement, he is sorrowfully shown the condition of the building, the dirty windows, leaky roof and dirty walls.

"All that is beside the issue. Look to the big things. Street repairs, sewage system, non-payment of franchise taxes by the Traction Company; a wallow of expenditure in building 'a hole in the ground,' popularly known as the proposed Rapid Transit plan. That is where the money goes, and it is time for the citizens to assert themselves.

"I for one believe that the time has come to cut out every extra tax levy, bond issue or anything else that will give the bunch a chance to squander money. Make them produce the goods on what they have or get out.

"The whole history of the organization has been a blot on the city. As far back as 1905 it was known that the then political leader here demanded of the three Judges of the Court of Appeals, then the District Court, that they reverse a decision in favor of the city for $280,000 against a large contracting firm.

"Yet for twenty years we have gone on supinely indifferent to our welfare, ready at all times to swallow whatever the gang put over.

"Some may say that 1905 is ancient history so far as the affairs of the city are concerned. But the same gang is in power and less than two years later a certain official overnight produced $214,000 when he was threatened with indictment for converting that amount to his own use from the taxpayers' money.

"I do not know where a copy of the report on the affair of 1905 could be found, but if it can be found I would like to make it compulsory that every member of this association read it. It gives a wonderful insight into how our city is run.

THE CINCINNATUS ASSOCIATION 39

"It is a crime what the people of Cincinnati are undergoing, not only in the matter of receiving nothing for their money, but in being drugged into a state of political lethargy that is fast making the city a laughing stock."

Is it any wonder that the burdened city fathers felt it essential that some answer should be made to this violent attack, especially in view of the amount of publicity it had secured? The mayor, George Carrel, for all his good qualities, was no speaker. The vice-mayor was a lawyer of ability, Froome Morris, one of whose distinctions is that he was a classmate of Calvin Coolidge at Amherst. R. K. Hynicka, the boss, was away at the moment, had seldom answered any attack, and as everyone knew was anxious to relieve himself of the responsibility of leadership. Morris was chairman of the Republican City Central Committee and was one of those who were looking with great interest toward the mantle of Elijah.

He was selected as the spokesman of the administration in the newspapers, and in a bland and lofty manner disposed of the attack as actuated by political malice and based on ignorance. "It is just such talk, decrying Cincinnati, that is handicapping the city. No man likes to vote taxes upon himself, and when someone like Seasongood poses as of profound wisdom and talks against taxes, the multitude is disposed to listen to him. The populace does not stop to analyze."

Mr. Seasongood was not one to sit quiet under abuse, and on the following day sent a letter challenging Mr. Morris or anybody else to a debate, propounding in advance a series of fourteen questions. Mr. Morris took a day to prepare a complete answer to each, again referring to Seasongood's appalling ignorance of city affairs. A few excerpts may be of interest.

Question 1 (by Seasongood):	Is it true there was an investigation by the so-called Drake Committee and that the disclosures made in that report were made in my address?
Answer (by Morris):	What has the ancient history of what the Drake Committee did fifteen years ago to do with the financial needs of Cincinnati today, for police, fire and health protection and civic administration?
Question 2:	Are the same persons connected with the Republican organization who were connected with it at the time that report was made?
Answer:	No, the Republican organization was completely reorganized in 1912 and for ten years has functioned under the direction of the Republican Executive and Advisory Committee, composed of 41 public-spirited Republican men and women, who, together with the Republican Central Committee, have conscientiously striven for honest, economic and efficient government.
Question 6:	Is it true that the county levy is too high in comparison with the city levy, and does not the same organization make nominations and supervise the activities of county and city political organization?
Answer:	I think that the county and school board levies are too high "in comparison with the city levy," although neither county nor school board is receiving more than is necessary to function properly. This is what the Taft bill remedies. The Republican organization makes no nominations and does not "supervise" city and county officials.

In the meantime the flurry of excitement had spread even to New York, for at this stage Mr. Hynicka was reported as returning to the city to discuss with "organization leaders" the state of the city's finances.

The invitation to debate was finally accepted and the event took place before the Walnut Hills Business Men's Association, one of the many active civic associations of the city. Mr. Morris was not permitted to forget the telegram about the gas ordinance, and by this time Seasongood had gone to the records for unfavorable comparisons of many types of Cincinnati expenditures with those in other cities. When Seasongood sat down, Morris refused to answer his arguments, and merely discussed the city's financial plight.

Soon Seasongood was digging into the county expenditures, for the basis of his story was the fact that the county had plenty of money, that it had the power to reduce its expenditures and give the city a fairer share and that since it was all one organization anyway it should be treated as one and refused any relief until it had improved this outrageous situation.

By this time the organization was frankly worried and called off all debates with Seasongood. One had been arranged by the Madisonville Welfare Association between him and E. E. Kellogg, a councilman from a neighboring ward, and Frank Lewis, deputy clerk of courts and Republican ward captain, called the president of the welfare association to instruct him that it was not to be carried out. The president, though mildly in Republican politics, told him they would do no such thing. "You'll not get anything more in the way of improvements from the city hall," said Lewis. "Good-bye," said the president. His board backed him up and that neighborhood of good Methodists and good Catholics from that day was a stronghold of rebellion against the machine. They enjoyed their debate, too, for when Kellogg failed to show up Seasongood placed a chair at the front of the platform and conducted the argument with his "invisible opponent."

I cannot resist another excerpt from Seasongood's last major address, on November 1, 1923, to the Cincinnati Real Estate Board, for it is in many ways characteristic.

When I went to school (I really did go to school once), I used to think that the feat of Horatius holding the bridge and Leonidas holding the pass at Thermopylæ were considerable accomplishments. For the past month, however, since I have been attempting to withstand the onrushes of the gentleman from New York and his cohorts, I have come to the conclusion the task must have been rather simple, if the character of the attack on those historic occasions was similar to that here. I am now of opinion that the severity of an attack does not necessarily depend upon numbers and that, in certain instances, the more there are, the more they interfere with one another and the easier resistance is made.

Apparently, I have been selected as Arnold Winkelried for the spears of the office-holders. I am entirely willing this should be so, as long as the spears are hurled in the daytime and not below the chest. I say to them in the words of Scott:

"Come one, come all! this rock shall fly
From its firm base as soon as I."

An orchestrion is an instrument played by one person and sounds as if it were a complete orchestra. The "sounding brass" of the campaign manager's trombone, the "sweet complaining grievance" of the mayor's violin, the high sharp notes of the editor of an afternoon paper's piccolo, all played by the master at the keyboard, are music to my ears. However, certain parts of the orchestra have not yet had their solo. I, therefore, call for the sheriff's double bass and the city engineer's percussion to complete the harmony.

First, as to the sheriff, the county commissioners by agreement with the sheriff pay him .65 per prisoner per day. The United States Government pays him .70 a day per prisoner. The city, I believe, pays him the same for its prisoners as

THE CINCINNATUS ASSOCIATION 43

the county pays. From these three sources he received for the year ending March 31, 1923, approximately $70,000. A sample breakfast at the jail is oatmeal, bread and coffee; lunch: soup, potatoes, hash and bread (sometimes meat instead of hash); supper: bread, coffee, apple-butter or dried peaches or prunes. An expert restaurant keeper in this city has given the estimate for furnishing a similar menu as .44 or, if guaranteed against loss, .40. The sheriff also furnishes the necessary equipment, such as plates, knives, and forks, etc., for which let us allow the liberal estimate of .05 a prisoner. Why should the sheriff from this one item (remember, whatever is saved in the county could be utilized by co-operation towards the relief of the city) apparently receive from $15,000 to $25,000 a year profits at the expense of the county on keep of prisoners? I say, apparently, because I do not know certainly. I await further information from the sheriff. . . .

It has been stated that I am a political partisan. If I am, I am a partisan Republican. I voted for our late lamented President, which cannot be said of the New York head of the local organization in the national convention. The vote on the extra levy has resolved itself into the question: Do the citizens of Cincinnati and Hamilton County like what has been done by those in power or do they disapprove? If they like what they have received, let them vote for the extra levy. If they wish to show their disapproval and their emphatic insistence on efficiency and economy, let them vote against the extra levy.

Seasongood precipitated the defeat of the extra levy, but there were other causes in the background. The city administration was, to say the least, inept. The director of safety, in charge of the police and fire departments, was a genial business man, pleasant and honest, but of no force in administration decisions. The director of public service was a lawyer of dominating character, set in his ways, who succeeded in creating a tradition, whether justified or not, of annoyance with the public. In the financial emergency, which was indeed desperate, it was decided by the powers that were, that the only way to get any money was to pound the public over the head by saving where it showed; that is, by permitting the streets to go unrepaired, by turning out street lights, by reducing the fire department and the police department, and forcing those whom they retained to take compulsory vacations without pay for as much as two days a week. Such a course of procedure only added to the public annoyance, and increased the margin of the negative votes. George Carrel deserved great credit for his refusal to approve any bond issues, the issuance of which, of course, made matters increasingly worse for the city, and his publicity produced public support for him in great contrast to the public reaction to the acts of some of his department heads.

The final result was 46,496 for the levy to 60,434 against. Not only that, but all the various city bond issues which had also been attacked were snowed under by a similar majority. At the same time the School Board in which the people had confidence secured on an extra levy for the schools a favorable vote of 61,780 to 48,836.

Another measure submitted to the people at this election by reason of a referendum was the Taft law referred to by Morris in answering one of the questions set forth above, together with a companion bill. These two were passed at the session of the legislature in the spring of 1923 through the efforts of my brother, Robert A. Taft, who had interested himself in the tax tangles of the Ohio laws. The Taft law raised the limitation from 15 to 17 mills, but was not likely in fact to raise tax rates, since it redistributed levies outside of limitations. It represented a sound attempt to prevent municipal bankruptcy through the state, but it was badly defeated. With it disappeared a special 2.45 mill levy given by the legislature which the city had had in previous years, equaling about $2,000,000 in money for current operations, or over a third of the budget, and the city fathers saw bankruptcy staring them in the face.

CHAPTER FIVE

HENRY BENTLEY AND THE NEW CITY CHARTER—1924

WITH the defeat of the extra levy and the Taft law, the city was certainly in a bad way. It was realization of this fact that had prevented more citizens from supporting Seasongood publicly, heartily as they agreed with his condemnation of the organization. "God help the people of Cincinnati," said Mayor Carrel to the press, and at once set about to find ways and means of economy. One of his first measures served mainly as the occasion for the entrance of another great leader of the reform movement into the arena, in a way quite different from that of Seasongood, but equally characteristic of the individual.

Carrel announced that the city would have to close the Branch Hospital, which was the city tuberculosis sanitarium, crowded to the attic with all of its four hundred beds full. Henry Bentley was the president of the Anti-Tuberculosis League and went at once to see the mayor.

"You are proposing to put four hundred dying people out on the street on January first," said Bentley.

"I know it," said Carrel, "but we have to do it."

Bentley, being a lawyer, investigated the Ohio General Code to see what measures he could take to force the city to continue, and found to his surprise that the law required the county, not the city, to operate the tubercular hospital, and the result was accomplished in Cleveland by having the commissioners of the county pay for all patients the unit cost on the theory that citizens of Cleveland were also citizens of Cuyahoga County. In Cincinnati, on the other hand, the county commissioners conceived of all their expenditures as being primarily for the benefit of the county outside of the city, and left the city, which paid 85 per cent of the county taxes, a very secondary consideration.

Bentley went to the mayor again and asked him why he didn't put it up to the county commissioners to operate the hospital. Carrel said he would be very glad to turn it over to them. Bentley then went to the county commissioners and put the matter before them. They submitted the proposal to their legal adviser, the county prosecutor, and he gave them an opinion, through his assistant, Chester Durr, to the effect that it would be illegal for the county to operate the Branch Hospital. Bentley went back to the mayor and the latter said he was going ahead to close the hospital. Bentley threatened to "raise hell." Carrel said, "How?" and Bentley replied that he didn't know, but he certainly would. He went back to his office and telephoned the Rotary Club, which was having a luncheon meeting at noon, and asked if he could have a few minutes on the program. He went and told the whole story. The club was very much wrought up, passed a resolution to fight the closing and appointed a committee of three to wait on the mayor and a committee of three to wait on the county commissioners, to try to get the county to take over the hospital.

The next day Bentley spoke at the Kiwanis Club on the subject. He kept that up for a week, speaking before every luncheon club he could reach, and in each case the club appointed a committee of three to call on the mayor and a committee of three to call on the county commissioners. At the end of the week, one of the members of the Anti-Tuberculosis League called on Bentley and said,

"What are you trying to do, wreck the Republican organization?"

Bentley said, "No."

Freiberg asked, "Well, you are certainly doing a lot of damage. Have you ever talked to Mr. Hynicka about the matter?"

"No."

"Well, have you any objection to going up and talking it over with him?"

Bentley said he was willing to talk to anybody about the matter. Mr. Freiberg then telephoned Mr. Hynicka, who seemed to be waiting for the call and said he would be glad to see them immediately. They went up and Bentley found Mr. Hynicka to be a very courteous gentleman. Bentley told him he was solely interested in keeping the hospital open, and Hynicka agreed with him and suggested he see the county commissioners; Bentley told him he had and that the prosecutor had advised them it was illegal for them to take it over. Bentley said he had looked up the law and felt the prosecutor had rendered this opinion because he had been told to do so. Hynicka asked him if he was sure of the law, and he said positively, that it was being done in other cities and, in fact, Cincinnati was the only city that was not doing it. Hynicka advised him to see the commissioners again and also the mayor. When Bentley returned to his office, his stenographer informed him the mayor's office had been calling him up every five minutes for half an hour.

He called the mayor and was informed that a meeting of representatives of the county commissioners, the county prosecutor, the service director, the safety director and the city solicitor was already being held at the mayor's office on the subject of the Branch Hospital, and that they would like Bentley to be present. He took a taxicab im-

THE NEW CITY CHARTER—1924

mediately to the city hall. The problem discussed was no longer, "Shall the Branch Hospital be taken over by the county?" but, "How shall the Branch Hospital be transferred to the county?"

In about thirty minutes the matter had been settled in favor of the county operating and paying for the Branch Hospital. To accomplish this purpose required action by the city council, which at that time consisted of thirty-one Republicans and one lone Democrat. The matter of how to persuade the council to support the decision was not even discussed. On the following day the council, under suspension of the rules, passed a resolution to lease the Branch Hospital to the county for $1.00 a year plus the cost of operation. The following Friday, at their regular meeting, the county commissioners accepted the lease. Since that time the Branch Hospital has been operated by the county.

This lesson in practical politics was not lost on Mr. Bentley. He and his associates had learned from their experience with the Cincinnatus Association the necessity of an open forum where public questions could be discussed and information regarding the dark places of municipal government could be broadcast to the citizens. They had learned through the experience with the extra tax levy that the Achilles' heel of the politician was real publicity, to which people would respond when they could. They had learned through this experience with the Branch Hospital that the individual political officeholder was helpless under a system of divided responsibility and that neither the mayor nor the county commissioners nor both together could accomplish a purpose both desired without the assistance of the unseen political leader in control of all public officials, including Democrats.

Was it not possible to unite the three lessons in one?

Was there not an underlying unity in the difficulties they had encountered? Would it not be better to use the public forum, and the denunciations of the orator, to rouse the people before election rather than to wait until after election and then to attack the shortcomings of the elected officials? If the hard-boiled politicians quailed before a storm of public disapproval, might it not be possible to utilize that same public opinion to secure the election of officials who would whole-heartedly support a program of civic betterment? Had they not been failing to see the forest because of the trees? Was not the first step to assure power and authority to public officials and commend them for exercising it properly and then to remove the handicaps that prevented the electors from selecting men desirous of accomplishing social objectives? Was not the way to secure reform through politics rather than despite politics?

This was the viewpoint expressed not long afterwards by Bentley before the Cincinnatus Association, when he reported on the progress in getting the county to take over a fairer share of its obligations to the taxpayer. As his platform for the next step forward it is of great importance and interest.

"We have made a beginning, and if we are to accomplish anything of permanent good we must give the credit to the politicians for every good thing done, and be content to have secured the accomplishment. Praise is the breath of life to a politician, and the only way we can pay politicians for doing the things we want done is by giving them a little praise. If we want to secure our own candidates it will be necessary to organize our own machine, arrange for our own precinct and ward captains, our own executive and advisory committee, and our own burlesque circuit. Unless we do this we cannot expect to name the office-holders."

THE NEW CITY CHARTER—1924

The attention of these amateur politicians was next turned to the necessity of a thoroughgoing investigation by some impartial body, of the city and county government, with a view to political reform. As the demand for such an investigation began to appear in print, the organization saw what must be done. If it was to be investigated, it determined to name the investigators.

The Executive and Advisory Committee appointed a subcommittee for just that purpose, but it made Colonel Wm. Cooper Procter the chairman of it. Colonel Procter insisted upon authority to appoint a real committee of citizens for the purpose of conducting an examination of the city and county governments, and on December 1, 1923, he notified of their appointment twenty-one men and women, including in the group all shades of Republican opinion and avoiding in appearance and in fact any control at all by the politically-minded.[1] It was nevertheless a conservative group.

The committee was to devise a plan to comprehend and solve the following: 1st. The coördination of the city and county governments wherever possible. 2nd. A united policy of construction of various public city improvements. 3rd. A proper financing of the city in the future. 4th. A thorough examination of the conduct and administration of the city and county governments looking to a reduction of the expense if possible, and at the same time maintaining an efficient administration.

The organization itself was represented by three mem-

[1] The committee consisted of Bolton Armstrong, Reverend Frank H. Nelson, James P. Orr, Charles A. Hinsch, Charles J. Livingood, A. E. Anderson, J. J. Burchenal, Mrs. F. E. Mackentepe, Murray Seasongood, C. L. Harrison, Mrs. A. C. Shinkle, Tylor Field, George H. Warrington, R. K. LeBlond, Charles P. Taft, 2d., Julian Rauh, John Omwake, Province Pogue, Gilbert Bettman, George D. Crabbs, Adolph Kummer, P. Lincoln Mitchell, and Herman Schneider. Dean Schneider and Mr. Crabbs were unable to serve.

bers of the Executive Committee. George Warrington, whom I referred to above as a suggested county commissioner, was selected as chairman. The committee, after investigation, employed Lent D. Upson, then the head of the Detroit Bureau of Governmental Research, to make the survey. Mr. Upson enlisted the support of a group of experts in their various fields, and produced what has since been known as the Upson Report. Of course, a man coming in from the outside to examine a political department, such as the Board of Education, or the county auditor's office, or the General Hospital, or to study the personnel policy of the city, could not discover all there was to be known in the brief period that could be allotted to the work. Nevertheless, the Upson Report reached a high standard in the accuracy and impartiality of its conclusions, to say nothing of the well-rounded picture it gave of the entire governmental set-up in Cincinnati and in Hamilton County. I may add that no member of the committee will forget it in a hurry, for after securing all possible subscriptions each one had to dig into his bank account to the extent of more than $400 to pay for it. No assistance came from the Republican Executive and Advisory Committee. Yet none of us regretted it at that.

The preparation of this report consumed a number of months. In January, before it was even under way, Bentley was asked to make a report to the Cincinnatus Association on the influence of the party emblem in the vote cast at the election just past. There had been only one office voted for under the Republican eagle and the Democratic rooster, that of city auditor, while there had been an election at the same time for the Board of Education of the city on a nonpartisan ballot upon which the names were listed alphabetically, and rotated. The report showed that in the residence sections of the city 95 per cent of the people who voted one way or the other for auditor also voted for the School Board, whereas in the downtown or basin wards there were many precincts where the number of persons voting for the School Board represented only 40 to 65 per cent of the persons who voted for the one office under the party emblem. The instruction of the Republican workers to certain types of voters was to vote for the bird with pants (referring to the eagle). The recommendation of the report was to amend the city charter by initiative to abolish the party emblem in city elections, Cincinnati being the only city in Ohio with a home rule charter which still retained the birds. Bentley insisted that the removal would not interfere with party strength, since each would put up tickets as before, but it would require the parties to appeal to the more intelligent part of the population and not to the element that votes the straight ticket without knowledge or consideration. The people would have to vote for men, not birds. Cincinnatus voted two to one for the report, but as it was not unanimous it was felt better to organize a new group to back the proposed amendment. So was born the Birdless Ballot League.

Six members of the Cincinnatus, including the president, added to their number two prominent civic-minded women and three men representing wide interests. I append a reproduction of the enlistment card, both because it is the first written memento of what became the City Charter Committee and because it illustrates the standard organization method of these new political amateurs. It calls for a signature on the dotted line below a statement of purpose; it calls for action and talk to one's neighbors; and it offers opportunity for a financial contribution.

The Birdless Ballot League of Cincinnati
EXECUTIVE COMMITTEE

Mr. Douglas Allen
Mr. Henry Bentley
Mr. Lawrence Bradford
Mr. John D. Ellis
Miss Agnes Hilton
Mr. Ralph Holterhoff
Mr. Guy Mallon
Mr. Anthony Mees
Mr. Murray Seasongood
Mr. Charles P. Taft, 2d.
Mrs. G. A. Tawney

PURPOSE—To bring Cincinnati in line with every other charter city in Ohio, by eliminating from the ballot used in the election of city officers, all party emblems, names and designations, thus compelling citizens to vote for MEN and not for BIRDS.

PLEDGE—I will do the things checked below:

☐ Circulate petition for the charter amendment.
☐ Interest my neighbors.
☐ Donate $..............

Full Name...................................... Ward............
Residence....................................... Precinct..........
Telephone—Residence.................... Office....................
Secured by ....

SEND THIS TO 2004 UNION CENTRAL BUILDING

Just about at this time the political forces which a few months later formed the backbone of the LaFollette movement of 1924 began to become active. One of their principal leaders urged Ed. F. Alexander, a capable lawyer who had been active in previous charter revision efforts, to draft a charter; he suggested that the securing of signatures to initiative petitions would be good political exercise for the cohorts of the Conference for Progressive Political Action, and it could then be voted on in November, 1924. Mr. Alexander went to work and by April of 1924 had his draft, following the general lines of the Cleveland charter drafted by Professor A. R. Hatton, and just going into effect in January, 1924.

Following a suggestion by Mr. Fenton Lawson, the two groups were brought together in the course of the next few months, and the Birdless Balloters were persuaded that without much more effort a charter change

THE NEW CITY CHARTER—1924

worth while could be brought about. It was pointed out that a mere change in the ballot would probably still leave the field restricted to nominees of the two parties, because of the fact that some vicious old laws were still in effect under the Cincinnati charter, although they had been repealed by the legislature. The assistance of the LaFollette people was offered in getting signatures, something of importance to the somewhat discouraged denouncers of the birds. Thereupon the Birdless Ballot League dissolved on June 9, and the City Charter Committee declared itself organized.

Discussion of the charter followed. Alexander for the LaFollette group insisted on proportional representation, rather to the dismay of some of the others, who without much opinion on P. R. felt it would be a handicap in the charter election. The same group were convinced of the necessity of a small council elected at large rather than the large council elected by districts, which was the Cleveland plan and the Alexander draft, and this time their view prevailed.[1]

By this time it was early July and time was short. It was definitely decided that the new amendment with the necessary signatures of 10 per cent of the voters at the last election should be submitted to council late enough so that it could not submit it to the organization vote at an August primary, but must submit it at the presidential election. Guy Mallon took charge of the circulation of petitions, and Miss Bessie Fennell ran the office. Provision was made for enlisting witnesses and challengers and

[1] Mr. Alexander's recollection is that I was for a city manager and against P. R. I do know that I was not satisfied with the proposed amendment and did not remain a member of the reorganized committee. However, in the campaign I remember addressing the Cincinnati Women's Club and telling them that the small council was good, that I was doubtful about the city manager, and that P. R. while new and strange to us was not of much importance one way or the other. Needless to say, my views changed with experience.

for the conduct of meetings for women in the homes. The signatures were readily secured and not long after the August primary the petitions with 15,000 names were filed with the clerk of council. The sponsoring committee, which with some others made up the City Charter Committee, consisted of Bentley, chairman, and Seasongood, two Republicans; Mallon and Alexander, two Democrats; and Miss Agnes Hilton and Mrs. Guy Tawney, both Republicans.

In the meantime there had been some fireworks for the edification of the populace. Seasongood was in great demand as a speaker among civic organizations, and pointed out with emphasis the number of improvements in governmental efficiency, described as impossible before the defeat of the extra levy, which had taken place in a few months since then. I have told of the taking over of the tuberculosis sanitarium; the same thing happened to the city infirmary (poor farm). The overcrowded county insane asylum, long the object of criticism, was turned over to the state, which should long since have had it, and the conditions were remedied. The attack on the sheriff's charges for boarding city prisoners started the safety director of the city on the same effort.

The Cincinnatus Association was blazing away under the leadership of its new president, Russell Wilson, the assistant editor of the *Times-Star*. Again the flavor of this modest group of good citizens can be given only by a rather full quotation from the letter which Wilson drafted and submitted to it on June 30, 1924. The contents explains itself.

Hon. George P. Carrel,
The Mayor of the City of Cincinnati.
Dear Sir:
The communication which you recently sent to the Cincinnatus Association consisted not only of your own letter,

but of a letter from Frank S. Krug, City Engineer, to Charles F. Hornberger, director of Public Service, and a letter from Mr. Hornberger to you. Mr. Hornberger's letter may be ignored. It is merely a gesture of martyrdom by one who is bored by the lèse-majesté of criticism by mere citizens. . . . But the form and matter of both your own and Mr. Krug's letters require them to be considered together. . . . It is too bad, for the purposes of intelligent criticism, that Council, too, did not contribute a letter.

As to matters of general policy, Cincinnati today has 108 miles of granite paving, as compared with 41 miles of asphalt. There are more miles of brick paving than of asphalt, 66, and there are 24 miles of wood-block, more than half that of asphalt. And yet there is a greater mileage of asphalt in the cities of the United States than of all other types of paving put together. Why this proportional neglect of asphalt as paving in Cincinnati, especially in favor of granite? . . . At one time in Cincinnati's history the city officials saw the greater advantages of asphalt as paving. . . . A municipal asphalt plant was constructed, a plant that is now operated only at ten per cent of capacity.

The truth is that the city has developed an inordinate appetite for granite. You may not be able to bite granite, to employ Bismarck's phrase, but you can consume it. You can pave a viaduct like that of Gilbert Avenue with granite at twice the cost of asphalt and cause amusement other than mild to visiting engineers, while you make the citizen who pays the bill grieve. To all appearance, somebody who is very anxious to sell granite to the city has found somebody among the city officials who is very anxious to buy granite. . . .

Mr. Krug's protest that outside contractors are encouraged may or may not be true. The fact is that they do not bid on Cincinnati street work, and there is a legend at City Hall that when outside firms secured contracts on subway work, despite Mr. Krug, his welcoming salutation was as rough as it was inhospitable. . . .

Let us say in conclusion as to the engineering department

that the technical proficiency of Mr. H. F. Shipley, the assistant engineer in charge of streets, and Mr. Walter Sullivan, the assistant engineer in charge of sewers, is beyond question. One of the defects of the administration of the city is that it does not permit the abilities of such gentlemen greater play.

One of the main subjects of attack was the diversion of trust funds derived from the automobile license tax, from street repair purposes, leaving necessary repairs unmade. Said Wilson to the mayor:

In 1922 only $108,000 was spent on street repair, leaving $91,000 worth of holes and ruts grow wider and deeper. In 1923 only $98,000 was spent, leaving $104,000 worth of holes and ruts to join the holes and ruts of the year before, now grown to rich maturity. Mr. Hornberger as a creator of holes and ruts was to have an even more prolific year in 1924 when Mr. Calerdine [of the Cincinnati Automobile Club] and Mr. Witten [of the Cincinnatus] proved that diversion of municipal funds, like murder, will out. To judge by the semi-annual allocation of funds, there would have been a diversion of $128,000, and a correspondingly large brood of holes and ruts, to join the two previous generations in our progressively disintegrating streets. . . .

What is the motive that has caused this wanton violation of the statute and the later concealment by the legerdemain of municipal bookkeeping? Is it that the people are to be chastened into a contrite spirit for having refused extra levies? Are they to be bumped into confidence in the city administration? Or is it that politicians are to be rewarded for the years of permissive disintegration of our streets by bond issues that would mean an orgy of municipal expenditure? Is the hand that withheld the hundreds of thousands to be entrusted with the millions of dollars?

Respectfully yours,
THE CINCINNATUS ASSOCIATION
RUSSELL WILSON,
President.

THE NEW CITY CHARTER—1924

The association voted to send the letter.

Is it any wonder that a motion that the association, as a predominantly Republican organization, recommend to the mayor that he request the resignations of Hornberger and Krug, passed with a whoop?

And is it any wonder that the bond issues referred to, including all the ones defeated in November, 1923, were again snowed under in the August primaries of 1924?

Mr. Hornberger's reply to all this excitement was the statement that the holes in the streets were 75 per cent propaganda, but for all that his name became the generally accepted term for such depressions as the citizens passing over the streets did find.

On July 26, 1924, the Upson Report was released. There is no place here to go into details as to what it contained. The important feature, so far as this story is concerned, was the report of Thos. B. Reed upon the city council.

The council of Cincinnati is not in the true sense of the word a representative body at all. It is, on all matters of general interest, controlled from the outside and the praise or blame for the results accomplished must belong to the outside authority which controls it. No secret is made of the fact that the authority is the Hamilton County Republican Committee. The impression seems to prevail among citizens of Cincinnati that this is an entirely normal situation. Comparison, however, with the municipal politics of other cities throughout the country justifies us in declaring that, while partisan and machine influences are conspicuous enough elsewhere, Cincinnati's situation is today unique in the completeness of organization control and the degree of helplessness of council. . . .

Party feeling is peculiarly strong in Cincinnati. This must for the present be regarded as a constant factor in any changes which may be suggested. Something, however, may be done to counteract the influence, met on every hand, of the doctrine of "party responsibility." Its advocates are able to point with some pride to the complete harmony which its application has produced between all the organs of the city and county governments. It is used, however, to justify a degree of party control which goes far beyond what is necessary to secure reasonable harmony—to the point, indeed, of removing the seat of government from the city hall to Republican headquarters. The idea of "party responsibility" is an English development. It grew up there as a result of the custom which required the king to select his ministers from among the majority party in the House of Commons. It has meant on its home soil an absolute identification of party leadership and official position. In Cincinnati the two are almost completely divorced. The party organization is something apart from and superior to the city government. Members of council and other city officials sometimes have a place in the management of the party, but it is seldom if ever a very prominent one. In consequence the city is governed, not by its elected officials, but by a party organization chosen by only a fraction of the people. . . .

Finally there can be no virtue in party responsibility as a government device unless there is an alternative party to which the people may turn. The Democratic party in Cincinnati has long been too weak to supply such an available alternative. While, therefore, the Republican organization is to be praised or blamed for the results of city government in Cincinnati, there is no effective way in which the public can hold that organization to account. . . .

At present it [Council] is composed of thirty-one Republicans and one Democrat, by force of circumstances inconspicuous and inarticulate. There is in council therefore almost no criticism of any organization proposals. Occasionally, and within well-defined limits, the two or three Republican members of council who have some leanings toward independence, express dissent from the majority view. They never, however, carry their opposition to extremes,—practically never, so far as a negative vote on a consequential matter. It is a truism that it is not healthful politically for

THE NEW CITY CHARTER—1924

any organization or party to possess absolute and uncriticized authority. . . .

It is furthermore quite obvious that, weak as the Democratic party is in Cincinnati, it is very much under-represented in council. At the last mayoralty election the Republican candidate polled 68,000 votes, the Democratic candidate 40,000 and an independent candidate 21,000. The Republican vote, however, was distributed over the city so evenly that the ward system of election gave the opposition elements practically no representation in council. It may be said without hesitation that this is unfair and in the long run detrimental to the interests of all concerned, including the Republican party. . . .

Considered from the point of view of their principal occupations the councilmen may be classified as follows:

Retired 2	Poultry Market 1
Professional:	Restaurant 1
Attorney 5	Saloon 2
Doctor 1	Tailor Shop 1
Veterinary 1	Business (Employees):
Business (Proprietors):	Auto Salesman 2
Barber 1	Brewery Manager 1
Butcher 1	Paper Salesman 1
Dance Hall 1	Shoe Salesman 1
Grocer 1	Clerk 1
Hay and Grain 1	Insurance Agents 2
Hotel 1	Workmen:
Laundry 1	Metal Polisher 1
Plumber 2	

Seven members of council were actively connected with the liquor business. Several of them conduct or have conducted resorts of disreputable character. Only one member is a workingman or in any sense represents labor.

In general, it should be said that the members of council are honest and well meaning. Under the present system there is almost no opportunity for a councilman to graft. They have too little independence even for that. . . .

For a body to be controlled from the outside the personnel of the present Cincinnati Council is admirable. It would be impossible for it as now constituted to be an independent legislative body.

The conclusion to which Mr. Reed came was a recommendation in favor of a small council, elected at large, and he proposed that it should be chosen by proportional representation.

The organization members of the committee did not even see the report of Professor Reed on the city council until it was set up in type, and in spite of their strenuous objections and insistence that it be suppressed, it appears in the report without the change of a word.

The Upson Report was of the greatest assistance to the proponents of the new charter. It is true that the Survey Committee had not endorsed Professor Reed's recommendation, but it had published it, which had nearly the same effect. In other respects the city's opinion was divided about the report, principally because Mr. Seasongood had not signed it. The letter transmitting the report to the Republican Executive and Advisory Committee simply stated that Mr. Seasongood had left for Europe on July 8, leaving a memorandum which he desired incorporated in the report; that the committee had decided not to incorporate it or to print it, and therefore the report did not carry his signature.

What had happened was this: At the first meeting of the committee Mr. Seasongood proposed as a subject of investigation the connection of vice in the west end with the Republican organization. The sentiment of the committee was in favor of leaving past scandals strictly alone, of washing no dirty linen in public, and of performing its services through the party organization, unless the party organization failed to carry out its recommendations.

THE NEW CITY CHARTER—1924

As the various reports were issued to the committee for review, Mr. Seasongood found that those on the city finances did not support at all the view he had taken in opposing the extra levy, in that they reported many city departments as sadly in need of revenue and in that they blamed the state laws governing the distribution of tax moneys as in large part responsible. Upson's own conclusion was: "It should be borne in mind that no government, good or bad, can be administered without funds. Were the city of Cincinnati governed by the most high-minded and efficient administrators in existence, they could not possibly give the citizens the type of government to which they are entitled with the funds now available for that purpose."

The committee decided to prepare a letter of transmittal giving its own conclusions, and Seasongood was appointed on the subcommittee to draft it, with Mr. Warrington, Mr. Bettman and myself. There were only two subjects of dispute. One was Mr. Upson's statement above quoted, with which all members of the subcommittee and of the general committee agreed except Mr. Seasongood.

Mr. Seasongood continued to insist, in the language of his memorandum on the subject, that

The real cause of Cincinnati's financial condition is the wasteful and inefficient city and county government, which has, with practically no interruption, prevailed for the past generation and manifested itself in the following ways, among others:
   (1) an excessive payroll in both city and county.
   (2) excessive allotment of funds to the county at the expense of the city.
   (3) neglect of streets and necessary municipal activities.

(4) improvident contracts and other unwise acts of officials.
(5) improvident issues of bonds.

The other subject of dispute was a clause approved in the draft by the subcommittee, except Gilbert Bettman, but stricken out by the general committee, which felt it was not a proper subject for the report. The minority thought of preparing a supplementary statement to accompanying their signature of the report and letter of transmittal, but after Seasongood left for Europe they finally concluded that the effectiveness of the many forward-looking recommendations of the report would be injured by any minority report. As a matter of interest the proposed minority report is given here:

July 9, 1924

To the Republican Executive and Advisory Committee
    of Hamilton County:

The undersigned members of the Committee of Citizens, insofar as they have signed the general report of the Committee, have intimated their approval of that report. They believe, however, that one paragraph should have been included in that report calling the attention of the Executive Committee to one point upon which they feel very strongly.

Reference is made on page 111 of the report to the need of intelligent planning in order to secure sound municipal finance. [We believe the following should have then been included:]

"There is an element wholly extraneous to the charter which demands consideration, which we trust will be treated as wholly impersonal. That is the power which your committee openly assumes not only to select the candidate for mayor and many of his appointees, but to direct in large measure his official acts and policies while in office. This is on the theory of party responsibility, which is carried further here than in any other city in the country according to the reports in this survey. Without strong men in office it might be for the best interests of the city to have a committee, such as yours, direct its policies for the time being, but strong men in office are desirable, and we cannot but feel that such a system, carried to the extent which now prevails here, is bound to keep such men from seeking or attaining it. It was evidently the intention of the framers of the charter to provide for a mayor who should have full power for a long term, in whom the people could repose confidence and at the same time hold to strict accountability for his official acts. His executive responsibility was not to be divided with anyone. It was hoped that such an office would attract men of commanding personality, and so we believe it would, had not the intention expressed in the charter been modified. Under present conditions the mayor is practically relieved of responsibility, which is assumed by the party through your committee. This is an obvious deterrent to independent men, even though they belong to the same party. Granting the capacity of your committee and its individual members, we believe, nevertheless, that better government can be secured by strict adherence to the purpose of the charter to make elected officials themselves, instead of a political party, responsible to the people."

What we have said must not be regarded as referring in any way to the present mayor, whom we wish to commend for the consistent attitude which he has taken in opposition to the issuing of bonds.

With the charter amendment on file in council the final step was to secure the votes of the people. It was a foregone conclusion that Republican organization supporters were against it: what of the Democrats? Two of the committee named on the petitions were Democrats, Mallon and Alexander; others were on the Charter Committee or assisting it, such as John Ellis and Robert Gorman. But these men were independents just as Seasongood and Bentley were, on the Republican side, and could not answer for the Democratic organization. At this stage Simeon Johnson was of service in discussing the matter with Thomas J. Noctor, the Democratic leader, and he was warmly backed up by the late John Weinig, who had been secretary to the safety director in the Hunt administration. Mr. Noctor, without any pledge or suggestion, specific or understood, as to patronage, offered to do all he could to help.

It now became necessary obviously to organize a campaign and to organize it thoroughly. Miss Fennell continued in charge of the office, which was opened on August 27. Mrs. Fenton Lawson was in charge of ward and precinct meetings and Miss Emily Kneubuhl was employed as executive to organize the women. There had been none or only a few who had been consulted in the actual drafting of the amendment, but their enthusiastic response to the publicity and organization work was instant and vehement.

It was necessary to have a speakers' bureau and to secure speakers who could address all types of civic and neighborhood groups. It was also necessary to make some provision for securing witnesses for the count, for there was no question what would happen in many precincts if witnesses were not there. Each precinct had a Republican judge and two clerks, and the same for the Democratic side, but granting the best of intentions on the part of Democratic leaders, their workers, especially in the downtown wards, were very apt to be in collusion with the Republicans.

This was the fall of the campaign of Calvin Coolidge for the Presidency. There was also, of course, a campaign in the County of Hamilton between the Republican ticket, nominated in an August primary for the county offices and also the state offices, against the Democratic ticket having the candidates for the same offices. In

THE NEW CITY CHARTER—1924

view of the furor of the national election, which always creates difficulties for those interested in local issues, the attention of the public to the local fight was surprising.

The old organization, having complete control of the city council, attempted to obscure the issues by proposing two other and different amendments themselves, at the very time they voted, as they were compelled to do by law, to submit the City Charter Committee amendment. They eliminated proportional representation, of course, and retained the mayor-council plan, but they did make various minor changes in the existing form. It was highly unimportant what the other two amendments proposed, for when people are in a mood to overturn what they conceive to be bad, and are presented with an alternative by a group in whom they have confidence, the details of the change do not greatly interest them. At least this is true of the large group of independent voters in the middle of the road, who really decide elections.

What was a most difficult problem was how to keep the people from being confused by the three proposals that seemed in the summary description so similar. Under the election laws as they then existed, these three amendments had to be placed upon the same ballot, or so the county prosecutor advised the Board of Elections. When it was discovered that the other two preceded the amendment of the City Charter Committee on the ballot, the effort was made to educate the public to vote "No, No, Yes"; "No" on the first two organization amendments, "Yes" on the charter amendment.

I have called them "organization" amendments, but the organization never formally endorsed them, or took formal action against the third. No one seemed to be guiding the regulars in any consistent plan of campaign. They seemed utterly disorganized. A purported Citizens Protective Committee to support one of the other amendments, and oppose the city charter amendment, a number of whose members had not authorized the use of their names, was said to have agreed to a debate, but it was called off by Mr. Hynicka without a meeting of the group. Finally, a week before election, he came out personally, but not officially, against the charter committee amendment.

This was one of the first of many instances where the City Charter Committee has been greatly aided by a few more or less fortuitous circumstances, or at any rate circumstances which its leaders had done nothing to produce. In every election the other side, the Republican machine, could be counted on to do the wrong thing at the right time. For instance, besides the two fake amendments, they attempted on the eve of election to prevent the Charter Committee from having witnesses at all. At once a number of lawyers interested in the Charter cause proposed to hire an airplane to send a representative to Columbus to file a mandamus suit in the Supreme Court of Ohio, to force granting the right which unquestionably existed under the statutes then in force. The threat was then withdrawn. All that resulted was fine publicity for the Charter cause.

It was difficult to anticipate in the course of this campaign how it would come out, although hindsight shows the result was inevitable. The organization with the tradition of many years of victory behind it was confident, really overconfident. The Charter Committee forces were active, eager and yet restrained by the deadening fear that somehow, somewhere the old crowd would again land on top.

The joint debates in this campaign were its high spots. Froome Morris and Gilbert Bettman were the protagonists of the existing order. It was as early as September 10 that Morris and Bentley met.

"The charter amendment proposes to destroy the present form of government which is fundamentally the type of government used in the United States and Ohio governments," said Morris.

"The first defect in the present charter," said Bentley, "is the divided responsibility, and that is a defect of business management. Every Ohio corporation is governed as we propose to govern the city. Under the Ohio laws it is run by a Board of Directors who are elected by a form of proportional representation, and they select the general manager, just as city council is to be elected in the same way and is to choose the city manager."

Bettman chimed in a week later. "The adoption of the city manager plan of government for Cincinnati would take away from the people the right to elect their own chief executive. The proposal is based upon the idea that executive government is a matter of expert knowledge," said he. A few days later he debated the matter with Robert Goldman, and afterwards with Guy Mallon, Bentley and Seasongood in order. Bentley and Morris met again, and Bettman closed the campaign by meeting Walter Knight and then Walter Millard.

On election day the City Charter Committee had men as witnesses in all the downtown polling places with full instructions as to the kind of fraud to look out for. My own report to the committee is perhaps typical of our experiences.

I went to the polling place of Precinct C, Ward 16, at No. 1155 Linn Street, on Monday night before election day. The Republican election officials were on hand but the Democrats seemed to have considerable difficulty in getting their quota. Those present obviously talked for my benefit considerably, and suggested that the clerks mark the tallies on many of the columns of the tally book up to 100 in order to save time. They also indicated that they expected to count two or three sets of ballots at once. Before leaving I indicated that I was going to object to this strenuously.

When I came back the next evening, it was suggested that the Charter ballots be counted first, but when I stated that I was going to stay until the end anyway, that proposal was dropped. I was acquainted with the Republican witness, who is the Precinct Executive, and a nice fellow, and I think that helped. As soon as I insisted on counting each ballot separately, there was no further objection, and this was done.

When we came to the Charter ballots, the last ones counted, my suggestion that each of the three questions be counted separately and each completed before the next was begun met with no objection, and the count was completed in that way.

The result was decisive. The charter which was supported by the City Charter Committee was victorious by a vote of 92,510 to 41,015, while the other two charter amendments were decisively defeated. Great was the triumph and great was the rejoicing among all good citizens of the community. The vote had been overwhelming and showed clearly the temper of the people, in a year when President Coolidge received the highest majority of any presidential candidate up to that time, and the Republican county ticket was elected by an equal majority. A new day had arrived in Cincinnati.

CHAPTER SIX

THE GREAT DECISION AND THE FIRST CHARTER VICTORY—1925

WITH this victory a difficult question was presented to the organizers of a successful revolt. They had before them the example of the city of Cleveland, where a group had prepared what was thought to be an ideal charter, and in planning for its first election in 1923 sought only to insure an independent representation in their city council, without attempting to elect a majority. The Citizens League and other civic organizations had indicated their opinion of the various candidates who presented themselves, but no one had made an effort to stimulate candidacies of capable individuals, and there had been no organization formed with the object of electing any such selected group.

The City Charter Committee had several alternatives. Should it, as in Cleveland, simply investigate and publish the results of such a study of the records and character of all candidates who should present themselves? Should it make an effort, on the other hand, to stimulate the candidacy of capable individuals, and yet make no special effort to elect them or any other candidate, except by a general endorsement and a description of their capacity? Or should it organize as it had for the adoption of the amendment, and work to elect a group, either nine, the number provided for the entire council, or a smaller number in proportion to its estimated strength? The question did not have to be decided at once, and was discussed for many weeks.

The first step toward the new day seemed to the Charter leaders the crystallization of public sentiment and goodwill into a permanent organization. It was decided to have a victory dinner in January, and Professor C. E. Merriam, that great civic warrior, was invited from Chicago to address what it was hoped would be a crowd. There had been many groups interested in the campaign for the charter, but they had never been really brought to a feeling of unity. They joined only in their protest against what they were called upon to endure at the city hall. When the night of the dinner arrived, there appeared a very interesting crowd, bearing somehow a strong resemblance in personnel and attitude to the group which had supported social welfare agencies.

Merriam struck the keynote:

Your vote last fall for the City Manager form of government will have no more validity than a New Year's resolution unless it is carried out. America is filled with the wrecks of charters that were shattered on the shores of public indifference and because the people ceased to care.

If Cincinnati's interest lags, this will only become another law to clutter up the statute book. Be very sure that greed and selfishness will not be asleep. Those who profit by misgovernment will be active and energetic. You who want a government, honest instead of crooked, efficient instead of wasteful, need not wait for the millennium. Your chance to secure it is here if you will but seize it.

And then that equally great civic warrior, John M. Withrow, started the permanent form of the City Charter Committee by moving the resolution that gave the existing executive committee of six power to add five more to its number, and to draft a constitution.

After that organization proceeded rapidly; a constitution was adopted (in accordance with the best American practice), and the Executive Committee was expanded into a Board of Directors of eighteen.[1] The new board went to work with the same staff, Miss Kneubuhl and Miss Fennell.

What was the new organization to do? Besides the question of its policy for the next year, there was the task of redeeming certain pledges made in the campaign. The committee backing the amendment had urged the abolition of the city primary, and the substitution of nomination by petition, as recommended by the Upson Report. This meant the elimination of $30,000 of useless expense, especially as there were no city officers to be nominated now, except personal property assessors, the municipal court clerk, and the municipal court judges. A bill was prepared and submitted to the Hamilton County legislative delegation to be introduced in the session that was to begin on the first of January. At the same time a bill was prepared to give the City Charter Committee or any similar organization the right to have witnesses and challengers at the polls to protect the interests of its candidates, something apparently restricted to the two national parties, or to the supporters of a state constitutional amendment or a city charter amendment. The legislative delegation pledged its aid in the passage of both.

But the pledge was never binding on the organization apparently, for it promptly set about to defeat both measures. That for the Charter witnesses and challengers never had a chance in spite of the good faith of some of the legislators, and that for the abolition of the city

[1] The first board consisted of Henry Bentley, president; John D. Ellis and Philip Ziegler, vice-presidents; Guy W. Mallon, secretary-treasurer; Edward F. Alexander, John M. Cronin, Harry Freiberg, Miss Agnes Hilton, Ralph Holterhoff, Julian A. Pollak, Mrs. Clara M. Pressler, Stanley M. Rowe, Murray Seasongood, Walter Schmidt, Charles P. Taft, 2d, Mrs. Guy A. Tawney, Carl H. Voellmecke and Dr. John M. Withrow. It was elected at a meeting of the charter members at Christ Church parish house.

primary was languishing in committee as the end of the session approached. It took a general letter to the members of the City Survey Committee, and their demand as a group upon Mr. Hynicka, to secure the passage of the city primary abolition bill. Such stupid obstruction on the part of the organization, beginning in 1924 and continuing through 1930, never accomplished its object and generally proved of assistance to the good government group. It seems to be an outstanding characteristic of intrenched political machines.

But this left the general question of policy unanswered, and the group was not unanimous by any means. Bentley's general ideas have been noted in one of his Cincinnatus addresses a year before. He wanted to organize in the wards and precincts. Seasongood was not so sure. It was early determined that members should be secured in any event and that a ward and precinct approach was a convenience in this regard. And, of course, finances were needed to do anything, to follow at all the suggestion of Professor Merriam. Action they were determined upon, whichever direction it took. So committees were formed on the fundamental problems of organization, membership and finance. Miss Kneubuhl was called to Rochester about the first of March, and on March 16, 1925, she was succeeded by Miss Edna Strohm, who has helped to guide the destinies of the City Charter Committee ever since. By the first of April there were nearly fourteen hundred members, and a ward and precinct organization was well under way among the women. A speakers' bureau was at work addressing civic associations, church groups and women's clubs, and literature explaining the new charter and the new method of voting was being distributed. Ward meetings were held, and with the membership campaign helped to promote finance. The newspapers, including those which had opposed the

THE FIRST CHARTER VICTORY—1925

new charter, were glad and anxious to publish all the material they could get.

By the first of May there were 700 ward workers in 18 out of the 26 wards, but membership began to slow down; only 106 were added in the month, and 112 in May, which was typical of the Charter Committee's experience down through the years. The goal of 10,000 set by the Board of Directors has never been approached. A résumé on July 1 showed 10 wards out of 26 at least fairly well organized, six and a half described as hopeless because of being in the downtown area, and the balance with good prospects as soon as the campaign excitement began.

Meantime discussion continued. An early proposal was to prepare a platform which every candidate who wished the endorsement of the City Charter Committee must sign. It was to contain a pledge that, the signer, if elected would not vote for anyone for city manager who was not approved by a committee of citizens, such as Dean Herman Schneider of the University of Cincinnati, some professor from St. Xavier College, a representative of labor, and a woman. The platform was also to contain a pledge to carry upon all the candidate's campaign literature all the persons endorsed by the City Charter Committee, and while requesting all his friends to vote for him for first choice, to urge them to vote for the others so endorsed for subsequent choices. This showed a thorough understanding of the basis of proportional representation, for it meant the pooling of a solid block of votes attracted by one or more of the candidates endorsed. There was no danger of loss by spreading the vote if everyone was urged to vote for all of them.

But the pledge plan was too complicated, and gradually the ideas of the group crystallized on the plan adopted: To nominate nine candidates, pledged to support each other but without strings affecting their independent judgment on any questions, especially the selection of the city manager. The platform was simple:

A NEW DEAL—BUSINESS METHODS IN GOVERNMENT—FREEDOM FROM POLITICAL BOSSES

The candidates selected were not to be left out on a limb, so to speak, to finance and run their own separate campaigns, but the City Charter Committee was to organize completely in wards and precincts to elect them, and run one main campaign for them all.

That was an epochal decision. At the time it seemed a natural result to reach, growing out of long discussion and preliminary decisions as questions arose. But it represented a political method theretofore unknown in municipal reform, and it marks the most distinctive feature of the whole Cincinnati experiment. If we have contributed anything to the permanent good of our nation, politically speaking, it is this plan, rather than the service of any particular individual.

Who were to be the candidates? The decision must be made quickly, for already hopeful aspirants were circulating petitions, and under the charter a citizen could sign only one. A general request was sent out to all civic groups asking for suggestions, and the nominating committee made up lists of all available timber. These were classified, for purposes of consideration, by political affiliation, nationality (German, Irish or American descent), residence and religion. There were certain outstanding candidates as to whom none of these considerations made the slightest difference, as, for instance, Seasongood himself; but the Charter group were sufficiently good politicians to know that the ticket should be well balanced. It was early decided that the proportion of Democrats and

THE FIRST CHARTER VICTORY—1925

Republicans in the city must be recognized by dividing the ticket six Republicans and three Democrats; of course, certain large and somewhat self-conscious areas must be represented; and finally the candidates proposed must accept; all of which suggests that if there is a more thankless and difficult job in the world than picking a ticket and getting the candidates to accept in what might be called a reform movement, I don't know what it is.

Nevertheless, the job was well done. At the head stood Seasongood. Then followed Tylor Field, a member of one of the old families, but popular with labor groups through his business as a general contractor (on private work). Cecil Gamble's name speaks for itself in Cincinnati and elsewhere, and his character stood equally high in business and charitable enterprises. All three were Republicans. Through the efforts of Bentley, Johnson, Ellis and Weinig the Democrats were induced to accept the three out of nine places and to suggest three names acceptable to the Charter Committee. Stanley Matthews was a greatly respected and able judge of the state court, a Democrat elected by a Republican town. Edward T. Dixon had recently retired from the same bench to private practice, a poor boy who had risen high in his profession, and one of the best known Catholic laymen of the city. William J. Higgins, a business man from the principal Democratic suburb, was not so well known, but stood well in his own community. Of the remaining three Republicans, Julius Luchsinger was the labor representative, being at the time the president of the street car men's union, and Mary Hicks was one of the leading social workers in the city, besides being active in women's clubs.

Charles O. Rose deserves a longer thumbnail sketch. He was a lawyer who had served in the prosecutor's office early in his practice, and then in 1916 again took an interest in politics and was elected to council from his ward, one of the better residence wards. But he soon proved too honest and independent for the organization, and when they redistricted the city in 1921 they gerrymandered him into a different ward where he was expected to be beaten. He went to work, and to the surprise of everyone came out on top again. He showed great interest in the subject of gas and electric franchises, opposing several of the dubious franchises that gave the Charter so much ammunition. There was grave doubt in the minds of the Charter Committee as to putting him on the ticket; they seldom made a better choice. He became the watchdog of the treasury and prevented what so often wrecks a reform administration, too much spending. Cincinnati's unique financial position is largely owing to him.

The announcement of the ticket came just about the first of June, and was greeted with acclaim. The great advantage of proportional representation was soon seen, because even the single one of the four daily papers that was against the Charter could not avoid endorsing a majority of the ticket, each man of which was running on his own personal strength in addition to the platform of the City Charter Committee.

Proportional representation permits an individual to support one or more of the candidates on a ticket even though he may be violently in disagreement with others of the candidates. It is conversely true that if a candidate draws the support of a particular individual or group, by doing so he makes it somewhat more likely that that individual or group will also vote for one or more of his associates on the Charter ticket.

These facts explain the general strategy determined upon by the City Charter Committee. It sought in selecting candidates to secure persons well distributed geographically. There are geographical areas which have acquired for one reason or another a strong sense of indi-

THE FIRST CHARTER VICTORY—1925

viduality and of community loyalty. That loyalty must be recognized in order to avoid stirring it to enmity against the whole ticket. The effort was made and made successfully to secure a ticket that was representative of differing racial and religious views, and of different economic strata of society. The general policy, then, was to urge every candidate to work hard for first choice votes for himself, but to speak in favor of all of his associates and to try to secure for them second, third, fourth and other choices up to nine. Even if it was likely that the City Charter Committee would elect only six of its candidates, nevertheless, the fact that nine were running and that the friends of all nine were interested in the campaign helped to produce additional votes for those who were most likely to be successful.

In contrast with this policy, the organization, evidently misconceiving the method by which proportional representation worked and its entire basis in theory, selected only six candidates, and then divided the whole city into six districts and allotted each of the districts to one of the six candidates. The results were most amusing. One of their candidates was Mr. Schneller, who was still the clerk of council under the old charter, a nephew of Lou Kraft previously referred to as holding the gambling franchise for Hamilton County in the early days, and successor to his uncle's place as the ward captain of the Eighteenth Ward, the center of the west end and the center of the black belt. Since he was one of the leading members of the Republican organization, it was obvious that he must be given a downtown area. One of the other six candidates, however, was Adolph Kummer, the German president of the Central Labor Council. Since he could not be given the downtown area, it was decided for some unknown reason that he should be given an area which included Avondale, the center of most of the Jewish vote, and Clifton, another one of the better residential districts. As a matter of fact, at that period Schneller lived in Avondale himself, and it was too much to expect that he should leave that area to Kummer. In fact, he did what might have been expected and cut under Kummer to the best of his ability in that neighborhood. Before election day arrived, the tempers of the six candidates on the Republican side were anything but pleasant and their failure to coöperate had its effect without any doubt on the number of votes they received.

Publicity in this campaign was easy. It must have seemed to the harassed leaders of the organization that some one of their cohorts was putting his foot into it just as they were pulling his predecessor's out. The Cincinnatus Association started early in the year. I was elected president in January, and immediately appointed committees on all the subjects in which we were or might be interested. There were committees on streets and street bond issues; on the street-lighting contract (both gas and electric); on the garbage contract; on county and city budgets; on the gas contract; on the sheriff and the roadhouse problem; and many others. And, of course, Mr. Seasongood individually and as a member of the City Survey Committee, was not letting the grass grow under his feet. On February 5 he addressed a letter to the badgered Mr. Hornberger, still service director, calling attention to various discrepancies between the request for bids for the collection and disposal of garbage and the ordinance which authorized the request. "As a matter of interest to you," wrote Mr. Seasongood, "to show you that the existing contract has been extremely profitable to the contractor, the Cincinnati *Post* of November 17, 1924, shows that the Union Reduction Company paid income tax for 1923 in the amount of $11,402.57. As the tax was 12½ per cent, this company therefore made net approximately $91,000. Doubtless this was after charging off liberal amounts for depreciation and paying liberal salaries. You have no doubt been informed that the residents in the vicinity of the plant held a public meeting and have complained very much about the odors."

A few weeks later council suddenly passed ordinances authorizing the advertisements for bids for a gas street-lighting contract for three years and for an electric rate contract for ten years. Laurent Lowenberg, a member of the appropriate Cincinnatus committee, investigated at once and the next day Cincinnatus through its executive committee sent a letter to the mayor condemning the period of the electric contract as tying up the city for too long a time, contrary to good municipal practice in view of the constant reductions in the cost of electricity.

At about the same time an ordinance was proposed to fix the rates for private consumers of natural gas. The Cincinnatus gas franchise committee, headed by John Ellis, at once condemned the proposed rates because they were fixed merely upon the useful value of the local company, the Union Gas & Electric Company, without any investigation as to whether the wholesale rate paid at the Kentucky state line to another one of the subsidiaries of Columbia Gas & Electric Corporation was justified or not. An independent report indicated that this was exorbitant. The association approved its committees' report and urged through the press that all civic associations be represented at the hearing before the council committee. The matter was debated several times in the next month before the association between the very genial and able head of the local utility, Mr. W. W. Freeman, and Ellis. Nevertheless, the ordinance was passed over the mayor's veto on May 19.

There had been some organization sympathizers in the association, and the effectiveness with the public of this constant pounding can be realized from this outburst from one of them who was a little behind in his dues. "I do not wish to have my letter or my check regarded as an application for reinstatement in the association, nor do I wish to be reinstated either automatically or on any other basis. I am so much out of sympathy with, and opposed to, most of the things which the association has done or attempted to do in the past few years that I am glad to be out on any terms."

During this winter of 1924-25 the United States government had prosecuted a large number of the Cincinnati police for violation of the prohibition laws, in particular for accepting bribes from liquor dealers. Most of them pleaded guilty, but a few stood trial, and in the course of the whole matter it appeared that one of the organization members of council, Mr. Joseph Reichert, a member of the council Committee on Light, and a saloonkeeper of the city, had taken an immunity bath by testifying against some of the policemen in the grand jury, to the effect that he had bribed them. Such an opportunity was too good to be missed and a special Cincinnatus committee headed by Russell Wilson wrote to the prosecuting attorney to demand state prosecution of Reichert for bribery. Here is a quotation:

Mr. Reichert stands guilty of this statutory offense. The evidence is available. The men he bribed are now in the Atlanta penitentiary. The detailed information against Mr. Reichert is in the possession of the United States government, whose Department of Justice holds no brief for Mr. Reichert and without doubt would release the evidence upon request from the officials of the State of Ohio, of whom you are one. Indeed, it would tax the legalistic ingenuity of any prosecuting attorney to fail in securing the indictment and conviction of a man who thus has confessed his crime that he might secure immunity of the Federal courts in exchange for the imprisonment of the men whom he bribed.[1]

This is more than a simple case of bribery. Mr. Reichert is a member of the Council of the City of Cincinnati. He is not only sworn to uphold the laws of state and nation, but on him rests the duty of helping to make the laws of the city. He who bribes is as guilty as he who accepts the bribe, and, by the same token, a man who will give a bribe will take a bribe. In his present position, Mr. Reichert is a menace to the community. His idea of public service evidently is that of one who helps his pocket by betraying his constituency and his city. Since he has stood before the community as a self-confessed briber, he has made no contrite move to resign the honorable office he holds. His silence is a defiance of common honesty and of the spirit of our institutions, and his retention of office is simply brazen notice that he is for sale. But there is relief for the City of Cincinnati if you take action. Section 12824 of the Revised Statutes of Ohio is as follows:

> "A person convicted under the next preceding section (12823) is disqualified from holding any public office or appointment under this state, and, if not a state officer, shall be removed from office or employment by order of court."

If you prosecute Mr. Reichert, as is your duty, he may become imbued with the spirit of resignation, and vacate the office that he is so unworthy to hold. Our City Council is a temple, from which a money changer like Joseph Reichert should be driven.

Your duty as an official of the State whose laws Joseph Reichert has violated is plain. To you there can be no alternative, if you realize the spirit and the letter of the law. And we have confidence that you will perform your duty, despite the political influence and cynical defiance of the law

[1] The prosecutor's problem was not so simple as Wilson stated, for Reichert's confession could be used only if the crime were proven, and there was considerable difficulty in getting other evidence.

of one who has proved himself not only unworthy of holding honorable office, but of enjoying citizenship itself.

The Prosecutor then announced that he had requested the Attorney-General of the United States to turn over the testimony, and Cincinnatus followed up the request with a personal letter to Hon. John G. Sargent. But nothing happened, and Mr. Reichert continued to serve in council and on the Light Committee. The listening electorate of Cincinnati did not miss a word.

The next important step involved the County Budget Commission which met in August and September. It was prepared to take what the county needed, give the schools what the law said they must have, and let the city receive what was left. Again the Cincinnatus Association came to the fore, and with Mr. Bentley, representing the Charter Committee, started a blast of publicity. The newspapers coöperated by following the hearings in a way that had never been done before, and half a million dollars more was pulled out of the hat, so to speak, to permit the city's proposed budget to balance.

The first move in the active campaign came from Mr. Hynicka. There had been an imposing Executive and Advisory Committee, and it was assumed that it would continue; but suddenly on September 19, without even a meeting, it was apparently discharged, as Mr. Seasongood remarked, like a lot of officeboys, and a new committee of eleven was announced, all good old political names, long known in the organization.

One more splendid campaign argument was furnished to his opponents when Mr. Hynicka permitted Wm. V. Dwyer, the well-known sporting man of New York, to come out to Cincinnati and raise the money from the organization people large and small to build and operate the Coney Island Race Track, about ten miles up the Ohio

THE FIRST CHARTER VICTORY—1925

from the city. The Ohio laws prohibited gambling at this time, but in a few counties of the state complaisant sheriffs and other public officials could be found who would either do nothing or gave administrative rulings that the contribution system of betting was not contrary to law. In Hamilton County Sheriff Witt, after a thorough investigation, said he could find no gambling at the track (which was operating under the pari-mutuel system); and the Prosecutor, who was also the campaign manager for the organization, said nothing. Again the Cincinnatus Association stepped forward and addressed the sheriff in protest.

The economic effect of one hundred and eighteen days of racing in the vicinity of Cincinnati is deplorable, and most of the additions to our floating population in that period are degrading. The merchants of Cincinnati are feeling the drain of money now, with the racing not yet over, and they will feel it even more in the Christmas shopping period. There is less money with which to pay cash and less money with which to pay bills. Savings accounts are being wiped out, homes will not be paid for, Christmas presents will not be bought. Peculations by employees are numerous, many of them petty and therefore not made public, but nevertheless the cause of blighted business careers and financial distress to relatives. Our streets have been adjuncts of what seems to be a political gambling device, and home-going citizens bumped over Front Street while the returning racegoers were directed to the comparative boulevard along Third and Martin Streets. The Coney Island racing season is over, but the chance still remains for you, sir, to do your duty and insure that 58 days of racing in Hamilton County in 1925 shall be reduced to none in 1926.

As if their mistakes would never end, the organization clerk of the municipal court proved to be a defaulter and disappeared to Canada, and he has never returned. An epidemic of rabies was blamed by the Academy of Medicine upon the failure of the sheriff to perform his duty upon stray dogs.

The high spot of the speaking campaign was the meeting at the Avondale School a week before the election. I quote much of the published part of Seasongood's speech.

This is the birthday anniversary of a great American, Theodore Roosevelt. Let us be glad that such a man lived and gave his strength to the betterment of government and let us cherish his memory in grateful remembrance. Let us hope, too, that November third will be for this city a day of congratulation and a new birth of freedom.

In the recent meeting of Mr. Hynicka with his clacquers and supes, the precinct workers, the *Enquirer* says I was referred to as a "loud speaker and chanticleer."

Perhaps I am a loud speaker, but it is necessary to be such to make my opponents running for office—and my gracious, how they are running (away)—hear me, because they will not get on the platform with our candidates, but content themselves with whispering slanders which cannot be checked or refuted. Well, if I am a loud speaker, I am right here and it is not necessary to get New York or California to hear what I have to say. As to chanticleer, our opponents simply will not recognize that we are dealing with a birdless ballot. Chanticleer, in the play, tried to protect his family and neighbors from the buzzard and so the characterization is not inapposite.

Mr. Hynicka still shouts for party regularity. What has he to say of party irregularity in the person of the late clerk of the municipal court?

Every branch of the public service is demoralized under the present system. Take, for instance, the sheriff. It is his duty to gather up stray dogs. That disgruntled band of reformers, the Academy of Medicine, have twice stated in the most positive terms that the present epidemic of rabies is due to his nonperformance of this office. I suppose the children who were bitten by mad dogs which the sheriff failed

THE FIRST CHARTER VICTORY—1925

to collect were Democrats and allowed themselves to be killed purely for "political propaganda," but if the sheriff cannot collect dogs, he certainly can collect fees for feeding city prisoners at .65 a day. There are about 40,000 city prison days a year with consequent loss in excess charges of about $10,000 to the city. No wonder we have not sufficient policemen. The organization state platform took cognizance of this graft and promised to remedy it, but, of course, nothing has been done.

Mr. Hynicka says he stands on the Upson Report. If so, he is likely to fall, for the Upson Report, which was signed by one of his present candidates for council [Adolph Kummer], besides calling attention to the profit made by the sheriff, says of council:

> "Ward representatives in the very nature of things are likely to overemphasize the requirements of their localities to the detriment of the city as a whole, and we think the evidence is clear that this has been done in the past."

Truly, as the sheriff is Witt, the council is humor, or rather tragedy, the surveyor saying:

> "The great majority are mere voting automata."

If Hynicka stands on this same report, this is very hard on one of his candidates [Schneller], because the report says distinctly that the city clerk's office is overmanned and extravagant. The committee, including one of the candidates who is running, says of his fellow candidate, in his official capacity:

> "The report on clerk of council shows that his staff could be cut down materially with resultant saving."

This same candidate, after an open primary had been promised President Harding, threw his ward, the eighteenth, so hard for Wood, that there was practically not a Harding vote in it.

What reliance can be placed on any promise they make?

A choice bit from Seasongood's last speech before the election was this:

A friend who is a great traveler recently told me of a striking similarity in the government of Constantinople and that of Cincinnati, as it has been administered. I knew we were in the same latitude, but I have not realized before that we have sunk to the same depth. Stray dogs roam the streets there in large numbers and the streets are full of holes. On one day each year, however, the Sultan rides from his palace to the Treasury. In preparation for that day, all the dogs are kept off the streets over which he rides and the holes are filled up to make his transit comparatively safe. In a few days thereafter, the dogs are again at large and the streets are again full of holes.

Such was the campaign to the public. But how was this new political method working? An examination of the organization as it was operated for the last month before election might be of interest. The general headquarters of the Charter Committee was in an office building, being the year-round offices expanded to fit the campaign need. A vacant store was secured in a favorable location with volunteers in charge as far as possible to answer questions and furnish literature. At the headquarters you would find either Mr. Bentley or his right bower, Max Hirsch, or both, at any hour from nine in the morning to six in the evening, and you would also often see John Ellis, head of the men's organization. These men were volunteers, although in most subsequent campaigns the executive of the men's organization has been paid for his time. If an ideal man had been discovered, he might have relieved Bentley and Hirsch of much detail, but our movement has always demanded the full time of at least two such leaders for at least the last three weeks.

They had as full-time head of the office and organizer

THE FIRST CHARTER VICTORY—1925

of women's work, Edna Strohm, whose devotion was at least equal to theirs, and whose ideas of method were similar. All three were glad to give publicity and credit where it did the most good, that is, to candidates, public officials and leaders in the organization.

Literature consisted of candidates' cards, miscellaneous pamphlets from outside sources and sample ballots. Upon the cards appeared the candidate's name and photograph and on the back "Vote for all Nine," with the complete Charter ticket.

The men's and women's organizations were quite separate and neither could be said to have jurisdiction over the other. There was in each a ward captain for all wards except downtown, and precinct workers in most precincts. The women tried to have a worker for each block and generally succeeded. The distribution of sample ballots and other literature in the last week of the campaign gave an excuse for them to poll the precincts, that is, talk to every householder or his wife, find out how they felt, and promote Charter ideas. The men took care of the polling place on election day, challenging voters if necessary, and in the afternoon checked off on a printed voters' list who had voted. This they turned over to the women precinct worker and with her assistants she chased the forgetful to the polls before closing time. None of this organization has ever been paid, a policy not easy to maintain in depression years, since Republicans and Democrats alike continued to pay their workers for election day.

A word should be said about the Democratic organization. In picking our own independent group we made no distinction either among the men or the women as to whether they were Democrats or Republicans. We did want true independents whatever their national party label. We did not want men or women active in the Democratic organization, for that meant consolidation in effect. The Democratic organization followed the general lines of the Republican, but with fewer jobs and less money for work on election day they were naturally weaker. The few jobs came from the Democratic Governor, and the money from a few local stalwarts.[1]

The regular Democrats followed the Charter loyally in this election and their literature, endorsement and personal work helped elect the ticket. But in many cases the election officials representing them were young and incompetent—quite unable to cope with the tough Republicans in the downtown wards.

In many of these wards we had no organization, and these were the dangerous ones. So, in one corner of the Charter office you would find an emergency squad of young men, mostly volunteers, telephoning madly to lists of men thought to be friendly and forceful, seeking to enlist them as witnesses and challengers for the downtown wards. A great chart on the wall showed a square for each precinct and they gradually filled up with names. Then the recruits had to be instructed and on the final day before election had to be given their credentials.

In another corner worked the speakers' bureau. The street headquarters held a meeting every day at noon and someone must be scheduled there, always candidates preferred. Each ward that was organized was apt to hold a general meeting and the Charter women invented "political teas" in the various neighborhoods. Two or three big meetings were worked up at various stages in the campaign. The radio was just beginning to come into use, and speakers had to be secured and trained for all these occasions, if candidates were unavailable.

Most of this was grist for the publicity mill, handled by some experienced newspaper man and doled out to the papers.

[1] They are at last reaping their reward in the new administration.

THE FIRST CHARTER VICTORY—1925

And all of it was directed and served by many men and women who sought no pay in money and no reward in jobs, graft, public utility retainers or other compensation, and refused them when occasionally there was opportunity to profit in that way.

The visitor to headquarters might see a conference going on about finances, but generally that touched the office only by way of the budget, carefully planned in advance and strictly adhered to. Outside the office the finance committee was busy raising the necessary funds. From the beginning the City Charter Committee was a permanent organization which engaged in an active campaign for only a part of every other year. For this reason it has always distinguished its normal and regular annual budget from the campaign budget. The director of its finance committee from the beginning has been Ralph Holterhoff; without his efforts the movement in the city would have failed just as surely as it would have without the distinctive abilities of Murray Seasongood and Henry Bentley. In the summer of 1925, Mr. Holterhoff did what he has done in nearly every year since that time, whether the campaign was for the charter in the city or for the Citizens Committee in the county; he resigned as chairman and induced someone else to take the job. But in every year including 1925 he has personally raised most of the substantial sums, amounting to a large part of the total sinews of war. The financial report for the year 1925 is typical:

Cash on hand Jan. 1, 1925........	$258.27
Total deposits for the year........	24,183.10
	$24,441.37
Total expenditures for year.......	21,482.84
Balance in bank Dec. 31, 1925....	$2,958.53

The plan at the beginning of 1925 was to raise $30,000 for each of three years to make sure of the success of the movement. That goal was not reached, the total expenditure in noncampaign years ranging around $12,000 and in prosperous campaign years $35,000 altogether.

The campaign, besides the fireworks and the machinery, contained one of the most thorough pieces of educational work in Cincinnati's history. The people had to be told what this new charter was that they had adopted, and they had to be shown how to vote. The change in the charter was fundamental, but not hard to explain. Only one of the 13 titles had been changed, that having to do with the mayor and council. The old council of thirty-two was wiped out, and in its place was substituted a small council of nine elected at large by proportional representation. The system of proportional representation selected was the Hare system, which eliminates party designations, and therefore requires nomination by petition. The charter called for between 500 and 700 signatures to nominate.

The mayor, formerly the chief executive of the city, elected by the people, became under the charter the presiding officer of council, elected by it from its own members, and the titular or official head of the city. He had no executive power, except that of appointing the city auditor, and the members of certain boards. The head of the administrative service of the city was to be the city manager, chosen by the council for an indefinite term, and removable by it only after a hearing. Council was forbidden to interfere with his appointments in the city's service, which were to be under classified civil service almost exclusively. On the other hand, the theory of the plan so splendidly carried out in the next years was that the city manager should not interfere with the decision of questions of policy, but should simply give his advice

THE FIRST CHARTER VICTORY—1925

when asked and carry out what council ordered. The general administrative set-up was to be under the direction of council.

Equally effective was the educational campaign on how to vote. Schools were held before every type of organization, with the surprising result that the invalid ballots were actually a lower percentage of the total vote cast than in any recent election.

The results of the vote could not be known election night, but enough could be known to foretell a great Charter victory, and Dixon and Seasongood had over 20,000 votes each in a total cast of about 120,000 [1] and were surely elected. In due time it appeared that the Charter had elected six of the nine on its ticket and missed the seventh by only 77 votes. The other three places went to the Organization. If there had been rejoicing after the election on the charter amendment in 1924, it was superlative rejoicing that followed the victory so won in the famous year of 1925.[2]

[1] Cincinnatians pointed with pride to the fact that Cleveland, a city of exactly twice the population, in their city election on the same day polled only 105,000 votes.

[2] An interesting side light on the election was the fact that a whole set of bond issues, many of them previously defeated, were passed by substantial majorities, evidently in the confidence that the new administration would have the spending of the money. But the old council was not through and made gestures as if to spend the money before they went out of office. Shouts of rage went up from the public, and the matter was dropped. In fact, it appeared after the election that as to a number, if not all, of the bond issues authorized, the ballot upon which they appeared required that they be not used until 1927, apparently with the idea that they could not then be carried out until too late to get any political benefit at the next city election. More shouts of rage.

CHAPTER SEVEN

PROPORTIONAL REPRESENTATION

I HESITATE to break the thread of my story, but I must describe the method of election that brought about our triumph, and this is perhaps the most convenient place to do it.[1]

Proportional representation has come into national prominence since it was proposed for the revised charter of the city of New York by Judge Seabury and incurred the dislike of Alfred E. Smith. It cannot be said that the distinguished editor of the *New Outlook* has added to the people's knowledge of this useful tool of democracy. I have remarked above that in 1924 I thought proportional representation a harmless element in the new charter for Cincinnati. There is hardly a supporter of the City Charter Committee today who does not feel that proportional representation is the most important single element in the success of good government in the city and must be preserved at all costs.

Proportional representation is designed to give representation in a legislative body to every group, in general thinking alike on political subjects and considered large enough to deserve representation. It is designed to prevent the situation that so frequently arises under majority rule, where because one slate has a small majority, the entire slate goes in, and the minority, with only a few votes less than the majority, has no representation. That

---
[1] If the reader wants to avoid rather interesting technicalities, let him skip this chapter. But he'll miss something good, if I do say it as shouldn't.

is not democracy or the rule of the people; it may be tyranny.

Let me illustrate. If a city such as Kansas City has a charter providing for a small council elected at large without proportional representation and if the Republicans have a majority of, say, 7,500 votes, it is likely that even the weaker candidates on that ticket will pull through, and the council will be entirely Republican. All those who voted Democratic are thereby disfranchised, and for the term of that council have no voice in the government of their city. A vote is not a voice in a democratic legislative body unless it results in the election of someone for whom you vote.

The more common form of city council is that elected by wards, what our English cousins call a "single member constituency." New York has it in the Board of Aldermen; Cincinnati had it until 1926, under its old charter. The city is laid out in small districts by the controlling machine, and the effort is always made to put as many of the opposition into the same ward as possible, and elsewhere to balance the opposition by a slightly larger number of loyal voters, no matter what strange shapes the wards may assume. The word "gerrymander" is a part of our political vocabulary, but it is not always understood that such an arrangement may give control of a city or state to a minority. In any event, the results seen in New York and in Cincinnati under this system are typical and inevitable. The last Board of Aldermen in New York had exactly one Republican out of 70 or more. Poor Joe Baldwin from the Park Avenue district had to be on every committee of the board as the whole minority in himself. If there were 69 Democrats in New York to one Republican, the result could not be complained of; but the Democratic majority, while substantial, is nothing like that. Is that democracy except with a capital "D"?

In Cincinnati the council elected in 1921 for a four-year term consisted of 31 Republicans and one Democrat—26 elected by wards and six elected at large, thus illustrating both forms of election at once. The one Democrat was from Price Hill where all the Democrats possible were collected into one area, and the six at large were all Republicans. Yet the Republican vote in 1921 was only 68,000 to 61,000 for the two opposition tickets, or 53 per cent of the whole. Democracy, if it means anything in this country, means that the policy approved by the majority must be carried out by an administration representing the majority, but surely the minority must be given representation and the opportunity for intelligent and restraining criticism. The system disclosed in these two examples is not "Americanism"; it rather resembles the single party domination of Italy or Russia or Germany.

A further investigation in either New York or Cincinnati discloses some more about what its defenders claim is the American system. The majority ticket is chosen at a party primary generally placed at a most inconvenient time for all except the organization vote. The machine cannot be beaten at that primary. The minority ticket is chosen in the same way, except that the majority organization is generally in control of the minority one through underground channels. Witness the regular Republican leaders in New York, battling this summer for their political lives against opponents making just that charge. Any sensible observer will always choose the majority organization as the lesser of two evils; there is never any real alternative. The machine in power, itself a minority, controls the city. Is that American democracy?

As stated, proportional representation is designed to give representation in a legislative body to every group in general thinking alike on political subjects which is considered large enough to deserve representation. Districting a city into wards is a geographical subdivision. But people who think alike may be scattered all over the city in many subdivisions, and, on the other hand, many geographical districts are anything but homogeneous in sentiment. A ward councilman represents a geographical constituency, or rather a part of it—the majority that elected him. A member of a council elected by proportional representation represents a constituency, a whole constituency, of people who think alike, at least in preferring him or what he stands for. It is a homogeneous constituency, but not geographical.

Under proportional representation a voter may like a candidate and vote for him because of religion, or color, or because he has the loudest voice, but surely he does that just as often without proportional representation. And if there are political organizations (as there may be under proportional representation and as there are in Cincinnati under proportional representation), whether amateur or professional, the voter can be educated to vote for the candidates of one of those organizations. If one of those political groups or parties enlists the support of a majority of the electorate, it will elect a majority of the council. There may be three groups or more, none with a majority, producing that bugaboo, government by "blocs" of which opponents of proportional representation talk. But for many years before March 4, 1933, we had just that division in the Senate of the United States into three blocs, none with a majority, and all without benefit of proportional representation.

What proportional representation does is readily seen by its results in Cincinnati. The first council when elected turned out to be four independent Republicans and two Democrats from the Charter ticket, and three regular Republicans. That meant that the voters of Cincinnati were about four-ninths independent Republican, two-ninths Democratic, and three-ninths regular Republican. Furthermore, the representation of the Democrats was not prevented because of the fact that there were more than two Democrats running, nor that of the regular Republicans because there were six candidates for the three places they secured. The three elected were the ones they preferred out of the six, the three who best represented the mind of the group. In this sense a primary to select preferred representatives was combined in the election, and with this advantage, that the entire electorate participated in it. In the elections since that time the vote for independent Republicans remained stable while the regulars increased until at the 1929 and 1931 elections there were only three independents elected to four regular Republicans, indicating what has taken place, a slight swing to regularity. The Democrats also maintained their voting strength at about the same level until 1931, when their first choice votes dropped suddenly from their average of 30,000 to only 18,000, and they only just elected their two.

Mr. Smith in his *Outlook* editorial in March, 1933, opposed proportional representation because the reformers through it proposed to do away with party government by eliminating party designations. I can hardly deny that the "reformers" to whom he refers have exactly that object in many cases, but I can assure him as one practical politician to another that proportional representation does not necessarily have that effect at all. If he does not trust my judgment, I can refer him to Newton D. Baker, who in addressing the Citizens League of Cleveland on February 4, 1930, after six years of experience, vehemently attacked proportional representation and the manager plan because, as he said, it was hypocritically maintained by the contention that it was nonpartisan, when in fact both the administration of Manager Hopkins and that of Manager Morgan, even more frankly, were political (both Republican).

The fact is that any existing political organization can continue to operate under proportional representation just as it has before if it can educate its supporters to a somewhat higher degree of intelligence. It can put up a ticket and can elect it, but the voters must be educated to know the ticket, and cannot vote for it by marking a cross under the bird with pants. The Democrats and Republicans continued to flourish in Cleveland under proportional representation, at first with an agreed division of the spoils, and then with the Republicans in and the Democrats out.

The great difference under proportional representation is that it is the only system of election under which it is possible for an amateur, independent, fusion organization, if you please, to function with any chance of permanent success. I agree with my distinguished Democratic countrymen in condemning *non*partisanship, because I believe it to be an illusion that has led innumerable reform movements in cities to ultimate defeat. But I cannot agree that the partisanship must take the form of support of one of the two national parties. There is no Republican or Democratic way of repairing streets or cleaning them, and no basis for a local division of parties along national lines except the necessities of national parties themselves, and the desire of local machines for national patronage.

We must have partisanship and a lot of it in our cities if we ever expect to get out of the slough of graft and corruption and crime in which we exist right at home in our cities where over half of our people live. But that partisanship must be in unselfish support of movements for good government, organized in the wards and precincts, without interest in political jobs or in national party divisions. And the only system of election which permits of the continued existence of such an organization is proportional representation. Proportional representation failed in Cleveland, because, as Mr. Baker said in that same speech, there were no groups that corresponded to the definition of the authors of proportional representation: there were no coherent minority groups with definite programs. In Cincinnati proportional representation succeeded because there was a coherent minority group that proved in fact by assistance of proportional representation to be a majority group: the Charter Committee. It surely can be said to have had a definite program and it has carried its program out.

So much for the general theories about proportional representation and experience with it. But is it not complicated and hard to understand? And does it not take a long time to count the ballots—to such an extent that its usefulness is destroyed?

The opponents of proportional representation, including Alfred E. Smith, in support of their affirmative answers to the first question select a paragraph from the original Cincinnati Charter Amendment and quote it without its context and without explanations of the terms used. I agree with them that it makes just about as much sense to the ordinary citizen as one page from the blueprints of the new Golden Gate Bridge or a selected paragraph from the specifications for the voting machines used in the City of New York. But the fact that I cannot read the blueprint is no reason for not building the bridge or for not riding over it when it is completed. Nor is the fact that the specifications of the voting machine make no sense to me any ground for saying it should no longer be used to stop most election frauds. I shall be able to see the bridge and I can readily understand what the voting machine does. So do the voters of Cincinnati see what proportional representation does and they are going to keep it in spite of Mr. Smith's fears for their intelligence.

It does take some days with us to count the ballots, but it makes a wonderful horse race. I am surprised that no one has introduced a bill at our last Ohio legislature to permit pari-mutuels at the count. Let me explain what happened at this first election.

The polls closed at six-thirty and within a few minutes the police messengers brought into Music Hall the first ballot boxes, from the nearby downtown precincts, sealed up, and accompanied by a sheet giving the total number of votes cast in each precinct.

At the central counting place long rows of tables were provided for the 26 wards. In each ward division was a set of bins, each approximately the size of the ballots, one bin for each of the thirty-nine candidates and one for invalid ballots. Each precinct box went to the proper ward table and was opened. The ballots were unfolded, counted and checked with the precinct report. Then they were sorted into the bins according to first choices; that is, they were put in the bin of the candidate before whose name the figure "1" appeared. The sorters were one Democrat and one Republican under the law, but the Charter was permitted to have witnesses outside a rail behind the sorters and two or three representatives for the whole count on the inside.

The first-choice ballots for each candidate were then put in envelopes marked with the ward and precinct and put in a large bin in the center for that candidate. The invalid ballots went to the Board of Elections to be passed on formally. The informal figures of first choice votes in that precinct went to the auditors to be tabulated. This process went on until fifty miscellaneous precincts were tabulated and then the results of those first-choice votes were posted for the benefit of the public who congregated by the score board, well away from the workers. And so, far, far into the night, until all but one or two stray precincts were heard from, and the workers adjourned until the next afternoon. Meanwhile the dopesters were figuring how many besides Dixon and Seasongood the Charter Committee would get, but everyone knew the victory was decisive, for the Charter candidates had 76,405 first-choice votes and the Organization only 33,304, and the twenty-four independents had 11,000-odd. The next steps were slow for the crowd. The division by wards at the tables was discarded, but the envelopes in the candidates' bins were placed in order by wards and precincts. Then each candidate was given a table and the two with surpluses several, and the official count began. At Dixon's, for instance, a team of one Republican and one Democrat sat down with rubber stamp "Dixon" and a numbering machine, and as they checked each ballot again in Ward 1, precinct A, stamped it 1, 2, 3, and so on. Any doubtful ones were sent to the Board of Elections for a ruling and those for Dixon thrown out the night before from this precinct as invalid, but upheld by the board, were restored and stamped. So for each candidate until every ballot was stamped for a candidate and numbered consecutively. The totals added to the invalids must equal the total number reported cast and no step further was taken till the balance was struck.

The total valid first-choice votes then appeared to be 119,730. There were nine places to be filled. It is obvious that ten candidates could each get 11,973 votes, and so be elected, but if each candidate be required to get 11,974, only nine could be elected ($10 \times 11,974 = 119,740$, or 10 more votes than there were). So the figure 11,974 was taken as the quota, or number of votes, that must be secured for election.

But I have stated that Dixon and Seasongood had,

respectively, 21,699 and 20,543, or a good many more than either needed for election. So, in theory, the Board of Elections said to the surplus voters for these two candidates, "Here, your man is elected without your vote and we'll let you cast it for someone else, the one you like best out of the other candidates, your 'two' man." [1]

That's fair enough, says my reader, but which of those 22,000 of Dixon's voters are you addressing? A proper question, say I. Dixon's surplus is 9,275, or 42.8 per cent of his total. Strictly speaking, I should count the second choices on all of Dixon's ballots and then give to each candidate 42.8 per cent of the second choices for him among them. But that is a terribly long process and I call to my aid Old Man Average who serves the life insurance companies so faithfully. He tells me that if I arbitrarily take out of Dixon's ballots numbered consecutively (and in order of wards) about every other ballot until I have withdrawn 9,275, I will have come within a very, very small fraction of a per cent of exactly the same result as if I followed the strict theory suggested above. And so the surplus is distributed to the other candidates who need it (of course, omitting Seasongood) and the same thing is done with Seasongood's surplus of 8,569.

Of course, that distribution changes the relative order of the remaining candidates, for now Field is third and Matthews has jumped from eleventh to sixth.

Now the board says to the lowest candidate's friends: "Here, your man can't be elected; we declare him defeated; don't you want your vote to count for someone who can be elected? Who is your second choice outside of Dixon or Seasongood?"

And here, of course, no theoretical step is needed, for the board simply takes all the ballots for that candidate,

[1] From here on I suggest the reader follow the table in the appendix, pp. 251-253, as he reads the text.

sorts them among the remaining candidates, and sends the new batches to the proper candidate's table to be stamped consecutively following his first-choice ballots and such additional ones as he got from the two surpluses.

So the process goes on until only ten are left besides Dixon and Seasongood, and only seven places. Field has reached the quota and Rose and Schneller are close. A Republican candidate is low and a Charter man next low, but the other five are bunched, three Charter and two Republican, and only 420 votes separate the top and bottom. Who of those five would get the four places?

The distribution of the low Republican's votes puts Schneller in, raises Daly well to the top and gives Lackman a lead of 1,400. The next low man, the Charter candidate Higgins, was a Democrat and he was sure to give Matthews enough to put him over. But would enough go to Gamble and Luchsinger to raise them above Lackman? Eager witnesses lean over the rail as those 7,709 ballots are redistributed among the four remaining candidates, trying to estimate the proportion going to each man. And gradually it appears that Lackman is getting quite a few, until in the final result he has 11,161, to Luchsinger's 11,265 and Gamble's 11,084. Gamble is low and loses out by 77 votes in 119,730. So the Charter has six (four Republicans and two Democrats) and the Organization three.

Just to check this result, a totaling of first-choice votes showed 76,405 for the Charter and 33,304 for the Republicans with the quota 11,974. The Charter had 6.38 times the quota, which would seem to indicate they were entitled fairly to only six places. The Organization had 2.78 times the quota, which would seem to justify their three representatives. As to the division between Democrats and Republicans in the Charter forces, Dixon, Matthews and Higgins together had 2.5 quotas and the six

PROPORTIONAL REPRESENTATION 105

Independent Republicans 3.88, so that the division into 4 and 2 again would seem as representative as possible of the true proportion among voters. Proportional representation lived up to its name.

I would add one more observation. In 1921, 61,000 voters out of 129,000 had no voice in selecting their mayor and at least that number had no representative in council for whom they had voted—47 per cent of the voters were in effect disfranchised. In 1925, 107,766 voters had at least one man in council for whom they had expressed a choice and perhaps three or more; that is, 90 per cent of the voters whose ballots were valid and 87 per cent of the total who voted. Which is the more democratic and American system?[1]

[1] As supporting this position, see editorial in the *Saturday Evening Post* for August 19, 1933, discussing Republican and Democratic representation in Congress.

CHAPTER EIGHT

THE CHARTER VICTORS IN ACTION

THE battle was over, and the victory won, but the real test of the Cincinnati experiment was only just beginning. Would the spoils be distributed or would these "hifalutin" reformers after a few fine gestures yield to the pressure of circumstances? Specifically, would they agree on a city manager? And what kind of one? Would they agree on a mayor from their own number and remain friends? And would they really run the city without patronage? How long would they present a united front to the enemy?

The six Charter councilmen and Bentley determined to get the best man in the United States. As they looked over the field in middle November, they decided that the places to find the experienced men were the City Managers' Association, soon to meet at Grand Rapids, the National Municipal League meeting at the same time in Pittsburgh, and in the municipal service of Washington, D. C., run by three commissioners under the direction of Congress. Tylor Field was sent to Grand Rapids, Bentley to Pittsburgh, Seasongood to Washington. Field brought back Edey of Berkeley, California, Bentley selected C. A. Dykstra of Los Angeles, and Seasongood's search unearthed C. O. Sherrill. Sherrill was lieutenant-colonel of engineers, formerly adjutant of the 77th Division, and at that time in charge of public buildings and grounds in the Capital. After thorough canvassing of the situation the six councilmen did agree and picked Sherrill.

Sherrill was deeply interested, but his friends had told

THE CHARTER VICTORS IN ACTION   107

him he was a fool to consider a job that was sure to be political and uncertain, no matter what the salary (already decided on as $25,000), especially as he was within a year and a half of retirement. He could never run the show on the administrative side, said they, for all the assurances of the councilmen, since the boss of the victorious party would insist on running it for the benefit of himself and his friends. When he expressed some of this feeling, Field went with him to see Bentley. Bentley assured him that he, as chairman of the City Charter Committee, would ask for no appointments and would back Sherrill against anyone else in the unlikely event that pressure might be brought on him by any such person for jobs or privileges; he was to be city manager in fact as in name. Sherrill on the spot declared his intention to accept, and the first hurdle was past.

The next question, the agreement of the six Charterites upon a mayor, was not so easily settled. Dixon had the highest number of first-choice votes and under some charters that would have meant his automatic selection. On the other hand, Seasongood had been the spearhead of the attack for three bitter campaigns. The very bitterness of his attack, inevitably upon persons, created now a most serious danger. For the Organization, to defeat the man they hated, and with some shrewdness, came to the Democrats with an offer to vote for Dixon or anyone the Democrats suggested except Seasongood, and an open split over spoils even before any work had been done was only too possible.

But Dixon and the Democrats proved stalwart in refusing to countenance a Charter split and cooler heads inside and outside the group finally brought harmonious agreement upon Seasongood. On January 1, 1926, he was sworn in as mayor and Sherrill as city manager in the old council chamber made famous, or infamous, by the execution of telegraphic orders of a nonresident boss. This new movement, its representatives youthful, clear-eyed, energetic and determined, took its place in the books of our history as the first reform enterprise of any permanence in a great city of the United States.

With these preliminary difficulties out of the way, the second civic dinner was held with all councilmen present, including the three regular Republicans. The jubilation was great and there were no clouds in the sky, but the ring of determination to live up to the campaign pledges could not be overlooked in the addresses of Bentley, Seasongood and the Charter councilmen. Again the audience of civic-minded leaders augmented by the amateur organization of women and men was an inspiration in itself to the observer.

The six Charter councilmen remained in office with one exception for the succeeding four years. Julius Luchsinger retired at the end of the first two-year term and was succeeded by Charles Eisen, not a labor representative, but a business man and former manufacturer living in the northwest district of Cincinnati. Those four years show a uniform pattern and it would do no good to follow through the various details of administration. It should be possible, however, to give a general impression of their effect under a few simple heads.

The first question presenting itself to any such group coming into a governmental organization which had been the tool of a political machine for many years, interrupted only occasionally for brief periods by comparatively ineffective reform movements, is that of personnel. That question is the first test of the sincerity of purpose of a movement which claims to stand for good government and to have for its object the reform of abuses. The Charter movement was sincere without any question. Its leaders, however, recognized that there were certain employees at the city hall, especially in a few executive positions, whose principal qualification was the ability, or reputed ability, to deliver votes on election day. Furthermore, in many cases official figures on the delivery of votes in precincts bore a questionable relation to the number of votes cast, which naturally threw considerable doubt on the honesty of the individuals concerned. It could hardly be expected that the new city manager and administration would receive any sort of service from such men, to say nothing of loyalty. Some of them were essential cogs in the Republican machine and soon resigned knowing that no further political activity on behalf of the old organization would be permitted, either actually or in spirit. At the general Victory Dinner, at which Colonel Sherrill was invited to be present and was called upon for an address, he announced what was practically agreed upon and what had been placed absolutely in his discretion, that there would be no dismissals at all at the city hall, and that all employees would be retained as long as they handled their jobs, but that under civil service requirements, political activity would not be allowed.

This announcement and this policy was a most desirable protection for the administration. The pressure for jobs from some of the Democratic portion of the coalition was great, especially during the first year and a half. The independent Republicans making such demands were fewer in number and their leaders were not at all interested in jobs. During that period the two Democratic members of council were constant pleaders at the doors of the city manager for openings for deserving supporters of the administration. The pleas were rejected except for the appointment of Higgins, the unsuccessful candidate for council, as treasurer when the incumbent resigned.

Civil service had under the machine been a dead letter.

110   CITY MANAGEMENT

The forms were complied with, the appointments were made temporarily pending an examination for the position in question; the examination was held some time later, or perhaps was never held, but in any case those who were occupying the positions had so great an advantage and the examinations were so designed that an outsider had little or no opportunity for the place. In the end no outsiders competed. Of course, there were certain instances, such as the positions under the independently elected Board of Education, and the positions under the trustees of the University of Cincinnati, where this was not at all true, and where the merit system was in full force. As the City Charter Committee came into power, the appointment of one member of the Civil Service Commission devolved upon the mayor. One member died, and the third member resigned. The result was that within a few months of the beginning of the Charter administration the Civil Service Commission had been completely reconstructed, its members appointed respectively by the new mayor, by the Board of Education, and by the trustees of the university, and it was able to institute at once personnel policies looking toward the complete and thorough adoption of the merit system.

This solution of the personnel problem had several results. In the first place, it was demonstrated that the old type of politician, selected because of his ability to produce votes on primary day and on election day, might be a thoroughly capable, honest and thorough public servant. On July 31, 1933, of the 4,400 employees on the payrolls of the city, including day laborers, 1,621 were in the service of the city on January 1, 1926. To put it a little differently, there were on the city payrolls on December 31, 1925, 3,096 persons in the classified competitive class, unskilled labor class and unclassified group. In addition there were approximately 500 in all these classes at the

General Hospital, making a total of 3,596; 1,621 of these, or 45 per cent, being still employed on July 31, 1933. This would indicate an average annual turnover of 7.3 per cent, certainly not excessive for any business the size of Cincinnati's, and in view of the low rate of pay in the earlier years compared to the rate in private business during Coolidge prosperity. In other words, all of the excellent routine work of the city administration was performed by a body of employees a large part of whom had been Republican appointees.

Another less desirable result was that a number of employees were retained whose work was adequate and satisfactory but who remained loyal to the individuals and principles under which they had been brought up and took every opportunity when unobserved, either at home or at their offices, to stir up hard feelings and enmity against the city administration. It was possible only after long periods of time gradually to eliminate the more objectionable of this type of employee.

One of the greatest changes in personnel policy was the enforcement of the new provision in the city charter, forbidding any person in the classified civil service of the city to contribute to the funds of any political organization. It had been a regular part of the Organization's methods to assess every employee, including even judges, 2½ per cent of his salary for the campaign fund. It made a sure source for the necessary sinews of war. With the advent of the Charter administration at the city hall assessments stopped, and have never started again.

I have suggested previously several happenings that were fortuitous so far as the City Charter Committee was concerned, but which made their task far easier. Two more such events need to be described in connection with the beginning of the new administration.

With the beginning of 1926 new state tax laws went

into effect which corrected the outrageous situation I have mentioned in city finance in Ohio. They were principally the work of Robert A. Taft, who did most of the drafting and was the principal leader in the Ohio House and Senate in securing their adoption. The foundation of the whole scheme was the removal of sinking fund and interest charges from all limitation so far as the tax rate was concerned, but limiting bond issues to a total amount equal to 5 per cent of the tax duplicate of the subdivision concerned, and requiring a vote of the people for nearly all such issues. It will be seen that this automatically limited the amount of the levy for debt service. To relieve the cities from the control of the County Budget Commission another law gave them the power to fix their own tax limit in their home rule charters. Budget procedure was codified and greatly improved. Without these laws the new councilmen and city manager would have been greatly handicapped.

The other fortunate occurrence was the settlement of the long dispute between the city, the Cincinnati Traction Company and the Cincinnati Street Railway, to which Mr. Seasongood made reference in several of the excerpts from his speeches mentioned above. The Street Railway Company was home-owned, but in 1901 it had leased the system perpetually to the Cincinnati Traction Company, a Philadelphia group sponsored by Morgan, Drexel & Co. A five-cent fare was profitable until 1918, when costs had mounted so much that the red figures appeared on the books. At that time a new franchise was granted providing service at cost. But political pressure was such that the fare was started at too low a point and it never was raised fast enough to catch costs. The result was that upkeep was omitted and by 1925 the tracks were in terrible condition, contributing more than their share to Mr. Hornberger's holes, and the company was not paying

THE CHARTER VICTORS IN ACTION 113

the annual franchise fee of $350,000 toward the repair of its share of the damage.

By the settlement, in which Judge Rufus B. Smith and Robert A. Taft represented the Street Railway Company, the Traction Company was eliminated, and the Street Railway took back the property and proceeded to operate it. I shall not discuss the equity of the settlement, as I might be considered somewhat prejudiced on the subject.[1] This, however, is true: The new company was able to raise new money, which the old Traction Company could not, and in the course of the five years, 1926 to 1930 inclusive, spent over $4,500,000 for the construction of 82.6 miles of single track, including the pavement between the tracks and for 18 inches outside, according to city specifications. This construction was synchronized with Colonel Sherrill's construction of streets, and formed an essential part of the city's public works program for that period, without cost to the taxpayer, except as he paid a fare not excessive in comparison with other cities. This represented an expenditure of nearly $3,000,000 more than the new franchise of 1925 called for.

The spotlight of the political interest during the course of the next four years in the city centered around a few of the outstanding members of city council, and especially around the figure of the city manager, Colonel C. O. Sherrill.

Colonel Sherrill found the physical condition of the city in a state of complete dilapidation. This gave him a fine opportunity, because his municipal experience had been greatest in the field of the construction and care of highways and other physical equipment.

In the course of the next four and a half years he literally rebuilt Cincinnati, to the point where he could say

[1] My brother is general counsel for the Street Railway Company, and our law firm represents it.

when he resigned in June, 1930, that he felt his task was done. And it was done without the slightest suggestion of graft or corruption, and with the justified feeling on the part of the people that they had received their money's worth. In addition the net bonded indebtedness of the city decreased in the process, and over $4,000,000 of the organization's deficit bonds were paid off.

The first thing that developed when Colonel Sherrill began to become familiar with his new job was the existence in unexpended and unencumbered balances at the city hall in the various departments of over $600,000, many of them in funds to finance functions that the old crowd had said had no money. For instance, the old service director had turned out street lights on the plea of having no funds, and it developed that the light fund had $45,000 left over at the end of the year. The retiring executives did not know what they had, and did not bother to find out, for their purpose was not service, but to bludgeon the people into giving them more money; so said the Charter supporters, and the argument seems reasonable.

New construction was to be by contract, and the first step was to revise the specifications to permit open bidding. The results were immediate. The prices in 1926 on asphalt, brick and recut granite were almost exactly 22 per cent under the prices for the same material in 1925, and certainly there was no general change in prices in the field of construction or in these materials to explain it. One of the contractors' rings in the city was in the field of sand, gravel and dirt; a contract let after election in 1925 had a unit price of $1.35 a yard for dirt, and when the city relet it under Sherrill, he got the same materials for .35 a yard.

One of the worst streets in the city was the main highway to the principal residence district of the city, Madison Road. It was an experiment in wood block and wooden street railway ties, and quite literally floated when it rained. One of the bond issues passed in 1925 was for $145,000 for the improvement of this street, but the joker was attached that it could not be used until 1927. After a study Sherrill reported to council that much of the foundation of the street was perfectly good and that an entirely new street was not needed, but that the paving was in such terrible condition that it should be rebuilt according to his plans at once. Council authorized it, and the new highway was finished before the end of the year for $71,000, a saving of $74,000 from the proposed bond issue, which has never been used. Furthermore, now, seven years later, the street is as good as new.

Street repair as distinguished from street building was done by the city itself, under Sherrill's direct supervision. Cincinnati had many streets like Madison Road which had foundations good enough for a great deal more wear, but whose surfaces were business-getters for automobile spring repair men. Sherrill devised the superheater scheme to meet this situation, heating the surface of the street before covering it with a coat of asphalt in order to provide a permanent bond, especially at the edges. It worked beautifully and made boulevards out of irregular collections of paving stones. Spring Grove Avenue was the outstanding example, but nearly every old street in the city now shows some sample of this type of repair.

By the end of 1926 the streets of the city were in good repair, and to the amazement of the citizens the cost of street repair for the year was only $751,000, or $36,000 less than in 1925 when they rode on holes. Where in the world had the money gone before?

Street oiling produced another amazing record. For 1926 it cost $9,039, whereas if the 1925 prices had been paid it would have cost $23,335. In the following year it cost $31,200, which at 1925 prices would have set the city back $92,302. To be accurate, it would have set the property-owners back that sum, for the cost was assessed. If it were figured out on the assessment basis, in 1925 a 50-foot lot paid $5.75; in 1927 it paid about .97. In that one item alone, the city manager saved his salary more than three times in two years. In later years the cost became so small and so much a part of upkeep that no assessment was made at all; it was absorbed as part of maintenance.

The traffic problem was an early subject of Colonel Sherrill's attention. Traffic lights had been ordered by the old administration and Sherrill installed them after some experimentation. I think I am correct in saying that he was the first to put in use the alternating red and green at successive corners that kept traffic moving, but slowly enough to be safe. He also trained pedestrians to obey the lights, which is perhaps unique to Cincinnati. Or is that too much to claim as a result of city manager government when it is more probably due to the law-abiding character of Cincinnati's German citizenry? There had been considerable complaint about the solid character of the traffic islands, and Colonel Sherrill developed a concrete safety platform that was a great improvement. These were installed all over the city with a substantial increase in the safety of pedestrians using street cars. There had not been a sign to be found on Cincinnati streets to direct the wayfarer, and a remnant of a bond issue, hitherto thought to be too small, was used to put them up inexpensively but permanently on every street corner in town.

There was a so-called central garage that took care of 75 out of 400 city vehicles. All police and fire cars were brought to a real central garage, where they were actually kept in repair, and if necessary rebuilt, all to the profit of the taxpayer. The streets were cleaned, many of them for the first time in years, and rubbish and litter began to disappear. An inventory of public property was made, and the city found to its surprise that it owned many things of which it had no idea. Many were the pieces of real estate that seemed to have been mislaid, and their rediscovery made their sale possible. Reorganization and motorization of street repair and street cleaning made possible the elimination of some unsightly yards. The total realized from such unused assets was over $109,000 that went to swell the sinking fund and reduce future levies of taxes for that purpose. The state of the city hall has already been referred to, and Sherrill at once set about a little obvious housekeeping. Within a few months the place could hardly be recognized, and when a little later the Bureau of Municipal Research made a study of office space, its layout was completely rearranged and it began to reflect the business methods at work in it. The "Sherrillizing" of the city hall, by the way, was done for the same amount of money that had left it dirty before.

A reference to the curb markets has been made. Subletting was forbidden and the city's income from the same tenants who had actually occupied the stalls before increased by about $20,000, which had gone before to the favored middlemen.

When you add to this record of accomplishment, nearly all of it within the first year, his very winning personality, touched with the soft accents of the South, you will readily understand the feeling of the people of the city toward Colonel Sherrill. He spoke at civic associations and luncheon clubs as often as he could, but finally had to restrict that, both on account of the physical strain and on account of his sound theory of the place of the manager as executive, rather than as interpreter of policy. A violent and bitter attack on him as a "carpet-bagger," which appeared in connection with the county primary fight in 1926 between his Republican supporters and the old crowd, only served to make friends for him among his enemies themselves.

Colonel Sherrill received the most loyal support from the Charter members of council. The two Democrats were under constant and unremitting pressure from their own party supporters, in matters of appointments, and yet their loyalty continued when he withstood such pressure, and on no occasion was the strength of the Charter line broken. Mayor Seasongood's theory of the operation of council was that the Charter majority should not caucus or discuss their problems except in committees or in council. The result was that on a few occasions disagreements between members of the Charter majority were aired on the floor of council when they might very well have been ironed out by equally vehement but less public discussion among the members of the group at some other place. But the Charter group rarely split, and even the Republicans seldom voted against Charter proposals. They are recorded in favor of all annual appropriation ordinances except in the most recent years.

In two fields of city administration, Colonel Sherrill had had comparatively little experience. These were welfare and police. He found the city welfare department consisting of two overworked women, the remnant of a larger and far more adequate department that had been developed and strengthened in the Hunt administration twelve years before. He found the police department underpaid, with its morale seriously injured by the revelation of bribery and corruption in connection with prohibition enforcement, to which I have already referred.

So far as the welfare department was concerned, after two years Colonel Sherrill reached the sound conclusion, urged upon him by private welfare executives, to appoint an able man as its head. He could have made no better selection than that of Fred K. Hoehler. Under Hoehler's guidance, the welfare department was gradually and carefully expanded. By 1929 the department was in a position to tackle the underlying problems even then existing, and in May of that year Colonel Sherrill, Mr. Hoehler and other civic leaders organized the citywide committee for the stabilization of employment.

In the case of the police department, the results were slower. The corruption in the department was greatly reduced if not entirely eliminated and the general morale and discipline greatly improved. The new Civil Service Commission gave special care to the problem of devising examinations and tests that would produce the best police material. The schooling process was greatly expanded and improved. The record system was overhauled and a new and complete system was installed, the first in the United States that was set up under the new uniform classification of offenses, adopted by the International Association of Police Chiefs, and now by the United States government. The city manager, however, was never willing to follow out the complete recommendations of certain studies made for him, perhaps rightly, and the problem of organization, training and development of the detective bureau was never adequately solved until more recent years.

Nevertheless such omissions were the very limited exceptions that proved the rule. The city manager installed a business-like, systematic and efficient conduct of public affairs and gained popularity in doing so. He used his own native ability, but he was wise enough to use expert advice, too, for the studies made at his request by the Bureau of Governmental Research revolutionized the conduct of many city departments.

Such an organization as this bureau is an essential part of good government. No public official has time to study the operation of his own office, nor has he the detachment of such a private, outside institution. This bureau was formed shortly after the Upson Report was issued, and as a result of the recommendations of that report. George Warrington, chairman of the Upson Committee, was its organizer and president. It brought from Newark, New Jersey, John B. Blandford, Jr., who directed its studies for the next five years. It raised from private sources a budget that enabled it to assemble all necessary information on any problem, and secured from public funds the special cost of any expert brought in from outside to study the information and work out solutions. A list of the formal studies made for the city might be of interest.[1]

One of the most important positions under Colonel Sherrill was that of city solicitor and no better choice could have been made than John D. Ellis. He was projected at once into public utility matters in connection with the electric rate referendum,[2] and a new schedule of rates asked for by the Cincinnati & Suburban Bell Telephone Company, from the Ohio Public Utilities Commission. He assisted in securing a decision from the Supreme Court of Ohio that removed the last basis for various attacks on the legality of the new charter. He was called on for innumerable opinions on the interpretation of the new charter which in many cases really involved questions of policy. His office had to draw all ordinances and his presence was always required at council meetings. It is simply an evidence of his indispensable service that he has always been acting city manager in the absence of Colonel Sherrill and of his successor, C. A. Dykstra.

[1] See Appendix.
[2] See Chapter Thirteen.

CHAPTER NINE

NOW THE COUNTY—1926

IN the meantime, while Colonel Sherrill was establishing himself at city hall, politics continued to boil and bubble on the outside, among the Republicans. After the success in the election of 1925, and the induction of the Charter majority at the city hall, it became clear that the great danger to the new administration was the entrenched Organization at the courthouse, in the county government. Among other things three of the county officers, the auditor, treasurer, and prosecutor, formed the County Budget Commission, which it will be remembered distributed tax moneys among the subdivisions. The prosecutor could often make the police look ridiculous, besides preventing coöperation by unfriendly legal opinions such as the one mentioned above with reference to the tuberculosis sanitarium.

The courthouse was especially important to the Organization because, with the city starved under the tax laws, the important cogs in the machine had entrenched themselves in the county offices.

The county was important in another way. Political parties are governed by law in Ohio, and the governing committee of the county is elected at the primary elections in the even-numbered years. The boards of election in the counties of Ohio were and are appointed by the Secretary of State as supervisor and inspector of elections, upon the recommendation of the respective county central committees, two Republicans and two Democrats for each county. This means that all the election machinery, even for the counting of the proportional representation ballots in city elections, is in the control of the two political machines.

Would the City Charter Committee do anything about this situation? By the middle of March its policy committee had decided that it should neither initiate nor lead a county movement either in the primaries or through an independent county ticket to wage a battle for its own defense. But on March 22, 1926, when Mr. Bentley addressed the Cincinnatus Association, reporting this action, he said:

"However, the City Charter Committee is deeply interested this year in the County Budget Commission and will watch with keenest interest the preëlection moves leading to the selection of the candidates for county treasurer, county auditor, and county prosecuting attorney.

"The City Charter Committee is also keenly interested in the make-up of the County Central Committees of both Republican and Democratic parties. It would like to see elected upon both of these committees, this fall, friends of the Charter movement so that next year when the new city council must be elected, there may be on the Central Committees of both political parties a group of citizens who will say there is no need of dragging political partisanship into a city election. We believe in voting for the best candidate for city councilman and insist that both parties keep their hands off the city elections in the same manner as they have kept their hands off the Board of Education elections. The City Charter Committee does not want to fight either political party but it is not for peace at any price."

Matters moved slowly. The primary was on August 10 and that meant that nominations must be filed by June 10, so that time was short. Yet it was not until May 13 that sentiment crystallized among independent Republicans, for on that day the third great leader in this movement, Victor Heintz, called together a group of them to discuss the matter. There was no difficulty in arriving at a decision; all were agreed that a ticket must be placed in the field for the county offices at the primary; and that the attempt should be made to run candidates for precinct committeemen, numerous as they were. The only question was whether a legislative ticket should be attempted. Among this Citizens group were B. H. Kroger, James P. Orr, Albert H. Morrill, Colonel P. Lincoln Mitchell, and others equally prominent in business and professional life. Captain Heintz was made chairman, Colonel Mitchell secretary, and Powell Crosley, Jr., treasurer. Mr. Morrill was made chairman of the nominating committee, and the group adjourned to meet a week later.

Some little time before the first meeting I happened to run into Mr. Bentley on the street and he said, "How about your running for prosecutor?" "That's all right with me," said I. And it was, for I had learned from my father how valuable in his practice and on the bench he had found his experience as assistant prosecutor of Hamilton County, with its constant service in court in the trial of all kinds of cases.

Fortunately the suggestion met with the approval of the first meeting, and that left only seven candidates to find. This task was far more difficult, for in the case of the other offices it meant real sacrifice for any citizen of the type desired to give the time to a kind of public service that meant perhaps a bitter campaign, and certainly no commensurate financial return. One name was agreed on at once, that of Mr. Samuel Ach for county treasurer, but it took considerable persuading to induce him (and his good wife) that he must accept. He had retired from the School Board not long before, after more than ten years' service, and had just retired from business also. He was approaching seventy, and was planning a vacation trip that he and his wife had long had in mind. It was typical of his sense of public obligation that he did accept the call within the week.

When the group met again, the fight was on, for the Republican Central Committee met on the same day, and after adopting a resolution not to endorse any candidates for the August primary (contrary to the invariable practice), but to back whatever candidates secured the nomination, it heard Rud K. Hynicka announce that he would not be a candidate in August for precinct committeeman, which meant, so he stated, that he would not be eligible for election as chairman of the Central Committee. Rumors of the proposed retirement had percolated to the revolters, and Captain Heintz promptly decided on vehement publicity, for the activity of the Citizens had been behind closed doors.

"A large number of true Republicans have become disgusted with the way the few in control of the Republican party locally have been conducting its affairs," said he. "In recent years these few self-appointed leaders have lost every fight they have made at the polls. They have lost all sense of responsibility to the public and all party conscience. We look for Hynicka to say he is going to step down and that he will pass his crown over to one of his few self-appointed leaders. But the public will not be fooled. They know that from New York he would rule Cincinnati and Hamilton County just as he has done in the past."

Mr. Seasongood was reported as saying: "I feel like Brown when told of the funeral of Jones.—'I did not attend, but heartily approve of it!' If it means that Hynicka is really relinquishing party leadership, it is good news."

By the following week, the announcement had been made of Mr. Ach's nomination and my own, and Captain Heintz had challenged Mr. Hynicka to a debate on the subject, "Should the Republicans of Hamilton County put an end to Hynickaism, for the good of the Republican party and of our citizens and taxpayers?" Needless to say the challenge was not accepted. In the meantime suggestions as to the remaining candidates were asked from the public, and the nominating committee went to work with a will. It took nearly all of the remaining two weeks to complete the slate, which was announced on June 8.[1]

With the announcement was a fiery statement declaring the policies of the Citizens Republican Committee, the name by which the new group was to be known, that bears the characteristics of Captain Heintz's style.

We can report to the public very definitely that the selfishness, greed and petty jealousies of the little group in control of the Hynicka organization have produced a condition approaching chaos. The panic and fear of impending defeat have prevented them, up to three days ago, from agreeing on any policy or on a single candidate. They realize that Hynickaism must have new faces to disguise its iniquities. Their frantic efforts to secure new faces as candidates have not produced one.

The efforts of the Hynicka clique to build up a veneer of reform are being carried on by two groups. One group consists of Mr. Hynicka's recently appointed [September, 1925] committee of eleven, which includes the little group

[1] For county auditor, Charles Eisen, banker and business man; for commissioner, Charles A. Meyers, Jr., insurance man (and Eppa Rixey's father-in-law); for sheriff, Charles J. Leverone, commission man and old-time athlete; for county clerk, Edward K. Hennegan, attorney; for county recorder, Robert Heuck, formerly in the theatrical business, and well known University of Cincinnati athlete; for coroner, Frederick C. Swing, physician. As in the case of the Charter ticket, the group was widely representative geographically and otherwise.

of four or five who have been using the Republican party for personal profit. In this committee one faction is urging that no candidates should be endorsed, another is urging that a full ticket be endorsed, and still another urges that a public statement should be made that no ticket will be endorsed, but that an endorsement should be made secretly. Each faction distrusts the other. Their last meeting presided over by and dominated by Chairman Hynicka, evaporated when Chairman Hynicka expressed disgust with the entire situation and abruptly left the meeting. The other group endeavoring to construct this veneer is led by Mr. Gilbert Bettman and Mr. Joseph Assel.

Both have been in frequent contact with Mr. Hynicka and both have been endeavoring, without success, to secure the support of prominent and misinformed Republicans. In all kindliness, we wish to say to these Republicans—"Beware!" If necessary, before the tenth of August, the mask will be torn off Hynickaism and all its ugly greed and selfish detail, with specific instances, will stare you in the face.

The object of the movement was declared to be the same kind of government in the county as already provided in the city, and it was announced that as in the city no capable public servants would be displaced. Yet the fight was obviously going to be more bitter than the city contest the fall before.

On July 5 the speaking campaign began, with an atmosphere differing in more than tone from a fall campaign. For it was Cincinnati in July, and that meant that a crowd indoors was hardly to be expected. So we set up soap boxes in every corner of Hamilton County and shouted a crowd together above the roar of trolley cars and the conversations of critical opponents in the background. I have never wished for Joe Humphries' lungs except once that summer, on a concrete schoolyard on Vine Street Hill, hemmed in by brick buildings, when the passing street cars seemed to jump down one's throat. A candidates' schedule might call for three or four speeches an evening at one- to ten-mile intervals.

The approach to the rural community was something new, and proved none too successful. The outlying districts were the very ones that had received the special attention of the county commissioners, although they furnished 10 per cent or less of tax money, while the city paid at least 85 per cent. The small neighboring cities, like Norwood, were a great deal more friendly.

There was plenty to talk about. While Seasongood in the previous campaigns had used county figures occasionally, as in the case of the sheriff feeding prisoners in the county jail, not much of the field covered by the Upson Report in the county had been gone over. The Organization made little attempt to answer arguments. Campaign Chairman Chester Durr's preëlection statement is perhaps typical of their arguments: "We of the regular Republican organization adhere and subscribe to four cardinal principles: party loyalty, party responsibility, party solidarity, and obedience to the mandate of the majority."

Their actions in some respects spoke louder than words, and furnished further examples of their ability to do the wrong thing at the right time.

As soon as the nomination papers of the precinct committeeman candidates of the Citizens group were filed, the Board of Elections set out to scrutinize them with the greatest care. Where the slightest deviation appeared from the statutes strictly construed, out went the papers. Immediately the Citizens Republican Committee denounced such tactics and started a counterattack on the regular candidates. The statute seemed to require residence in the precinct, and in many cases in the downtown wards the executives were known to live in the suburbs in fact, but to make some pretense of keeping a room in the precinct. Protests were filed against many of these, and as the Citizens candidates appeared in defense of their nominating petitions, these old-time regulars had to come in also and testify. Dan Bauer, for instance, swore that he was staying temporarily in Mount Washington for his health, but that he had rented a room on John Street which he intended to make his permanent residence. Another was staying in Kennedy Heights with his son, because of his son's health, but his real residence was downtown in the Sixth Ward. A third had been for eleven years on the hilltops, but he had had a bedroom suite sent to his room downtown. A few withdrew under this pressure, but most of the explanations were accepted. All of which made interesting reading in the papers.

Among those petitions thrown out on the Citizens side were those signed in pencil, and another group some of the endorsers of which had withdrawn. We subpœnaed these last and one of them swore he had a small retail business and had been threatened with loss of trade if he did not take his name off the petition of the Citizens candidate. A stinging editorial in the *Times-Star* condemning such political blackmail was reprinted and broadcast.

The opportunity of a suit to test the validity of these rulings was too good to miss, and it was promptly filed in the Ohio Supreme Court by Sanford Headley, vice-chairman of the Citizens and one of its leading supporters. The court had adjourned for the summer, but when Headley at the Chief Justice's suggestion wrote its members, enough came back to hear the case specially on July 10, and decided pencil signatures were good. More headlines and more material for speeches.

Meantime Henry Bentley, who had supported the Citizens since their ticket was announced, threatened appropriate action if 309 of the county employees who were running for precinct executive on the regular ticket were elected, because he claimed they were in the classified civil service of the state and forbidden to join in any political activity. An inconclusive answer was forthcoming. More headlines.

After the suit was filed and before its decision, Captain Heintz announced that in any event the Citizens Committee would have candidates in every precinct who would seek to have their names written in. The Board of Elections, relying on the county prosecutor's opinion, announced it could not be done. Protest was made to the Ohio Secretary of State, the head of the election machinery of the state. On July 18 he reversed the local board.

Nothing could have been more helpful than this continuous effort of the Organization, well publicized, to prevent a fair fight in the primary. That is, nothing could have been more helpful except a good outstanding issue, and the Organization furnished that in the Coney Island (Ohio, not New York) Race Track, already referred to in the previous city campaign.

Since that time the principal stockholder, Wm. V. Dwyer, had been convicted of conspiracy to violate the prohibition law with a rum fleet and was in jail awaiting the affirmance of his conviction in the upper courts. The Attorney-General of Ohio had secured a Supreme Court ruling that the track was more or less illegal, but it proceeded to open just the same, as soon as Latonia, across the river in Kentucky, closed its spring season. The Citizens Committee demanded that it be closed. A show was made of prosecuting on the part of the sheriff and the prosecutor. Amid the clicking of movie cameras, deputy sheriffs bought contribution receipts (pari-mutuel tickets) and made arrests. Trials gradually got under way, while the defendants, waiving their own presence, went on with their duties at the track, of course still in full operation.

All of us in our speeches had been referring to this open disregard of the law. At the Citizens dinner, July 26, Seasongood, sounding the keynote of the campaign, described the situation in characteristic vein:

Now as to the prosecutor and the sheriff and gambling in the county, and particularly gambling at Coney Island. Why all this pother now? What has opened the sheriff's eyes and roused the prosecutor from slumber? The Coney Island Race Track operated all last summer, undisturbed. Can anyone rationally say that the race track gambling scandal of last summer was not due to the sheriff's and the prosecutor's nonperformance of duty, and that that nonperformance was not related to the interest of Hynicka and Schott in Coney Island? If they had been in earnest, why could not the test case they initiated just before the primary election this year have been begun and completed at the opening of the track last year? In the Civil War "smooth-bore" was the name for imitation cannon planted on forts to deceive the enemy. The prosecutor and the sheriff in their friendly present attack on Coney Island, are nothing but "smooth-bores." They are making a great noise and pretense of action, whereas if they had been in earnest, gambling would not now be going on at the track, and the retail merchants would not be clamoring for relief against loss and defalcation.

But the trial droned on, and the pari-mutuels clicked on. At last, on July 29, Sanford Headley, at Terrace Park, smoked them out. I quote a good deal of his speech because it shows how to avoid the greatest danger in such an issue as this, often present in municipal campaigns of reform movements—the liberal sympathies of a large mass of voters in cities:

You will all, no doubt, recall that when Mr. Hynicka and his associate, Mr. Wm. V. Dwyer, also of New York, the same Mr. Dwyer who was sentenced to two years in the penitentiary by Federal Judge Mack of New York, promoted this enterprise, he stated to his prospective investors that there would be two years of racing. You will recall the result of the racing season of 1925, when the gamblers, touts and parasites brought here to conduct the races, took literally millions of dollars out of this city, and you will likewise recall that no word was uttered and no move made by any official of this county to stop this evil.

Some two weeks ago, the prosecutor and the sheriff became extremely busy. The public press was filled with interviews, manifestoes and fulminations—in fact a veritable war of words was declared against the race track gamblers.

The uninitiated would have assumed that none but a fool would brave the wrath of such active, earnest, alert officials as these, but the race horses came; with them came the usual gang of touts, parasites and gamblers. Since that time there has been a suggestion of legal gestures. But the race track still continues, and I make this prediction, that it will continue to operate until the full length of the meeting has been concluded, and Mr. Hynicka's original promise will be carried out, namely: that there will be two years of racing—one to pay for the cost of the plant, and the other to put hundreds of thousands of dollars into the pockets of its owners.

During all of this gesturing we have the prosecutor appearing as an avenging angel. But what has he accomplished? Nothing but to follow the will of the boss to whom he is subservient and without whose endorsement he never would have been prosecutor of Hamilton County.

If the prosecutor is sincerely and truly desirous of closing the Coney Island Race Track, he knows of a section of the Ohio Code that would have put it out of business immediately. Or if he is ignorant of this section of the law, I shall be glad to tell him where it can be found.

That could not be passed unnoticed, and the next day bright and early an assistant prosecutor was at Headley's residence to demand what was meant by the speech and what section of the code could be resorted to. Headley demonstrated. The next day the track announced it would close for the year. More publicity and more food for triumphant speeches.[1]

To complete the story, the next spring, when I was prosecutor, word came to me from the Tammany backer of Dwyer, who was being asked to put up $100,000 more to put the track in condition. He wanted to know if I would permit it to operate. I sent back word I would not. The track remained closed until the 1933 legislature made pari-mutuel betting legal, and a meeting has been conducted during the summer of 1933.

The Organization helped out just as much by a weekly sheet the County Central Committee published at its headquarters in the Strand Building, called the *Hamilton County Republican*. In it they called Sherrill a carpetbagger, referring to his original home in North Carolina, and held up to abuse and ridicule everything done by the city. This led the City Charter Committee, late in July, to urge its Republican members to support the Citizens ticket, and in many other ways it produced a natural reaction. At the Citizens dinner Seasongood referred to it:

Now, I understand, I am expected to be a kind of civic gladiator, always ready for a fight, and so to take cognizance of the gentle castigations and weekly bilge water emitted from the Strand Building.

So far as concerns myself I intend to take no notice of the "slings and arrows of outrageous journalism." I have cultivated the disease known as ichthyosis, which gives one a hardening of the skin without internal disturbance. I am having the time of my life. My assertions of the past three years are being proved true; we are accomplishing things in Cincinnati to its lasting benefit. It will never lapse to

[1] I understand the prosecutor deserves personal credit for the closing, for the rest of the old crowd wanted to go right on permitting the track to operate, and he incurred considerable ill-will from the regulars. He told them he was not going to take any more blame by pulling their chestnuts out of the fire for them.

where it was before this movement was begun, and so I repeat the couplet:

> "Sticks and stones will break my bones
> But names will never hurt me,"

and grin at headlines such as "Mayor Misleads Women Voters."

But the malevolence and mendacity of this sheet towards the city administration are worthy of notice; first, as showing the low character of the Hynicka leadership and, second, its plain hostility to a successful city administration although predominantly Republican. The Hynicka paper states that it is published by the "Republican County Central Committee." Its object is to advance the candidacy of the Hynicka organization candidates. They must take responsibility for its attitude, which is one of blind hostility to the city government and the city manager. Privately a number of the Hynicka candidates have come to the city manager and to me and said they disapprove of this paper and consider it both untruthful and stupid. But they do not dare to make such expressions publicly, and, if they make such objections at all to the publishers, it shows the truth of what we assert, namely, that the candidates themselves are mere lay figures under the Hynicka system and the actual planning and work are done by the boss.

The mayor went on with a telling comparison of prices for canned goods paid by the city in running the General Hospital in 1926 as compared with prices paid by the county in 1925. He ended with a call to attack those who would destroy what had been accomplished, and in particular a call to all good citizens to volunteer as witnesses and challengers to prevent election frauds.

There was increasing bitterness as the campaign wore on. Two rather strong editorial expressions in the *Times-Star* about my opponent, Mr. Ed. D. Schorr, brought a violent attack on me. It was characteristic of the Citizens movement in this and later years not only that my answer was immediate, but that there were two more replies from others of our stalwarts the same day. We never allowed the ink to dry on the other fellows' speeches before our comeback was in print.

The enthusiasm of the last week led to several predictions by my supporters about the number of public officials I would put behind the bars if elected, something I did not have particularly in mind as the principal job of the prosecutor. The excitement rose continuously, and the campaign ended with a free-for-all out in the country at Peach Grove, between Leverone, Swing and Mumby, our supporters, and three young Organization hecklers. A victory for us in the primary was indicated by the result of this curtain raiser. Albert H. Morrill was sued for slander by Chester Durr because Morrill said inaccurately Durr was profiteering as a printer out of the *Hamilton County Republican,* the scandal sheet above referred to, and Heintz called on the United States Attorney-General, besides the city police, to watch for election frauds.

Behind these exciting pictures thus reflected in the public press was something different and equally important, the amateur organization of men and women. The appearance of headquarters was a good deal like that of the Charter the fall before, but the personalities were quite different. Heintz and Headley were those most continuously on hand instead of Bentley and Hirsch, but the difference in atmosphere was deeper than a mere change in faces. The campaign was directed by a considerably larger group of men than in the city. Decisions were reached on the policies to be followed in almost daily conferences of candidates and campaign committee, in which all shared to a greater degree than in the city. While the note of idealism was no less dominant, the number of active participants with considerable political experience was somewhat greater. Heintz himself had been a Congressman and in 1920 had managed the Chicago office of Harding's campaign under Jim Good. Headley had been brought up in Athens, Ohio, where he had seen General Grosvenor in action, and he had conducted the Republican affairs of Ohio State University as a student there. This is not to say that the leadership was any more capable, for that may be a matter of opinion, but it clearly was different.

Headquarters was different in other respects. This was a county campaign and that meant an approach to communities embracing over 100,000 people outside the limits of Cincinnati. We found great difficulty in getting workers in some places like Norwood, even though we managed to get a majority there when the votes were counted. A number of such communities were still under the fear complex created by the Republican organization.

Another difference was in the men's organization. It had been hastily enlisted before, more of a flying battalion to protect us downtown during the count. Now we were looking for a resident in each precinct to run for executive, and we sought to build up an even more complete citywide organization. That meant bringing into headquarters far more men early in the campaign, and it was bound to include more of the type not seen in the city fight—old-timers who for one reason or another had left the regulars—all of them with considerable political experience. The number of these was not great, but it was enough to give some trouble of a kind the Charter Committee had not gone through. The new political plan, omitting the few undesirables, was now in this process really developing into the unique type of political organization conceived by Bentley two years before.

The election itself was as hot as the campaign. The downtown wards, where the Organization was strong, came in first, and we thought we were licked. We had heard all day of difficulties at the polls because our good women voters, and some of the men, too, did not like to have to say they were Republicans, for all the world to know, as of course they had to in order to vote for us. And many, we heard, had refused and did not vote. By midnight there seemed no hope for any but Swing, the coroner, and Heuck, the recorder, neither thought of as the more important offices. With only 88 out of 638 precincts to go, Ach moved ahead, but the Organization people drifted home toward 2 A.M., much relieved. We were sick. But our noble witnesses in those 88 precincts on the hilltops, who had watched the count with eagle eye and thereby prolonged it until three and four in the morning, escorted downtown such a vote at the very end that apparently Charles A. Meyers, for commissioner, and I, for prosecutor, just got in under the wire by majorities of 222 and 845. And we elected about one-third of the Central Committee, besides the two members of the State Central Committee. For clerk and auditor we had no chance, but we lost the sheriff by just about the votes of the fourth independent candidate. The total vote was over 60,000, more than double the usual primary vote.

Then began a sad story. For as the official count started on Thursday it appeared that working in these early morning hours many election officers had failed to fill out the tallies in the poll books, the little vertical lines, one, two, three, four, and a cross line supposed to indicate five votes as counted. Everyone knew that tallies were always kept on scratch paper and transferred to the poll books later, but the Organization representatives seized on it and seemed to have the law on their side. Gradually with other errors Meyers's lead and mine were cut down and down, and it began to look as if we would both lose. After long conferences among ourselves, and

NOW THE COUNTY—1926

with the attorney, representing Krollman, the Organization candidate for commissioner, we concluded a compromise was the only solution, and my election and Krollman's were conceded. We may have made a mistake not to demand a complete recount, but that was not easy under the old election laws, and I think we did the best we could. At least we had a majority of the Budget Commission, with Mr. Ach and myself, and that was one of our principal objects. We elected only 80 or 90 of our candidates for precinct committeemen as it finally turned out in the official count.

NOW WHAT?

The situation confronting both factions at the close of this primary was fraught with political danger. The fight had been bitter. It was the expectation of each side that it would win a complete victory. The result being what it was, the ticket was composed of 8 candidates, 4 endorsed by the Hynicka organization and 4 by the Independents, whose ideas and ideals were as far apart as the poles, and whose only common attribute was the label "Republican."

It immediately became necessary to devise ways and means of managing a campaign whereby those two opposing groups and their backers on the same ticket would not be flying at each other's throats. Conferences looking to this end were immediately initiated by persons on the Organization side who had not been particularly active in the primary campaign, John V. Campbell, Nicholas Longworth, Fred Schneller and many others; for the Independents, Captain Victor Heintz, General Mitchell, A. E. Anderson and Henry Bentley.

In addition to getting the Independents' nominees elected, these representatives had to look forward to the municipal election of 1927 and to have a care that they were not building up an organization that would overwhelm them the next year, thus defeating one of the main purposes and objects of the primary fight they had just made.

After ten days of conferences, it was agreed that the party management should be committed to an executive committee of nine, four of whom were to be Independents and four Organization, with the chairman of the Central Committee as the ninth. This committee, as finally constituted, consisted of Fred Schneller, chairman, John V. Campbell, vice-chairman, Clifford Brown (the county commissioner), William E. Hess, Ferd Bader, Jr., representing the Organization; General P. Lincoln Mitchell, A. E. Anderson, Charles O. Rose and Sanford A. Headley, representing the Independents. At the time the last four were named by the Independents as their representatives they agreed among themselves and with the managers of the independent movement that they would stand solidly against any interference by the Republican organization in the next municipal election. Unfortunately the matter was not made a definite part of the agreement between the two factions.

This executive committee, upon its organization, immediately proceeded with the selection of a campaign committee on which practically every important Republican in the city, Organization and anti-Organization, consented to serve. A vigorous campaign was conducted which resulted in the election of all of the candidates on the Republican ticket.

The most interesting feature of the campaign was the part of it involving the women's work. The influence of women in Republican or Democratic politics had ceased to be a myth and became a formidable reality in this 1926 primary, when for the first time in the political history of the parties in Hamilton County a full ward and precinct volunteer organization of women was formed. Their work was so vigorous that the Republican women's vote in this primary was approximately five times as great as in the contested presidential primary held in April of 1924.

During the entire primary campaign, the Citizens women were under the impression that their forces were stacked up against a similar force in the regular Republican organization. Later developments revealed that the organization Republican women were very much unorganized, wholly unsupported in organization by the men and made up mostly of a few women jobholders. In contrast, the Citizens roster contained the names of the leading members of greater Cincinnati's philanthropic, social and educational organizations.

The partial victory of the Citizens ticket in the primary necessitated a united front of Republican women against the Democratic organization, but the Citizens women approached this step reluctantly. They were eventually convinced of the expediency of the coalition.

The skepticism with which the Citizens women entered the Strand Building, still the official headquarters of the Republican organization of Hamilton County, was exceeded only by the suspicious attitude with which the Republican organization women accepted them. This suspicion, while more carefully concealed, was apparent, and a similar hostility was not so well concealed in the attitude of the men, extending from the elevator men to the head of the organization. There was no mistaking the fact that they resented having women enter their hallowed portals, except as scenery pure and simple. To go to the Strand Building represented to the Citizens women a genuine sacrifice which they consented to make only because through this united effort would the Budget Commission be under the control of the Citizens Republicans, if the fall campaign succeeded.

For obvious reasons, Mrs. Florence Benham, a Citizens woman, was chosen chairman of the women's organization in this campaign. In order to weld these two extremely militant forces of women into a harmonious working force, she called a meeting at the Sinton Hotel early in September, which was attended by approximately two hundred women, about two-thirds of whom came from her side. It was quite evident that the Citizens women were there "to be shown." Captain Victor Heintz, chairman of the Citizens Republican forces, and Mr. Fred Schneller, the newly chosen chairman of the Central Committee of the Organization, were the principal speakers, each presenting points in favor of the union of the two groups. The one deciding influence of that meeting was, so far as the Citizens women were concerned, the statement which was read by Captain Heintz and had been written by Mayor Seasongood, who commented upon the work of Mr. Schneller in city council and described him as the laboring oar. Another factor that prompted many otherwise militant Citizens women to enter this campaign was the pledge given them privately, of Mitchell, Anderson, Headley and Rose, Citizens representatives on the executive committee, to maintain a "hands-off" policy in the city government by the Republican organization.

One of the amusing sidelights in the campaign was unconsciously revealed by John V. Campbell, who had been made chairman of the campaign committee. On the first day that Mrs. Benham entered her office, she was showered with every known courtesy and convenience, but at about noon Mr. Campbell approached her and said that that afternoon, at a meeting of the precinct committeemen, her precinct chairmen would be appointed. Mrs. Benham informed Mr. Campbell that she was there for that purpose herself and that, while she would appreciate the coöperation of the precinct committeemen in building up the women's organization, the selection of the women chairmen would not be the men's affair. Somewhat stunned, Mr. Campbell bowed out of this embarrassing situation and invited her to attend the meeting of the committeemen anyway, which she did. This meeting merely emphasized the reluctance with which the women in politics were endured by the professionals. Nevertheless, the women's organization was built up separate and independent of the men's organization and of the women jobholders. And all the women joined hands and worked admirably together to the end of the campaign.

This volunteer organization of active workers was an innovation whose worth was noted, and the men decided to form a permanent Republican women's organization. Some two months after the close of the campaign, Mrs. Benham was summoned to the office of Mr. Schneller, where a meeting was held for the purpose of formulating plans for it. In the interval between the close of the campaign and this meeting, which occurred about the first of the year, rumors were abroad that the Republican organization would again oppose the Charter government in the coming city election in spite of the early assurances that they would observe a "hands-off" policy. This meant the end of coöperation with the Republican organization so far as the Citizens women were concerned, but Schneller went ahead with his plans anyhow, and did form a permanent women's organization of a sort.

One other matter that was voted on in the 1926 election was a city charter amendment, which was in fact a new charter. The original amendment of 1924 provided that after council had been in office six months it should appoint a Charter Commission of three with a secretary to revise the entire charter. Accordingly, in June, 1926, council informally agreed on Bentley, representing the Charter Committee, Robert N. Gorman (the son of Judge Gorman of Hunt days), representing the Democrats and the Charter group, and Robert A. Taft, representing the Republicans, with Howard Bevis (recently Ohio Director of Finance and now a member of the Ohio Supreme Court) as secretary. Within a few months this able group revised the charter throughout and produced an excellent piece of work. The only mistake was in the retention of the independent boards, the Park Board, the Health Board and the Recreation Commission, whose employees are not under the city manager. The whole commission agreed that this was unsound in theory, but, especially in view of the Republican primary fight that was raging, they did not want to submit a charter that would raise any additional opposition. When the revised charter was submitted to council, two of the Charter councilmen happened to be away, and the Organization trio moved to strike out proportional representation. A four-to-three vote defeated the motion. Up to this date that is the only attempt to do away with what Charter supporters believe is the best protection for the believers in good government.

At the election the new charter carried by a two-to-one majority, and won in all wards and in a large majority of the precincts of the city. The abolition of the various boards, therefore, could hardly have defeated it, but that is hindsight and the commission deserves no blame for its decision.

At the beginning of January, Heuck, Swing and I took office.[1] The staff in each of our offices was small, and we carried out our pledge to let no one go who was doing

[1] Mr. Ach's term did not begin until September after the August financial settlement between treasurer and auditor. This was unfortunate, as it left me a minority member of the Budget Commission until 1928 and, as it happened, left him a minority member in August, 1929.

his job satisfactorily. So far as concerns the legal staff which I inherited, I retained only two out of ten, but I kept all the office force. The secret service officer resigned to go as bailiff with my predecessor, then a judge, and to replace him I brought an experienced detective from the city hall. I picked my staff of assistants with difficulty because so few of those I wanted had had criminal trial experience, but I found to my surprise that my best men were those with character and thoroughness, quite irrespective of previous experience in the particular technical fields called for.

When I had made my selections with the help and advice of Headley especially, I submitted the list to the Republican Executive Committee. Mr. Schneller, the new chairman, had asked me to appoint as my secret service officer, in place of the city detective referred to above, one of his precinct executives in the Eighteenth ward. This I had refused to do, and hearing nothing further from the committee, I proceeded to announce my proposed appointments. Incidentally, I had caught the judge of elections in the precinct of Mr. Schneller's nominee creasing the council ballots along Mr. Schneller's name while his nominee was instructing the illiterate voters, before they came in, to put the mark at the crease.

Heuck had found a group of copyists chosen for their supposed vote-getting ability, and he gradually weeded out many of them and replaced them by expert girls. One, for instance, after recording a long mortgage with over 125 mistakes, was asked his previous experience, and admitted he was a horseshoer by trade. In spite of a steady and real improvement in the service of his office to the public and to the lawyers who used it, Heuck was subjected to a constant guerrilla warfare of carping criticism, especially from Organization lawyers, who, while not in the majority, were the most vocal.

I had expected something of the same kind from the judges before whom my office had to present criminal cases, and from the county commissioners whom my civil assistants advised. It is a matter of lasting gratitude that nothing of the kind developed. I must add, however, that none of them ever went out of his way to support us when our office was unjustly attacked.

CHAPTER TEN

THE GREAT TEST FOR THE CITY CHARTER COMMITTEE—1927

WHILE Heuck and I were busily engaged in finding our ways around the courthouse, the Charter Committee was going through its greatest test. Although it was only a short twelve months since January 1, 1926, it was already necessary to plan for the election in November, 1927, the councilmen's terms being for only two years. One would think that the course would be clear and that everything should proceed as in 1925—the selection of candidates, the organization in wards and precincts, the campaign, the election. But it was not so simple as that at all.

The policy of Bentley and the Charter Committee had been to leave the conduct of affairs to the elected officials and to give them the credit. "Praise is the breath of life for a politician," is what Bentley said three years before, and at the Third Civic Dinner held in January, 1927, he lived up to his theories. "I shall not speak of the accomplishments of the new city government; I shall leave these to his honor, Mayor Seasongood, and City Manager Sherrill. These gentlemen and the other eight councilmen constitute the officers of that government and to them is due credit for the remarkable achievements of the past year."

That very policy had its serious dangers, if it meant that the public officials were going to be removed from contact with their political backers. It was only too easy for them to lose touch with public sentiment, favorable and unfavorable. In the spring of 1926 an effort had been made to avoid this danger by creating a contact committee of the City Charter Committee to discuss questions of policy and public opinion with the councilmen. It took a real effort, for the contact committee was made up of busy men, and the councilmen were busy, too, forced almost daily to decide important questions on their own sole responsibilities. Small wonder if by the end of the year they felt the City Charter Committee members were a little outside the stream of action. Small wonder if some, in council and out, felt that having started the ball rolling, the committee should now retire and become simply an endorsing body, rather than grow into a self-conscious municipal party.

The Republicans took advantage of this feeling and of their union with the Independents for the 1926 election to attempt to split off the Independent Republicans from the Charter ranks. They (meaning Schneller) offered, privately of course, to endorse all the Charter Republican members of council except Seasongood, and to name no others on the ticket who were not acceptable to Bentley. Lincoln Mitchell was taken into Schneller's confidence and felt this was a fair offer that should be accepted. The discussion spread to the whole of the new Republican Executive Committee, up to that time harmonious. The division stood six to three in favor of putting up a Republican ticket under those conditions, that is the five original Organization members and General Mitchell.

This will explain why Schneller planned to endorse Field and Rose, Charter councilmen, to approve of the city manager form of government and to pledge the Republican candidates to retain Colonel Sherrill. It was a serious threat to the new movement.

Bentley met the situation and won through with the backing of the great majority of Charter supporters. He began by defending the theory of the City Charter Movement at the same Civic Dinner of January:

The City Charter Committee has interested in municipal affairs citizens who never before regarded politics as within their sphere of action. It has created the mechanism through which they may function, and has furnished them a medium of political expression. There is no doubt that political organization must exist. Government without political organization is impossible. Without organization the citizens are helpless to make their will felt. But there are good and bad forms of organization.

The City Charter Committee was organized as a protest against that form of political organization that demanded merely followers and not thinkers. It relies for its services upon the volunteer efforts of men and women interested in good government. It cannot command service, it must win it by fair play. It has appealed to a new motive in political action, the responsibility of the individual for the government, the possibility of using the government for public purposes and for public good.

It has drawn to its support that great body of public-minded men and women, who have heretofore found their only opportunity of public service in social service activities. It has held before them the vision that a municipal government properly administered can do more than any private philanthropy.

It has given a new vision to Cincinnatians of the power of idealism in practical politics. It has drawn men and women into service of the public, service of hands, service of minds, service of soul. It has shown a new form of political organization, for the City Charter Committee is unique in America. It is the only purely municipal party that not only endorses candidates, but maintains a complete volunteer ward and precinct organization and which has for three consecutive years carried the elections by a two-to-one majority.

The problem of American democracy is the problem of municipal government, and we in Cincinnati are again leading the way towards its solution. The eyes of America are upon us.

Bentley followed this up by carrying with him the members of the committee itself in the determination to place their own ticket of nine in the field, and to organize to elect it. Incidentally he mitigated the bitterness among the Democrats toward Seasongood because of his open comments on their pressure for patronage, and they were kept safe in the Charter group.

Nevertheless, the Republicans went ahead with their ideas, apparently thinking Bentley could not retain control of his people. The discussions on the Republican Executive Committee went on. By the middle of February, Mr. Anderson joined General Mitchell, and from that time on the matter stood seven for and two against a separate Republican ticket. By the middle of March, the plans had gone to the point where the personnel of the ticket was under discussion, and the Republicans of the Charter Committee were still expected to follow along in spite of the opposition of Headley and Rose. The formal action finally came on April 6, 1927, by a vote of seven to one, Mr. Rose being absent as he was a candidate and Mr. Headley voting in the negative. The next morning, April 7, Mr. Headley set forth his views on the subject in an interview printed in full in all the morning papers. Most of the Independents active in the county agreed with him, but a few followed Mitchell and Anderson. The committee, as organized, virtually ceased to function for the rest of the year. Mr. Headley was thereafter excluded from the meetings until after the close of the municipal campaign. The reading of his speech shows clearly enough why:

Since I am unable to agree with the majority of the Republican County Executive Committee on the question of placing a councilmanic ticket in the field at the forthcoming municipal election in Cincinnati, I deem it fair to them and to the public that I give my reasons for my disagreement.

In the first place, it must be remembered that this committee is a county committee, the members of which were chosen as the result of a county primary. Three out of the nine members are not residents of Cincinnati and would be ineligible themselves for any elective office in the city. If there is any good reason why the committee should put a ticket in the field in Cincinnati, the same reason requires the committee to put a ticket in the field in every other municipality in the county. This would require a ticket in Norwood, Elmwood Place, Newtown, Glendale and Cleves. The response of the citizens of the City of Norwood, for example, to such action on the part of the committee may well be left to the imagination.

In the second place, the citizens of Cincinnati, by adopting the charter amendment in 1924, placed an emphatic disapproval upon political partisanship in municipal government. They reaffirmed this attitude in the councilmanic election of 1925 and again and just as emphatically when they adopted a new charter in 1926. That the citizens were right in this attitude is evident to everyone who stops to compare the present city government with that which went out of office January 1, 1926. The economies effected, the efficiency demonstrated, the morale of the administrative force of the city bear eloquent testimony that there is no place in municipal government for partisan politics. The City Charter Committee is a nonpartisan group of high-minded, unselfish citizens who are responsible for the original charter amendment, for the present city council and for the new charter adopted in 1926. They deserve support at the hands of every person interested in good government so long as they maintain their present attitude of noninterference with the administrative and legislative officers of the city.

In the third place, the action of the committee will necessitate the raising of a large campaign fund. I am sure that the business men of the city interested in municipal government will be averse to contributing this fund. The only source remaining from which it may be obtained is the levying of an assessment upon the elective and appointive county officers at the courthouse. Our committee has gone on record as being opposed to the levying of any such assessment even for the conduct of a county campaign.

I understand that the committee expects to endorse Colonel Sherrill individually and the present form of city government. They only express the hope of maintaining the present high standard of administrative efficiency. Such a platform begs the question and misstates the issue which is, Shall the city officials continue to serve the city according to their individual or collective best judgment unhampered and untrammeled by outside political interference and control? Any such interference or control would be a distinct backward step and would destroy the progress made in the last three years towards better government.

Lent D. Upson in his report on city government in Cincinnati made June 1, 1924, uses the following language:

"I am convinced that great improvement in the government of Cincinnati will come from the introduction of a strong critical minority into council, the independence of that council from national party affiliation, and the destruction of the theory under which the political organization in power usurps the authority and annuls the independent judgment of elected administrative and legislative officers.

"Further, the present system of party organization does not facilitate the entrance into the government of energetic individuals not inherently politically inclined. Cincinnati is the only large city in Ohio in which it is extremely difficult for a citizen to run for an office independent of a recognized party. It is one of the few cities which still cling to the idea that national politics have a place in local administration."

I wish to observe further that the last three appointments made in the county government were Jack Rubenstein, Charlie

Cowie and Sam Blythe. If the committee follows the plan proposed and succeeds in the election of its ticket, I wonder how many Rubensteins, Cowies and Blythes will be on the payroll of the city one year from today.

In the meantime the Citizens officeholders at the courthouse, and Mr. Ach, treasurer-elect, were watching proceedings with interest. Headley kept us in touch with events, and a few days before the final vote in the committee we issued a joint statement opposing the proposed action. Dr. Swing refused to join in the statement and from that time on was not altogether sympathetic with the Citizens group.

Here again was something new to Cincinnati and we were all severely criticized by the regulars. Up to then members of the Executive Committee or public officials elected by the Organization's help kept their mouths obediently shut when questions of policy were decided contrary to their views. We believed the organization had supported us the fall before because it had to, and did not deserve endless gratitude for its action. But this issue we felt was something different from the political policies of the county, and we put our own city's good and its good government ahead of any national party.

Meantime the Charter candidates' committee set to work and in due time presented four names in addition to Field, Rose, Seasongood, Matthews and Dixon. Anthony Mees replaced Luchsinger as the labor candidate, a union man and a social worker. Three well-known business men completed the ticket, Charles Eisen (who had run for county auditor in 1926 on the Citizens ticket), Edward Imbus and John H. Dickerson.

There were new faces on the Organization side, too. The ticket, of course, included the three incumbents, Schneller, Lackmann and Daly. In addition, the Organization had endorsed Rose and Field, which put a majority, five, of the existing council on their ticket. General Mitchell had shown the courage of his convictions by accepting the sixth place. Fred Hock, of the Building Trades Council, was the labor representative, and L. J. Bradford and Chase Davis, as well-known business men, completed the slate. These last four were all new in politics.

Schneller, as a gesture of goodwill, had been made chairman of the important Highways Committee of council in January, 1926, and in this campaign he did not fail to capitalize on the work he had done. The fall before in the harmony campaign to elect the combined county ticket, Seasongood had written in answer to a request from Heintz:

I am glad to say that Mr. Schneller has been most assiduous in the performance of his duties. He has devoted a great deal of time and intelligent effort to his work as councilman and has been very helpful and dependable. I have found him entirely frank and anxious to make the administration a success.

He was not allowed by the Republicans to forget his statement.

Seasongood explained his position by a strong attack on Schneller's conduct of the Organization since November, 1926, without qualifying his approval of Schneller's handling of his councilmanic duties. The attack was based on Schneller's instructions as chairman of the Executive Committee to the Hamilton County delegation in the 1927 legislature to defeat the permanent registration bill, the bill to permit Heuck and other recorders to use photostatic recording, and various other measures the city was interested in, after a show of supporting them.

And with usual vehemence, Seasongood attacked the employment with Schneller's consent by county officials of various bitter Organization supporters as soon as they were let out at the city hall for disloyalty or inefficiency. They were not many but the names were well known to the public. As always, replies were immediate and denials and accusations flew back and forth.

A more important statement of the plans and issues came from Bentley in addressing the Charter women as they began their work of organization:

> When we beg our ward chairmen to secure efficient precinct chairmen and our precinct chairmen to secure efficient block workers, and our block workers to visit every voter on the street, you sometimes balk and say, "Everyone in my neighborhood is in favor of the Charter anyway, what is the use of all this work?" . . .
>
> There are people who say that there is no issue in this campaign; that the changes in the city are due to the city manager, Colonel Sherrill, and since the Republicans have adopted a platform pledging their candidates to retain Colonel Sherrill there is no real issue except that of personal choice among the candidates.
>
> Without in the slightest degree detracting from the greatness of Colonel Sherrill and of the marvelous work he has performed for Cincinnati, however, you and I know that Colonel Sherrill is not the cause of the change, that his work and his presence in Cincinnati are not the causes but are one of the effects of the change wrought in November, 1925, by the election of the City Charter candidates for council.
>
> For the first time in the history of Cincinnati a majority of the councilmen elected to that office were under no obligation to an invisible government. The six Charter councilmen were actuated by the same motives that actuate you ladies, a desire to make the city government an instrumentality of service to the citizens. They were not hampered in their conduct of affairs by an organization that was com-

pelled to consider every action in the light of its effect upon the next election for county, state or national offices. These men were free to decide issues upon the basis solely of the advantage to the city we love. . . .

Colonel Sherrill would never have come to Cincinnati had he not been assured a free hand in the selection of his employees. Colonel Sherrill could never have performed the miracles he has performed in Cincinnati were his hands tied by demands for political patronage and jobs. Colonel Sherrill will not and cannot continue to render the same service to Cincinnati if the councilmen elected this November restore the old conditions of political employment and patronage.

It is this information that your neighbors must have and it is your duty and your privilege to carry it to them.

To this he added an effective comparison of the Republican platform with its record:

Do you remember the words of Patrick Henry, "I have but one lamp by which my feet are guided and that is the lamp of experience. I know of no way of judging the future but by the past," and judging by the past of the Republican organization, I ask, what shred of hope is there on which to base the fulfillment of the pledges made in its party platform?

Look at the record. In 1924 the Republican organization fought desperately against the adoption of the city charter.

In 1925 the Republican organization fought the nine candidates for council on the City Charter ticket.

The Charter councilmen selected Colonel Sherrill as city manager. Last year the Republican organization subsidized the *Hamilton County Republican* and every issue of this paper contained scurrilous attacks upon City Manager Sherrill.

Last fall the revised charter was presented to council and the three organization councilmen voted against it.

Judging the future by this past, can you rely upon the platform of the Republican organization in its declaration of

GREAT TEST FOR CHARTER COMMITTEE

the sudden conversion of that body to the cause of good government in Cincinnati?

One matter of greatest importance to the city proved also of advantage to the Charter cause in the following six years. In July, 1927, it was announced that the seven railroads entering Cincinnati had signed an agreement for a union passenger station, long sought by the people of the city to replace the two unsightly stations in use. This meant also new freight terminals for most of the railroads and the ultimate expenditure of nearly $75,000,000 in the metropolitan community. This great accomplishment was largely the work of George D. Crabbs, a prominent Cincinnati manufacturer, assisted by my brother as the representative of a group of Cincinnati citizens interested in the project. The agreement was a sign of confidence in the future of the city and also in the possibility of accomplishing the project without the shakedown by city officials usual in other cities when large terminal projects are undertaken. While the Charter had done nothing to bring about the terminal, it rightly claimed credit for creating an administration to whose mercies the railroads were willing to entrust the project.

The heat of the campaign was too much for the Organization's endorsement of Sherrill. At least when they tried to explain away Charter success as due only to the expenditure of large and greatly increased sums of money, they found the quick answer that Sherrill had spent that money, that they were endorsing a majority of the existing council and that all of those five, including all three of their own particular representatives, had voted for every item of expenditure of which they complained. The debate, which was largely between Seasongood and General Mitchell, is of current interest because the same statements as to the year 1926, and the same comparisons with 1925 are being made again in 1933, when people are far more likely to listen to matters affecting the taxes they pay.[1]

By this time the Organization was wishing it had never endorsed Rose and Field. It could not very well issue a marked sample ballot without including them, and so for the only time in its history it issued sample ballots unmarked, and left it to the ward captains to mark the order of choice according to the ideas of each. Furthermore, it printed the names of all candidates so that an outsider (like Yeatman) could be backed at the last minute. In some wards just that was done and in most wards Rose and Field were not marked at all. Even an independent Democrat was backed in some instances.[2]

In this year the Charter was better organized than in any previous campaign. The record of its accomplishment was set forth in a most effective booklet of twenty pages or more, mostly prepared by the faithful John Weinig. In fact, his death in the following winter must be traced largely to the strain of overwork in this contest. Many others like him came to the fore as ward captains and precinct men, and the women were militant, their faith completely justified by what had occurred in these few brief months at the city hall. Many business

[1] Especially in recent years a so-called Research and Publicity Commission which seems to be connected with the Republican County Central Committee has furnished the opponents of citizen movements in other cities that have followed Cincinnati's example with these same statements and with other attacks on the quality of our own city's government, which they are careful not to publish in Cincinnati. For this reason I am adding as an appendix a full statement of receipts and expenditures of the city for the years 1921 and 1932, inclusive. These figures were prepared by the Cincinnati Bureau of Governmental Research at the instance of the Cincinnatus Association. A later chapter discusses the city's present finances and the Republican charges.

[2] This is not unusual. The St. Louis Republican organization was generally thought to be responsible for the newspaper advertisements in 1932 showing how to vote for the Republican local ticket and Franklin D. Roosevelt.

men, however, were still reluctant to stand up and be counted, and the few that did, like B. H. Kroger, L. A. Ault and J. P. Orr, were still the exceptions among the city's business leaders.

Even such men were not generally able to devote much of their time to the active work of the City Charter Committee, much as they desired to do so and willing as they were to give every support in their power. The active group in the enterprise was made up, generally speaking, of lawyers and insurance men, sometimes doctors and those in other similar occupations, whose time was to a greater extent their own. Such groups might have occasion to meet as often as once a week in the course of the year, especially during the nine months preceding the campaign. As the campaign drew nearer it required more time from a small group of three or four, and during the last six weeks of the campaign there probably were in 1929 and in each year that number of men devoting more than half time, perhaps as much as full time, to the political development and direction of the campaign. If an executive director had been found early in the movement who developed any unusual flair for political strategy, some of this time might have been eliminated. No such director was found and these men worked without direct compensation and without the expectation of payment by any indirect means, such as patronage. None of us in Cincinnati have shed tears over this circumstance, for we believe that the success of the movement has been due to the attention, devotion and intelligence of these few, with additions, making a group of probably twenty men who have been the executive committee, so to speak, discussing and deciding upon principal matters of policy. The word "men," I hasten to say, is used in a generic sense, because a number of women have been most active,

158 CITY MANAGEMENT

and their advice and support have been constant in the highest councils of the City Charter Committee and the Citizens movement.

When the time of the election arrived a persistent rumor going the rounds proved true, that the Organization was also "knifing" the business men on their ticket. Schneller evidently did his best for Mitchell, for when his own surplus of about 7,500 votes was distributed, Mitchell got nearly 2,000. But 1,300 went to Daly and nearly 700 to Yeatman, the leading Independent candidate. Bradford had some 2,500 first-choice votes (he needed 12,429) and got a few more before he dropped out; and Davis had only 428.[1]

It was also clear in this election that the Organization had knifed Lackmann in favor of Yeatman. Yeatman was a municipal court judge who was well liked but was left off the ticket to give room to the "business man" candidates. He had considerable following even among Charter supporters, and after being fourth in first-choice votes he was finally elected on the transfer of Imbus's votes, a Charter candidate. So the only changes in the council were the substitution of Eisen for Luchsinger and Yeatman for Lackmann. Charter supporters breathed a sigh of relief as they found their majority of six to three retained. The most serious test up to that time was successfully passed.[2]

[1] Complaint is made of proportional representation that it has this result, the defeat of the so-called "respectable" candidate on the Organization tickets. But the ones elected are those who truly represent the Organization vote, and these business men did not and do not. The Cincinnati councils since 1926 have been truly representative in the best sense; they have not been "silk-stocking" or visionary on the Charter side; while on the Organization side, admitting some variation in ability, there has been no member of the disgraceful type that often prevailed before 1926, and in many cases their coöperation and service have been excellent.

[2] This election also marked the first race of a colored man, Frank A. B. Hall, a retired city detective with an excellent record. With

I would add by way of postscript that they breathed another sigh of relief on January 1, 1928, as these successful candidates were sworn in, for the holdover Organization city auditor finished his four-year term of office and the mayor's new appointee, Henry Urner, took charge. Not only had employees, fired for inefficiency or worse elsewhere in the city hall, found refuge in the auditor's office,[1] but it had been a hotbed of intrigue against the administration. Confusing and deceptive figures were furnished to Organization speakers in the 1927 campaign and three or four of his men on city time addressed political cards; for which the Civil Service Commission promptly fired them.

When Urner came in as auditor he found plenty to do. For example, two ledgers upon examination appeared to be identical. He asked the clerks what they were for. They replied that both were kept so as to check each other. He asked how they knew which was right if there was a discrepancy, and the reply was that they didn't; they checked through both till they found it. Needless to say, one was eliminated. The whole bookkeeping system of the city was revised, and Urner became a real auditor of the city's finances.

no backing and not much of a public campaign, he stood eleventh in first-choice votes; but his total moved up too slowly, only 50 votes each count, and he was eliminated. It forecast, however, a difficult problem for the Organization to solve, with its large colored vote. For of his 4,200 votes less than one-third went to the Organization, while another third were for him only, and nearly a quarter went to the Charter. Eleven per cent of the population was colored in the 1930 census.

[1] The expense of his office rose from $56,035 in 1925, a high average year, to $69,272 in 1926 and $67,753 in 1927. A rearrangement of functions between auditor and treasurer in 1928 raised the combined cost from $94,590 in 1927 to $99,718 in 1928, but then the economies of operation began to show and the combined costs of the two were: 1929, $76,653; 1932, $64,832, or less than the auditor's alone in 1926 and 1927.

CHAPTER ELEVEN

NATIONAL POLITICS FOR THE FIRST TIME—AND THE SECOND COUNTY BATTLE—1928

AGAIN in our seesawing between city and county, we return to the Republican County Executive Committee, and the background changes to the national scene for the first time.

It will be recalled that in 1928 Ohio was the first state to hold a presidential primary in which a candidate must personally sign a declaration that he was a candidate. In January, Dr. Work, Secretary of the Interior, and an old acquaintance of Captain Heintz, requested him to come to Washington for an important conference. Upon his arrival, Dr. Work wanted to know whether, in his opinion, Herbert Hoover should contest for delegates to the National Convention from the state of Ohio, and asked what the Republicans of Hamilton County would do for him should he decide to do so. Captain Heintz immediately wired to Headley, as vice-chairman of the Citizens Committee, who found, after conference with men and women prominent on the committee, that they were enthusiastic for Hoover. He replied by wire that Mr. Hoover could carry Hamilton County by 25,000 votes.

In this conference between Captain Heintz and Dr. Work, Captain Heintz stated that it would be distasteful to him and his associates to carry on a campaign wherein it would be necessary for them to take orders or follow the lead of Walter Brown, of Toledo, long known as a machine politician. Dr. Work advised him that, while Mr. Brown was interested in Mr. Hoover's candidacy and was engaged in organization work for his nomination, he would not have anything to do with the work in Hamilton County.

Captain Heintz returned to Cincinnati while the Secretary of Commerce puzzled over the situation. Senator Frank B. Willis, of Ohio, was an avowed candidate for the presidency, and obviously a declaration of candidacy by Hoover meant a bitter fight in the Senator's own bailiwick and a possible defeat that might nip Hoover's chances in the bud. Responses from other parts of the state were not so enthusiastic as that from our group, for the organizations distrusted Hoover as not an "organization" type of man, and there were no independent groups active elsewhere. But the heartening effect of our guarantee to send four Hoover delegates to Kansas City helped turn the scales, and press dispatches from Washington announced that Mr. Hoover would contest for delegates in Ohio against the favorite son candidate.

Mr. Schneller, chairman of the Hamilton County Executive Committee, was quite perturbed at this turn of events, and shortly thereafter called a meeting of the Executive Committee in the Cincinnati law office of Senator Richard P. Ernst, of Kentucky. It was in this office that Congressman Nicholas Longworth had his headquarters in Cincinnati. The meeting was attended by eight members of the committee, Mr. Rose being absent.

Immediately upon the committee coming to order, Mr. Longworth made a short informal talk advocating the endorsement of Senator Willis. Mr. Schneller followed this by a talk to the same effect, and notwithstanding the fact that all the members of the committee were personally opposed to Senator Willis's candidacy, principally because he was an extreme dry, there was an immediate concurrence with this view by all the members present except John V. Campbell and Headley. Mr. Campbell offered to resign from the committee, stating that he had no desire to embarrass the majority, but that his views were too much at variance with the Senator's on the question of prohibition to permit him to endorse him for President. Mr. Headley stated that in his opinion nobody in Hamilton County desired the nomination of Senator Willis for President, and that his endorsement by this group, which was supposed to represent the sentiment of the Republicans of Hamilton County, would be a betrayal of the trust imposed upon them. Mr. Longworth then stated that he was a candidate for President of the United States; that he would be at the convention; that a great body of the delegates to the convention would be Members of Congress; that the plan of strategy was to kill off Mr. Hoover with the favorite son candidates of the type of Willis of Ohio, Watson of Indiana, and Curtis of Kansas; and after this was accomplished his own consolidated and secondary strength would appear and he would be the residuary legatee of Willis's strength in Ohio. This suggestion was concurred in by all the members of the committee except Campbell and Headley, Campbell stating that he would resign but that he would not endorse Willis. Headley stated to Mr. Longworth that if Longworth was a candidate for President, he, Headley, would support that candidacy for what the support was worth; that he recognized Mr. Longworth's ability as a statesman and had a proper pride as a Cincinnatian in his achievements; but that he would not enter into a political deal for the purpose of making him or any other person President of the United States. To the further insistence that Willis be endorsed, Headley announced that he would not concur and that he would make a public announcement of his opposition and the

NATIONAL POLITICS FOR FIRST TIME

reasons therefor were the proposition carried by a vote of the committee. This, with the memory of a previous public dissent and the threat of Campbell to resign, effectually barred the adoption of the resolution, and the meeting adjourned.

Shortly thereafter the Cincinnati papers announced the presence of Mr. Schneller, General Mitchell and Mr. Anderson in Washington for the purpose of supporting the candidacy of Senator Willis. The meeting took place at the residence of Speaker Longworth and facetious reporters remarked in dispatches to Cincinnati that the Senator partook of nothing stronger than grapejuice. The upshot of the whole matter was, as stated by Mr. Schneller, that he could not control "those Indians" back home and no endorsement could be made. Not only could no endorsement of Willis be forced through, but it was soon evident that we Independents could elect four Hoover delegates of our own if the regulars put up four for Willis. Thereupon, the Organization fell in line with the endorsement of Mr. Hoover already given by the Citizens Republican Committee. We were disappointed to lose such a good chance to defeat the regulars, but in loyalty to Hoover we went along.

After it was determined that Mr. Hoover was to have the support of both factions of the Republican party in Hamilton County, the matter of choosing the delegates became the next thing in order.

Under the law of Ohio, no person may stand for election as a delegate pledged to a presidential candidate without that candidate's consent. Without warning or notice, Walter F. Brown appeared in Cincinnati with a power of attorney to give or withhold Mr. Hoover's consent to any candidacy for delegate. Furthermore, he had in his pocket a complete list of candidates representing both the Independents and the Organization men, obviously prepared after conference with someone in the Organization. He can hardly have failed to confer with the chairman of the Executive Committee.

He called into conference Captain Heintz and Headley, representing the Independents, in his room at the Gibson Hotel. He stated that they must accept names given by him for delegates. Heintz and Headley absolutely refused to accede. After spending most of the afternoon in fruitless argument, a compromise was hit upon whereby neither side would send a delegate obnoxious to the other, but within this limitation each side was to choose its own candidates.

Immediately another bone of contention appeared. The Organization selected Gilbert Bettman as one of their candidates. This announcement by Brown to Heintz was equivalent to a slap in the face to the leaders of the Independent movement, as Bettman had frankly and openly attacked the charter itself and all its works since 1924, and the suggestion met with an immediate and emphatic "no." The fight on this point was long and bitter. At one time it appeared certain that no compromise could be reached and that the Independents, notwithstanding their espousal of the cause of Mr. Hoover, would have to withdraw from the joint campaign and put up a ticket of their own, which they threatened to do. However, when the fact that their decision was final and unalterable reached the inner consciousness of Mr. Brown, he forced the Organization to live up to the terms of their compromise and substitute another name. All four thus agreed on were nominated and elected as Hoover delegates.

The sequel may be of some interest. While the Citizens group were not looking for patronage of any sort, they felt that they were one of a few important influences early in his candidacy that led to the nomination of Mr. Hoover, and they had worked equally hard for his election. But after he was elected there was not only no acknowledgment of their support, but the federal appointments made in Cincinnati were dictated by the Organization, and were of a type that could hardly give encouragement to the supporters of good government. A much-needed federal investigation of delinquent officials in a neighboring city stopped suddenly just before indictment without any explanation, and the responsibility for this interference with justice was laid at the door of a non-resident Republican prominent nationally.

Not one word came to the Citizens group until January of 1932, four years later, when the National Convention was again looming up. Inquiry was then made of Captain Heintz as to whether the Citizens group would support the President. Heintz replied in effect that there was no reason why they should in view of what had happened, but that he thought they would in the primary and probably would against any Democrat but Baker. In that, from my personal observation, I believe him to have been correct, but the enthusiasm of many was restrained. No further word came from the White House, although the Citizens group then held eight of the eleven county offices and the Charter administration was still at the city hall.

With the presidential primary of 1928 over, we began to look forward to August when the county primary would take place. And we all had to review our records in preparation for it, for the possibility of a harmonious settlement of Republican differences had evaporated with the city fight of 1927, and the compromise on the Hoover delegates had not improved anyone's temper.

The records of the Citizens officeholders may be of interest. Heuck's work as recorder in his first year carried out the promise of its beginning against the meanest type of opposition. But it was not spectacular and his office had contact with only a restricted public, in the legal profession mostly. His predecessor, with expenditures (including his own salary and supplies) of $83,003 in 1926, had secured a budget allowance of nearly $2,500 more for deputies' and clerks' compensation for the succeeding year; but Heuck reduced the actual expenditures for that item by $1,000 for 1927 and by $16,000 for 1928, and was going at a rate that ended his year in 1928 with a total of $72,415, the lowest since 1922. His office did more business and reduced the charges to the fees fixed by law in addition.

Heuck, however, did not have to run again, as his term was for four years. I had been the object of our opponents' principal attention in 1926, and so I was again, but for different reasons. When I went into office I found a large group of pending cases left by my predecessor, or rather by his staff, and naturally they were the least attractive cases to try. We set out to get rid of them and we did so in the first six months, thanks to the excellent coöperation of Judge Frederick L. Hoffman, Judge Caldwell, until his death in May, and Judge Charles S. Bell. The latter's fine attitude was worthy of note, in view of our violent political battles of the previous years. I can say with modesty the record was good, for I soon found that the press of detail upon the prosecutor himself and the necessity of seeing the many citizens who had or thought they had business with me, forced the assignment of most criminal cases for trial to my assistants. A murder occurred the morning my term of office began, and in March we tried the three adult defendants in three courtrooms at once and sent them up for life within thirty days of their arrest, about the minimum time possible in a contested first-degree case in Ohio.

But October, November and December saw two trials that probably caused the loss of the 1928 primary for nearly our whole Citizens ticket. The first was the trial of Fat Wrassman for the murder of another bootlegger in a typical gang killing. The case came over from police court as a second-degree charge, with the defendant out on bond (i.e., homicide in a fight, without premeditation), but I heard by the underground that it was cold-blooded and intentional, and the bullet holes in the body were all from the rear and above. Then I heard that all the witnesses (in a beer flat) had been threatened if they talked. That got my dander up and we subpœnaed those we could find out about, pressed a little out of them, and indicted Wrassman for first degree. That meant no bond and Wrassman disappeared until a little before the trial. The trial went fairly well with a good German citizen named Emmert, formerly in politics, as our only witness who really stood up; but it was clearly shown that the deceased was not worth much. A gun had been found beside his body which formed the basis for a self-defense story, but during the trial we traced it by a hidden number to a leading sporting goods house in Cincinnati. The name of the purchaser was not Wrassman, but we subpœnaed in the proprietor, a supposedly prominent business man, to have a look at the defendant. The deputy sheriff serving the subpœna found that the gentleman and all his family had suddenly left on a trip. The result was an acquittal, and as it was the first prominent case I had lost myself, the courthouse employees, all of the opposition, hailed it with delight and the story lost nothing in their telling.

I may add in passing that while some of my friends criticized me for changing this indictment to first degree and pressing it to trial, because it is a type of case so difficult to win that most prosecutors allow them quietly to die, I am convinced that it was sound policy, after much more experience than I then had. If you put gangsters on trial for murders they commit among themselves, even if they are acquitted, they quit committing murders in your jurisdiction. They never know when they might get a bad break in the evidence or in a hard-boiled jury, and it costs them money for lawyers and time in jail. We tried two more of the same kind a year later and again both were acquitted, but from that time there was not a gang killing in Hamilton County for nearly four years. They do their murdering elsewhere.

During the trial of the Wrassman case came word that George Remus had shot his wife at Eden Park. The next eleven weeks were about the most wearing I ever put in. I have elsewhere [1] discussed some of the issues in that case. Suffice it to say that public sentiment in Cincinnati was almost entirely in favor of Remus and against the dead woman. It was clear that it was a first-degree murder and equally clear that Remus would set up insanity of a temporary and impulsive character as his defense. All of which meant that the only chance of convicting him was in delay, in the hope that public sentiment would swing. I am frank to say that I had not had sufficient experience to realize that, and when the judge on the criminal bench, only in office since January, insisted on going ahead during his three-month term on that assignment (ending December 31), I did not oppose it.

The result was almost certain in view of the feeling of the people when the trial began. It was only the courage of the judge in refusing to submit a "not guilty" verdict that prevented Remus's complete release. The shift in sentiment that began as soon as Remus started to perform in the courtroom could not reach the sequestered jury, as was indicated by their conduct after the verdict, wishing Remus a Merry Christmas in the jail and attending a party given by him. The reaction in popular feeling was completed when the Cincinnati papers for several weeks

[1] *World's Work*, May, 1928.

printed editorial after editorial from every city in the United States condemning the result and the jury. The prosecutor who tried the case was the natural object of popular resentment locally and again the Organization employees in the courthouse took pains to increase the feeling. It was extended to cover the whole movement, and none of the solid accomplishments of my staff could redeem the situation.

I would record one most desirable result of the Remus verdict. The outcry against the system that could produce such a jury was so loud that the Common Pleas judges revised the system completely and called in two well-known business men to draw the names that went into the wheel for the sheriff to pull out. Ever since that day our juries in both civil and criminal matters have been of high average ability and integrity, and the system of handling them is most economical and satisfactory.

Mr. Ach, as treasurer, was the outstanding star of our team. The first thing he found when he came into office on September 1, 1927, was a tremendous lot of delinquent personal property taxes. It must be understood that this was not a case of property concealed or not reported for taxation to be ferreted out by the tax collector. It was rather a matter of property reported for taxation and tax bills utterly disregarded. In the case of real estate, delinquent taxes will probably be collected eventually unless the value drops out completely, as perhaps in the collapse of a land boom. But in the case of tangible property reported by individuals and corporations, the very fact of the tax being unpaid may indicate the likelihood of disappearance or insolvency, and after such an event the county can whistle for its money.

The delinquency in many cases went back for six years and more for the same person, and left the inescapable inference that the obligation was not enforced because of political favoritism. Where that was not the case, still the taxes were not collected because the treasurer and the prosecutor feared the unpopularity of strenuous measures. This was frankly admitted in Cuyahoga County (Cleveland), where the delinquencies in these taxes amounted to millions of dollars at the time the new intangible tax went into effect in 1931, ending the uniform personal property tax.

Mr. Ach went after these accounts as if they were receivables of an ordinary business, and he arranged with me to add a man to my legal staff who would put in full time on the job, bringing suit where necessary. In the month of September the treasurer's office took in $20,000 from this source, and Seasongood did not fail to call attention to the fact in the city campaign then going on. Of course, there were many accounts that had to be charged off, but the money poured steadily in. In February, 1927, of the current personal property taxes then due there had been $208,359 unpaid. The effect of Mr. Ach's work was such that of the current taxes due in February, 1928, only $18,889 was allowed to become delinquent, and nearly half of that was in litigation.

By June 1, 1928, nine months after he took office, Mr. Ach had collected $166,419 from delinquent personal property taxpayers other than estates, while the amount collected by his predecessor in the similar period the year before was $21,785. Mr. Ach figured the average annual loss to the county by the former neglect of duty at no less than $75,000 per annum.

The surprising thing about this collection was that it produced great popular enthusiasm. Those who had paid on time were, of course, far more numerous than those who reported but did not pay, and they quickly realized that the failure of others to pay made them pay more the next year. The long-time results are reflected in the

Cincinnati attitude toward payment of real estate taxes during the depression, referred to later.

Besides all this, Mr. Ach found all tax bills being prepared in duplicate by hand, some 200,000 or more of them. The opportunity for mistakes was naturally very great. He had a study made by the Bureau of Governmental Research and soon installed a system of typewritten bills with carbons and stubs; then he promptly reduced the size of his office to what was really needed to do the work.

As the 1928 county campaign approached, Mr. Ach himself refused to run again, but an equally strong candidate was found by the Citizens in Edgar Friedlander, a retired broker with a wide following among social-minded people. Dr. Swing was by this time decidedly on the Organization side and was endorsed by them, but it was not considered worth while to put up an opponent for coroner.

On the Organization side one event had taken place which proved of lasting benefit to the cause of good government. One of the county commissioners resigned early in 1928, and with the prestige of the victory in the matter of presidential delegates, the Citizens group were able to defeat any candidates of the objectionable type. When A. E. Anderson suggested Charles H. Urban, the forward-looking members of the Republican Executive Committee were able to force his recommendation, and the public officials concerned promptly made the appointment. He also was endorsed by both sides in the 1928 primary and was, of course, elected in the fall. He made it possible, among other things, to designate Fred Hoehler, recently appointed city welfare director, as what amounted to county welfare director as well. This combination proved a great advantage when the pressure of unemployment arrived later.

The other offices were bitterly contested. My opponent in the 1926 primary, Ed. D. Schorr, was made campaign manager, and he put together a machine of greater strength than had been seen in Cincinnati for a good many years.

The Citizens Republican Committee started their campaign for their ticket of sound business men with a dinner on July 19, and, as before, Seasongood sounded the tocsin. This time he went after the local agent for the tar of the Barrett Company and his attorney on the ground that they were in politics for their business and were both paid on the basis of the number of gallons sold in Hamilton County. He followed with attacks on his old enemy, the Rapid Transit Commission, because Schorr had been its counsel. And he continued by going after various right-hand men of Schneller's in the colored wards. He recalled that the sanitary engineer had a fee contract rushed through in 1926 for fear the Citizens candidates might win and question it. This particular individual had been brought from Toledo for the job. The last heads to be swatted were those connected with the clerk of courts, for he had charge of the police court clerk, too, and the city had been having a great deal of trouble with that office in connection with police matters. A clerk of police court who had done a good job in clearing out some of the questionable characters had been fired by the Organization clerk of courts, apparently for that very reason.

The Organization had nothing much to say by way of defense, and many of the attacks were unanswerable. A rabies epidemic had made dog-catching important and the legislature finally provided for a county dog warden. In ten months, in redemption money and from sale of animals, the warden collected $2,643 as compared with $467 brought in by the sheriff in the same period the year before; and the increased activity brought about the receipt of $33,914 in dog licenses in the ten months, compared with $21,430 for the entire previous year. It will be observed, I might remark in passing, that we don't overlook many bets in Cincinnati political campaigns.

But however valid the arguments might be, especially those having to do with a contractors' ring on county road jobs, an August primary and the revived Organization were too much for us. Only Swing, Urban and Friedlander on our ticket pulled through, and Friedlander was the only one in a contest. Whereas I had won in 1926 by about 30,000 to 29,000, I lost this time by about 27,000 to 37,000. Again all records for a primary vote were smashed, but that was not much consolation, and Heuck, Ach and Friedlander looked forward to a lonely time at the courthouse. The glee of the Organization could not be restrained, and in the winter after the election Schorr told the Cleveland Republicans the experiment in nonpartisan government in Cincinnati would not last long, and a partisan Republican administration would soon occupy the city hall. He seems to have convinced even Cleveland Democrats, for Newton D. Baker made the same prediction in February, 1929.

One interesting by-product of our battle was that Cincinnati candidates in state contests profited largely by the size of our primary vote in 1926 and 1928 compared with that in other places. Two Cincinnatians won out in August, 1928, Myers Cooper for Governor (for the second time) and Gilbert Bettman for Attorney-General. Both won largely by the Hamilton County vote and were elected in the fall. As Bettman had been a violent Charter opponent, his vote demonstrated how strictly separate Cincinnatians keep their local and their state or national votes.

Another result was the elimination of the Citizens Committee from representation on the Republican Executive Committee, as well as the elimination of a large part of those precinct representatives elected to the County Central Committee in 1926. We had learned our lesson about primaries and it was the last time we ever tried to beat the Organization at that game. Our earnest advice to other civic gladiators is to stay away from them. They are generally placed at the times most inconvenient for everyone except politicians. Ours are still in August except in presidential years, and Cincinnatians either take their vacations away in that month or take them on the front porch and won't move for anybody. The weather is hot and people won't work unless their jobs are at stake. Everything in the primary system is "fixed" against the amateur. It is the one time when the jobholder and his three or four relatives, friends and debtors are absolutely invincible.

However, the fact that we had learned a useful lesson did not cheer us up much. It was in a way the low point in the morale of the Independent movement and we looked forward to 1929 with some misgivings.

CHAPTER TWELVE

THE THIRD CAMPAIGN FOR COUNCIL IN THE CITY AND THE RESIGNATION OF SHERRILL—1929 AND 1930

As the year of the next council election opened the record of accomplishment had expanded greatly. A second brief review may be worth while.

By 1929 Hoehler had been able to get his welfare department in shape, and in the spring Colonel Sherrill formed his Permanent Committee on the Stabilization of Employment, certainly the first step anywhere to combat the coming depression. An increase in unemployment was noted from May to September, and it was more rapid thereafter. The Cincinnati interest in this problem had been stimulated by the Community Chest, and the depression of 1920 had produced at least one successful experiment, the Procter & Gamble scheme of guaranteed employment for forty-eight weeks a year. The subcommittees of the permanent committee are given in a note.[1]

The city manager had also reopened the workhouse and reconditioned it, after which all the city prisoners were removed from the county jail. They had been rotting there in idleness and now were put to work on useful city tasks, much to their physical and mental benefit.

One of the curious results of the new administration's

[1] (1) On state-city employment bureau; (2) on continuous employment; (3) on temporary employment; (4) on public works; (5) on coöperation with social agencies; (6) on relief of transients; (7) on state and national coöperation; (8) on fact-finding (census, etc.); (9) on publicity and education; (10) on budget and finance.

policy of discipline in the police department was the great increase in the number of streetwalkers downtown. Where before payment of petty graft by favored individuals with support from the police court had limited the number, now all restrictions were off and the police judges either would not or could not handle the problem. Fortunately someone conceived the idea of treating it as a health problem, and prostitutes after an examination were quarantined in the women's ward of the workhouse. When the courts sustained the practice, the problem disappeared overnight.

The police even succeeded in preventing open violations of the prohibition laws, so that the public flouting of the Constitution, so characteristic of the large cities in the United States during these last years, never developed in Cincinnati to the same degree. Our people resent prohibition so far as the large majority are concerned, but they are law-abiding, and Sherrill's popularity was not affected at all by his insistence that the police should go after bootleggers and beer flats.

All city activities had expanded since 1927. The rebuilding of the streets with no section slighted was, of course, the most obvious feature. Sixty-one miles (on a uniform thirty-foot basis) of new streets had been laid down in three years, as compared with fifty-four miles in the previous ten years under the old Organization. Streets laid in 1928 at 1925 prices would have cost $263,000 more. The city hall had not only been cleaned inside and out, but had been so rearranged and remodeled as to give one-third more space.

Cases of sewer relief in 1925 had been eighty-nine. In the next three years they averaged over ten times that number, and this was typical of other similar services. Twenty-nine miles of sewers had been built in the three years as compared with a mile and three-quarters in 1925,

THE THIRD CAMPAIGN FOR COUNCIL

and again the cost per mile was down 50 per cent. The old sewer plans of the Hunt administration took on new life.

All this rebuilding cost money, but some of it was assessed on benefited property and the balance was made part of a joint bond improvement program, worked out by an unofficial committee representing city, schools and county. Over $25,000,000 in bond issues were voted by the people in 1925, 1926 and 1927, and there were many issues voted in years before but never used. But that did not mean these would be used. The Bureau of Governmental Research studied the trend of the tax duplicate and forecast also the probable future levies both for current expenses and for debt service. Then the committee fixed a maximum rate beyond which they would not allow taxes to go, and the bureau told them how many bonds could be issued each year for the next five years without exceeding that rate. The committee sat down with all the projects proposed by any department or subdivision before them and sorted them out in accordance with their importance and immediate necessity. Then they were assigned to the programs for each of the next five years. In that way an improvement association or property owner could tell just when the improvement he was interested in would be reached.

The program was reviewed each year, and because it was informal and flexible it could always be revised for the succeeding five years. This presented great advantages over the so-called blanket bond issue, for a change in circumstances could readily be met by a change in program.

Included in these bond issues was one for a municipal airport which was bought and built up to be one of the best in the country, only twenty minutes from downtown. Its cost was a minimum.

Parking privileges on vacant city property downtown, formerly handed out to deserving Republicans, were let out on bids for some $15,000 a year or more. Employees, formerly brought in from all over town on city time to draw their pay in cash, were now paid by check, and, as I have mentioned, the entire city bookkeeping system was revised so that a financial statement of every fund could be given the city manager every morning as of the close of business the day before.

The new charter had provided for public advertisements in a city newspaper instead of in the daily papers. What had cost $25,000 a year could now be done at a profit, and with far greater convenience to those interested in bidding on public contracts. One by-product of this was that the *Commercial Tribune,* one of the two morning papers (now defunct) immediately lost its friendship for the Charter administration and the Citizens, and became the only invariable supporter of the Organization among the Cincinnati dailies. The advertising payments had gone almost entirely to it, and their loss meant the difference between breaking even and losing money, between life and death.

The new Union Terminal had been progressing well, especially in its dealings with the city. Its chief engineer, Colonel Henry M. Waite, had formerly been city engineer in the Hunt administration, and then city manager of Dayton, and his tact and ability were matched by the straightforward and business-like attitude of council. Many streets had to be vacated and traffic across the new location provided for; all went forward with only minor disagreements and without the slightest suggestion of corruption.

A new record system had been installed for the police department in January, 1928, and the department had new and roomy quarters. The problem of political sabotage in both fire and police departments had come to the fore, nevertheless, and trouble was beginning over the unsound actuarial condition of both pension funds, referred to in the Upson Report. The payments for the police relief had ranged from $130,784 in 1922 to $197,080 in 1925, while the Charter had appropriated $318,000 in 1927 and $334,000 in 1928. For fire pensions payments had ranged from $153,780 in 1922 to $172,223 in 1925, while the Charter had paid out $261,239 in 1927 and $266,982 in 1928. But the pensioners continued to fight the administration bitterly.

The Charter administration had motorized one of its own public utility services, the collection of waste and ashes, and was furnishing greatly improved service at slightly lower cost. The feature most liked by the housewife was the innovation of collecting from the house-line instead of requiring her either to take the cans to the curb or to tip the collectors to come and get them.

During the period the city council had provided for a classification of all positions in the city service and had established standard rates of pay for the same work in different departments with a rising scale upward for length of service. This study showed how low were the rates in comparison with wages paid in business and in many cases paying the minimum meant a raise. The morale was, of course, greatly improved, although in these branches, as in the fire and police, political sabotage continued. If Colonel Sherrill had any fault, it was his faith in all city employees, and a few heads of departments were kept too long. On the other hand, nearly all this good work was done by the old city employees under fresh intelligent direction. A study made by a Cincinnati paper in 1933 showed surprisingly little politics in the city service in the seven years from January 1, 1926, confirming the figures already given on the 7 per cent turnover per year.

These and many other topics were the subjects of discussion in the 1929 campaign, but the Charter record could not disguise the fact that it was a difficult year, and four of the Charter majority were retiring—Field, Eisen, Dixon and, above all, Seasongood. This left only Rose and Matthews as veterans. Nevertheless, the two Democrats and five Republicans added proved a strong ticket. Julian Pollak was a steel manufacturer who had been active in the Community Chest and especially interested in negro work. Russell Wilson has been referred to as assistant editor of the *Times-Star* and president of the Cincinnatus Association. His gift of speech was quite as happy as that of Seasongood and his biting editorials had on occasion helped the Charter and Citizens' cause greatly. William Licht was a wholesaler well known from Rotary, and Harold Murray was a greatly respected member of the Typographical Union. Ed. Imbus had run two years before, but failed of election. John Druffel was a widely known and well-liked Irish lawyer, and Harry Garrison was a retired executive of Procter & Gamble.

The Republicans had opposed to this ticket a full slate of nine for the first time. Yeatman was now a recognized candidate and Daly ran again, but Schneller had withdrawn. Joseph H. Woeste was another municipal court judge, and Alex Patterson was the former city treasurer let out in January, 1926, and a candidate for sheriff in the August primary that year. Max Friedman was named on the theory that he would take a supposed Jewish vote from Pollak. The rest of the ticket had a combination of business and Organization affiliations.

This Republican ticket was not arrived at without difficulty. The problem of a negro candidate has been referred to in connection with the 1927 election. The colored population of the city was 11 per cent of the total, as the 1930 census showed. Inasmuch as there are nine members of council, it will readily be seen that if the colored voters united upon a candidate, and if they all voted for him (as colored voters often do not), they would elect one member out of nine, according to the theory of proportional representation. Colored voters are traditionally Republican and had been under the domination of the Republican organization, providing a block of votes that often constituted the balance of power. There was, therefore, no great pressure upon the City Charter Committee to nominate a negro as one of its ticket. It is hard to say what efforts were made within the Republican organization for representation, but it is sure that such efforts resulted only in the denial of a place. When their plea to the Republicans was refused, the colored group agreed upon two candidates, Hall again and George W. B. Conrad, a respected lawyer on the staff of the Pennsylvania Railroad, and proceeded to educate their people to vote for those two, and then to vote for no further choices.

The atmosphere of the campaign was not especially different from the prior ones. Again large increases in expenditure were the burden of the Republican story, but they had no siege gun like Seasongood to make their points effective. He opened the Charter campaign at the Avondale school as he had before and he was able to point out some of the effects of good government on goodwill in the outside world. "It is now a colorful city and is reaping the advantage of good government in improved credit and attractiveness to new industries." It was generally rated as the best governed city in the United States. One of the principal answers to the cry of expense was the tax rate, which was the lowest in nine years, and the net bonded indebtedness, which after three and one-half years of Charter government was $2,585,864 less, or a reduction of about 6 per cent.

A new turn was given to the Republican attacks by their pointing out that there was an increase of over 1,000 employees from January, 1926, to January, 1929; to which the Charter candidates replied that it was made up: police 112, firemen 18, Recreation Commission 57 (established by vote of the people in 1926 with a mandatory levy of $1/_{10}$ mill), workhouse 48 (closed in 1925), street cleaning 125, airport, building commissioner's office (to meet building increases), State-City Employment Bureau, welfare, City Planning Commission, hospital staff (100 under county in 1925), and health department.

But the most telling Charter argument grew out of certain happenings in the 1929 session of the Ohio Legislature. In 1928 it was discovered by the Charter group that the law probably put the employees of the municipal court clerk under civil service. The Civil Service Commission promptly proceeded to enforce the law. Immediately after the legislature met, the new legislative delegation from Hamilton County introduced a bill given the name of its author, E. G. Schuessler, to remove them from civil service. All the city administration and other Charter supporters opposed it, but made no progress at all. In the course of the debate in the Ohio Senate, Cliff Martin, formerly floor leader of the old council, was reported as saying, in explaining why the bill should be passed, "We want the jobs!" He denies having said just that, but it did represent the Machine attitude, and the remark was seized upon as a burning issue of the campaign.

One always wonders whether individual campaign arguments really affect general trends in sentiment. The Charter group was losing some Republican votes, but was

THE THIRD CAMPAIGN FOR COUNCIL 183

gaining back most of the loss. At any rate the vote on election day showed nearly as good a majority of first-choice Charter votes as two years before. Russell Wilson showed an amazing strength and nearly equaled the vote of Seasongood or Dixon in previous years. The real battle was for last place between Pollak and Daly, the Charter having made sure of five places and the Organization of three. Hall, the colored man, was the eleventh after getting Conrad's votes, and had reached over 8,000. Would his supporters follow instructions and express no more choices, leaving Pollak winner by the 2,277 votes he was ahead, or would the votes go back to Daly and the Organization as the old crowd hoped? The interest of the people in the Hotel Gibson Roof Garden was intense as Hall's ballots were distributed according to next choices. There were 4,410 who had no choice, having followed orders of their group. But even the balance, if properly distributed, could elect Daly. He did get nearly half, but over 600 votes went to Pollak and his lead was still more than 1,200, a clear victory. One could not help thinking what would happen in the future if Hall were on the Organization ticket, and if, when he was not elected, the regulars should get all his second choices. But sufficient unto the day—and the Charter was in for another two years with the same safe majority of six to three.

It should be noted that the six places were achieved perhaps for another reason. Only three of the Charter six were Republicans this time instead of four, and three were Democrats. Unless the three Democrats—Druffel, Matthews and Imbus—had all had about the same number of first-choice votes and increased at about the same rate, one of them probably would have been in tenth place instead of Daly when he was eliminated. Such an even distribution was intentional and is the usual practice on the part of the Democratic organization, so I have been told, but if so, it is certain that it could not work this way more than once in 100,000 times. The Republicans had found it impossible in 1925 when they tried it. It probably would not work again even with the same candidates.

When the council organized, Wilson's fine surplus vote made him the sure choice for mayor, even though it was his first term, for it reflected his leadership in this and previous campaigns. Pollak succeeded Field in the difficult public utilities assignment, Imbus went into the committee on highways, and Druffel to law.

I should have stopped before this to mention the outstanding service of Charles O. Rose as chairman of the Finance Committee of council. He was the brake on expenditures that kept the vehicle at a steady rate of progress and avoided the pitfalls that have upset so many reform movements after their first successes. Not a detail escaped his eye and he knew the budget as well as the city manager did. In 1927 he accepted the endorsement of the Organization and as a result he lost considerable Charter support; so that he was tenth in first-choice votes and was the ninth man elected, just under the wire. By 1929, however, he had established his place in the minds of Cincinnatians and was third in first-choice votes, and elected next after Wilson on the latter's surplus. In 1931 he tried to retire, but was drafted to run again, and again he was the second elected, on Wilson's surplus. The forcefulness of his "No" to those who wanted money spent, while often it was not graced by much tact, evidently did not up to that time diminish his own political strength on the Charter side.

The quality of this council at once began to demonstrate itself. Wilson was a most tactful leader and arranged for the Charter members to meet for lunch each Wednesday noon before the weekly council meeting and a little later invited them for a longer conference at dinner at his house once a month. At various times the Organization spokesmen have attacked these practices as secret caucuses, which is about the silliest criticism ever leveled at the Charter administration. A more valid criticism would be that these conferences have not included various representatives of the Charter and Citizens group more closely connected with our own amateur organization. Some such unofficial advisers bring fresh viewpoints and can serve as political scouts in a most useful way. In this respect the Citizens officeholders by meeting at fairly frequent intervals with the entire group have kept in closer touch with current public sentiment.

In June, 1930, like a bolt out of the blue, came Colonel Sherrill's resignation as city manager. Lehman Brothers, the bankers for the Kroger Company, came to him to ask if he could suggest anyone for an executive position as vice-president with that company, which was then going through a reorganization. The conversation led to an invitation to the Colonel himself, and the matter was closed and announced almost immediately. Many were the guesses ventured as to why the change occurred, but the fact seemed to be exactly what Sherrill said in making the announcement, that he felt his task was finished. He had undertaken and carried through with amazing and outstanding success the complete physical rebuilding of the city and that had carried with it an equally amazing spiritual change in the people of the city. His popularity was at its height, but already there were signs that the constant pressure of the opposition seizing hold of local issues, such as the building of an incinerator in the Camp Washington neighborhood, was beginning to affect public opinion. Colonel Sherrill was undoubtedly wise from his own viewpoint and, great as was the loss for the Charter, it was probably for the best in the long run. The Colonel retired as the greatest city manager in American municipal history, and so he remains in the public mind.

With Cincinnati's reputation for municipal government the candidates for the vacancy were innumerable and, besides the volunteers, nearly any able man in the governmental field could have been secured. That, however, did not make the task any easier, and the entire Charter group joined in the effort to sift those available and to search out good material in addition. The choice finally narrowed down to U. S. Grant, who had succeeded Colonel Sherrill in Washington, and C. A. Dykstra, head of the personnel division of the Los Angeles waterworks, one of the great municipal public utilities of the country. Dykstra had been considered when Sherrill was chosen, and when Grant on second thought eliminated himself from consideration there was no doubt about the selection.

It took some time, of course, for the public to form an opinion of the new man; but for those closer to the administration his prompt and tactful handling of a difficult problem in connection with the reorganization of the waterworks, for which his most recent experience qualified him especially, was all they needed. They felt the Charter movement had surmounted its most severe test and had demonstrated that it was something permanent, not dependent on the character, ability and popularity of a single individual.

CHAPTER THIRTEEN

PUBLIC UTILITIES

EXCEPT for a few incidental references, I have not discussed the record of the Charter administration on the subject of public utilities. The omission was intentional, for it is a matter so easily confused that a single clear story covering the whole period is essential.

There have been a few contests with the Telephone Company. It is one of the Bell System, but happens to be the only subsidiary which the American Telephone & Telegraph Company does not control, for it owns only 24 per cent of the common stock. That may explain why the relations have been good, for the company is home-owned. These contests took place before the Ohio Public Utilities Commission and were of no great importance.

The new street railway service-at-cost franchise went into effect in November, 1925, for twenty-five years, so that the Charter government had only to administer its terms, complicated a little at first by the development of buses and later on a great deal by the taxicab muddle. But the street lighting contract and the gas and electric rate ordinances have been constant sources of debate and discussion. It must be clearly understood that these last issues are still open questions and may not be finally settled for some time.

The opponent of the city in this controversy was the Columbia Gas & Electric Corporation through its local subsidiary, the Union Gas & Electric Company. I am not the one to write the history of the Columbia System, but I can give a brief history of its relation with the City of Cincinnati for the last six years. About all that newer arrivals in the city know about its past is that it was organized over twenty-five years ago by Archibald White to distribute natural gas from the West Virginia fields to Southern Ohio, and especially to Cincinnati. After a slow beginning it became a profitable enterprise and in more recent years has devoted the greater part of its attention to the development and protection of its electric business in the Miami Valley (Cincinnati, Hamilton and Dayton districts). Since the early days its executive direction has been from New York. It has not been a home-owned utility like the Street Railway Company or the Telephone Company, although its local operating subsidiary some years back engaged in one of the usual campaigns to sell its preferred stock to consumers. The Cincinnati property is owned by the Cincinnati Gas & Electric Company, a locally-owned corporation, and it is leased to the Union Gas & Electric Company perpetually.

In the field of regulation it has been the general policy of the Columbia Corporation to stay out of Ohio except through the necessary presence of its operating subsidiaries. The gas destined for Cincinnati was brought through Kentucky by the Cincinnati Gas Transportation Company and delivered at the state line on the north bank of the Ohio. The company's position for many years was that it was not a utility but a mining company, mining natural gas, and that not only was it not subject to the jurisdiction of the Ohio Public Utilities Commission, but that a city in determining what was a fair rate to pay for gas could not examine what it cost the Columbia Corporation or its subsidiaries to bring the gas to the state line. The Supreme Court of the United States removed

PUBLIC UTILITIES

the ground for this position by its decision in the Western Distributing Company case.[1]

There have been three phases to the controversy: consumer electric rates, consumer gas rates, and city street lighting (which is a small amount of gas and a large amount of electricity).

CONSUMER ELECTRIC RATES

On August 11, 1925, in spite of the rumpus stirred up by Laurent Lowenberg for the Cincinnatus Association, the council of "voting automata" passed an ordinance fixing the electric rates for a period of ten years. Charles O. Rose registered the sole negative vote.

Mayor George Carrel vetoed the ordinance on August 20, and stated the situation as he saw it in his veto message. In the first place, said he, the term was for ten years, obviously too long in view of the steady decrease in the cost of generating electricity all over the United States. In the next place, the rates were the asking price of the Union Gas & Electric Company, Columbia subsidiary, and council had accepted them without any expert investigation. Finally, provision was made for a charge for incidental power used in commercial establishments, but a householder, to get a power rate for his washer, icebox, irons, etc., had to pay for an extra meter and various other charges that gave him a minimum rate of $3 a month.

Council passed the ordinance over the mayor's veto (and Rose's "No") two months before the election in that year. But Rose and the Charter group circulated and filed a referendum petition and suspended the opera-

[1] *Western Distributing Co.* v. *Public Service Commission of Kansas* (1932), 285 U. S. 119.

tion of the ordinance until a vote set for the November election in 1926.

When the Charter administration came in, Rose introduced an ordinance repealing the 1925 ordinance, but the repeal was no good unless the referendum was effective. To test this point a suit was filed attacking the signatures on the referendum petitions. After winning before a master commissioner, the city lost in the Common Pleas Court, and was on the way to the Court of Appeals.

The whole question was finally disposed of after two years when John Ellis negotiated a settlement of the suit and council passed a five-year rate ordinance on May 17, 1928, promptly accepted by the company. The saving to the consumers was estimated at $750,000 per annum.

Now that ordinance has expired and a new study by Burns & McDonnell has been completed as to a new rate. Council has just passed a new ordinance, which the company will probably appeal to the Public Utilities Commission. Incidentally, the company did not improve their position with the public, whatever may be the merits of the question, when it was disclosed this summer that the generating plants were burning gas at an excess cost over coal of $1,500,000.

CONSUMER GAS RATES

I have already mentioned the telegram from Hynicka about the gate rate ordinance of November, 1921. That ordinance operated on the step-up theory, that the more gas you used the more you should pay per 1,000 cubic feet. There was an increase from 30 cents to 50 cents in the rate for the small consumer. Then in the spring of 1925 came the proposed five-year ordinance that went back to the step-down theory, a lower rate per 1,000 cubic

PUBLIC UTILITIES

feet the more gas you used, but it carried an average rate of 66 cents per thousand.

The ordinance was passed by council on April 28, 1925, 23 to 8 (Rose again in the negative), and after Mayor Carrel's veto was repassed on May 19, 1925, over his veto. A referendum was had on the ordinance, and it was voted down 53,596 to 51,404. But the company promptly brought suit and on the strength of a previous decision on the same franchise it was held that no referendum was legal and the ordinance went into effect.

As soon as the Charter group came in they employed W. J. Hagenah to investigate and determine what was a proper rate, and on the strength of his report passed the ordinance of May 14, 1930. The average rate fixed by this was approximately 59 cents. The company refused to accept it and brought suit to enjoin its enforcement in the United States District Court. When the court would not grant a temporary injunction, they dismissed the suit and appealed to the Public Utilities Commission.

In the meantime the city had employed A. S. B. Little and he was just beginning his work when the 1930 ordinance was adopted. When his full report became available, the city passed a new ordinance on January 14, 1931, for an indefinite period, the average rate of which is about 50 cents. The company also appealed this to the Public Utilities Commission. The effect of these appeals was to suspend the operation of the ordinances, but the company was required to give bond for refunds in sums which now total $5,000,000.

Little died and the city employed H. R. Allensworth to succeed him, the same expert who also represents the City of Columbus and the City of Cleveland. The Cincinnati case has dragged on and will not be reached until this fall (1933).

The Columbus case was older and the decision of the

majority of the commission was handed down before election day of 1932 for a 55-cent rate.

With that decision there was considerable political pressure in Cincinnati for a settlement. The two Cincinnati ordinances in question had been published in the *City Bulletin,* a newspaper put out by the city for that and similar purposes, to which I have already referred. The Supreme Court of Ohio, in an assessment case, held publication in the *City Bulletin* invalid, and that threw doubt on the validity of both gas rate ordinances. Since the company had itself appealed, it could not question the jurisdiction of the commission on this ground, but the chairman of the commission raised the jurisdictional question himself. It did seem a time to settle.

The company was asking 66 cents, that is, the existing rate, and the city offered 50 cents. The company indicated it would compromise on 62 cents and, after considering the relative distances of Cincinnati and Columbus from the gas fields, the city offered temporarily the rate fixed for Columbus, that is, 55 cents, and ultimately 2 cents less than the Columbus rate finally fixed. But the company rejected the offer.

The situation was dangerous politically. It was over two years since the new ordinances had been adopted and people were still paying the old rates. Furthermore, while the conduct of the negotiations by the company officials had been most unsatisfactory according to the Charter councilmen, the publicity on the part of the city had been badly handled and the true situation was rather obscure to the public.

At this crisis the city filed a suit in the Supreme Court of Ohio to prevent the Public Utilities Commission from dismissing the appeals. The Supreme Court reversed itself and held the *City Bulletin* publication valid and the appeals properly before the commission. Furthermore, at about the same time the court decided the Columbus rate case by supporting the minority member of the commission and holding that a 48-cent rate was not confiscatory. On that basis the Cincinnati ordinance with the 50-cent rate was equally valid in all probability, as a differential of 2 or 3 cents in favor of Columbus seems about right. But the company has appealed the decision to the Supreme Court of the United States.

STREET LIGHTING

A contract entered into in 1925 expires in 1935. In a recent survey of the City waterworks by Burns & McDonnell they called attention to the Western Hills Pumping Station, showing that some additional capacity was needed. Following this report, the Union Gas & Electric Company offered figures to show that electric power bought from them would be cheaper than steam power generated by the city. This question was investigated by Burns & McDonnell, who disputed the economy of buying electric power, and the suggestion was then offered that the real economy might be for the waterworks to generate the necessary power at the main pumping station on Eastern Avenue, which apparently had excess capacity.

This led to a complete investigation for the city by Fosdick & Hilmer, who have reported, in effect, that the generation by the city of electric power as proposed would not be economical for the sole use of the Western Hills Pumping Station. However, as a loop would have to be installed for safety, it was found possible to pick up on the loop a number of city services, which taken together would show considerable saving. This conclusion the company has disputed, but it came in and offered reductions to the city, schools and the university of about $30,-000 per annum. A further study was then made to see if the downtown boulevard light area and traffic signal area could not be served also. The report on this states that a considerable saving can be made, and incidentally claims that the present charge for street lighting is excessive.

At once the cry was raised that the city was going into public ownership, to which Rose replied that it was not, but that what was proposed was exactly what a number of manufacturing plants and office buildings in the community did already—to use excess steam capacity to supply its needs or those of its neighbors in the way of electric power.

In the meantime some of our professional taxpayers have initiated an ordinance to be voted on in November, 1933, calling for municipal ownership of the gas and electric systems. None of the political groups have endorsed it, but both have condemned it.

CHAPTER FOURTEEN

FUSION IN THE COUNTY AND ITS RESULTS FOR THE CHARTER—1930-31

To go back a little, as the Depression (with a capital "D") came on us and the year 1930 opened the question before the Republicans of the Charter group was the puzzling one, "What shall be done in the county?" Robert Heuck's term as recorder was running out at the end of 1930, and Edgar Friedlander's the following September. Should we give up and let the Organization take over these two offices and restore them to the patronage system? All of us were definitely convinced that a fight in the August primary was impossible; we had all we wanted of that in 1928. We knew we could not finance it, and, even if we could, there was no chance of success with the increased effectiveness of the Organization, and the prestige of its previous victory in 1928. Return to the Organization itself did not seem likely to produce a satisfactory regular ticket on a platform upon which we could stand, and a threat to contest the primary would not be a particularly effective bluff.

That left only quitting or coalition with the Democrats as possibilities. The Democrats might be unwilling because a fusion ticket would have to be in a separate column on the ballot and that might injure the Democratic state ticket. From our standpoint it meant the first break away from the Republican party in an election involving a partisan ballot, and we knew that some of our own people would shy away from it even while they supported the

Charter. But as our Citizens group met, we were inevitably driven to this combination and a meeting was arranged with leaders among the Democrats.

Somewhat to our surprise the Democrats were favorably impressed with the idea and ready with a plan to solve the difficulty caused by the election laws. They suggested putting up a ticket in the primary, which would then withdraw. That would leave open and unfilled the places in the Democratic column for county officers, and the fusion or Citizens ticket would be in a column of its own. The scheme of such a ticket was made necessary by a growing insurgency among the Democrats fostered perhaps by the Republican organization, but at any rate representing dissatisfaction with the Charter alliance.

Furthermore, the arrangement for a division of the seven places, four to the Republicans and three to the Democrats, was readily agreed to, the sheriff, prosecutor, and recorder going to the Democrats, and the commissioner, auditor, treasurer and coroner to the Republicans. The nominating committee faced a difficult task as always, for not even Friedlander would agree to run again. Nevertheless, when that grand old warrior, Samuel Ach, consented to run for commissioner, Friedlander could not refuse, and Heuck undertook the auditor's job. That took courage, for he knew that he faced a reappraisal of all the property in Hamilton County, which, if done conscientiously, could not fail to stir up all kinds of hornets.

Nothing happened during the summer, of course, until the announcement of the ticket after the August primary and the withdrawal of the seven candidates already nominated by the Democrats. And on September 3, 1930, the usual Organization blunder furnished a splendid start for the campaign. For on that day Captain Heintz, again the campaign chairman, appeared at the Board of Elections with petitions bearing 5,000 signatures nominating the seven candidates for the "Citizens ticket." "Brother, I have to refuse to accept these," said the clerk, an organization Republican of long standing. But the two Democratic members of the board were on hand and promptly called down the clerk for assuming to speak when the board had not yet acted. So the petitions were accepted. Then Ferd. Bader, Jr., secretary of the Republican Executive Committee, but claiming to act in his individual capacity as a citizen, and as a friend of the board, promptly filed a protest that the law did not provide for any such designation as "Citizens ticket," and the board fixed the next day for a hearing. The Citizens Committee appeared through Seasongood, Headley, Robert N. Gorman, the candidate for prosecutor, and Rose, and they denounced those back of Bader's effort to rule the ticket off the ballot. What better issue could have opened the campaign?

The board voted 2-to-1 to disallow the protest, but, being a bipartisan board of four, it took three to carry any proposal, and the motion was lost. Thereupon it was voted to refer the record to the Secretary of State, Clarence Brown, the head of the election boards and in effect the fifth member of the board in each county. As he was a candidate for reëlection and aspired to be Governor, it gave him a pretty political problem as well as a legal one. The scene of the pother was transferred to Columbus.

Meantime the Republican candidates and the decent element on the Republican side were apologizing for the mess and stating frankly they wanted to win fair and square, or not at all, while officially the Central Committee tried, without much success, to disown Bader's efforts.

After another hearing, in Columbus this time, Brown tried to compromise by letting the names go on the ballot, but under the caption "Independents" where apparently any other independents of any stripe would also be grouped, and the Citizens promptly announced an appeal to the courts for a separate column and a circle at the top to permit the voting of a straight ticket. However, they shouted pæans of triumph at the partial victory, and the Democratic State Convention, by chance in session at the moment, denounced the suppression of a free ballot, and charged a conspiracy between the "notorious Hamilton County Republican gang" and Brown, aided and abetted by the Attorney-General (Bettman). They also gleefully denounced the Republican Assembly and the Governor for passing a law that permitted it.

The appeal was filed the next day in the Supreme Court, and heard a week later with all the Citizens forces arguing for a liberal interpretation of the election laws. The court decided it at once, refusing a circle to the Independents but allowing them a separate column and the designation they sought. The Republicans announced that they had accomplished all they wanted in preventing the circle and establishing that the Citizens were not a party. But that was an acknowledgment that Bader's protest was official and not individual, and it gained the Citizens many votes.

Mr. Ach, running for county commissioner, and Seasongood were the headliners of the campaign effort itself, with Mayor Wilson as a strong assistant. The former sounded the keynote in addressing the Citizens women on September 9, telling of the record of the Citizens office-holders as treasurer and recorder, and going on to tell from his own recent experience on the Budget Commission of the high rate of expenditure in the other county offices. He made the prediction that a million dollars could be saved, and that was the text of a running debate that lasted till election day.

Seasongood as usual added something new and different by attacking the sheriff for allowing the slot machines in the county that had been harried in the city by the

Charter administration. The argument was most effective, at least when the defense had little to say except that this was an effort to destroy national parties. Although both Heuck and Friedlander had been elected by united Republican campaigns, the Organization, in reporting the accomplishments of its nominees in county offices, carefully omitted both, and that served for further campaign material.

The election was a complete victory for the Citizens, with Friedlander leading by 19,000 votes. Even Swing, now on the Republican ticket for coroner, was amazed to find himself beaten by 5,000. It meant that only the clerk, surveyor and two county commissioners, none of whom were running, were still Organization, and one of the commissioners, Urban, was of most independent mind. The gloom at the courthouse was funereal.

The most astounding thing in this election from the standpoint of the experienced politician was the fact that the Republicans who lost had a circle in which their supporters could vote a straight ticket for national, state and county offices, while we had to educate Democrats and Independents to mark their state tickets and then to go over to the last column of a big ballot and mark seven X's before seven names down near the bottom. Politicians from out of town are usually incredulous.[1]

It is worth noting that in the same election both Bettman and Brown carried the county by large majorities and were reëlected. It is true that Cooper for Governor, having lost the county when he ran in 1926 and carrying it in 1928 when he was first elected, had lost it this time. But there were a good many other explanations for that, and certainly he was far less anti-Charter and anti-Citizens

---

[1] Mr. Seasongood commented on this in connection with the 1932 election and printed a copy of the ballot. Seasongood, *Local Government in the United States.*

than Bettman. Longworth's majority was one of his lowest for Congress, but Hess, the Republican, won in the other congressional district, which is usually very close, and there again it was not the local fight that affected Longworth's vote. McCulloch, Republican, was swamped by Bulkley for United States Senator, but the growing wet tide was ample to explain the defeat when added to McCulloch's weakness as a candidate. So that the Citizens could claim with reason that their local fight had not injured the Republicans in state or national affairs.

Butterfield, Gorman, Kearns, Beckman and Ach went into office at the beginning of the year. Ach and Urban made a majority of the Board of County Commissioners in all matters in which they agreed, which included all questions of good government and many matters of policy. Beckman stepped into Heuck's shoes in the recorder's office and went forward to equal efficiency and a gradual reduction in expense as the collapse of real estate reduced the amount of work. Gorman kept the same office force as prosecutor, almost entirely inherited by me from Republican sources, restoring one clerk whom I had secured from the city civil service list, but whom my successor had promptly let out. His staff was entirely new. Kearns immediately set to work to get the office of coroner abolished entirely in favor of an appointed medical examiner, and as a preliminary arranged to move the morgue to the City Hospital, and to have the assistant pathologist of the University Medical School do the post-mortems.

Butterfield, as sheriff, took over an office which certainly needed shaking up. His predecessor had begun a county patrol system, and this was now formed into a real police force with the head of the Indian Hill Rangers, a semi-public body in one of the wealthier neighborhoods of the county, as the captain. This man has recently been appointed head of the state highway police. My former secret service officer, also let out by my successor in the prosecutor's office, was made county detective. The two chief office men, both capable, were retained. But Butterfield was under tremendous pressure from the Democratic organization for the jobs that did not seem to be available anywhere else, and to some degree he yielded to it. He did conduct something in the nature of a civil service examination for the county police, and besides scrutinizing those suggested to him by the Democrats, he had no hesitancy in firing them when they proved undesirable. There were a few appointments recommended by members of the Citizens group. Butterfield's family is high in Democratic councils in Hamilton County and it is to his credit that his handling of appointments was such that for a while at least some of them were not on speaking terms with him.

The best thing about the new Citizens officeholders was that they worked together just as they had pledged in their campaign. Ach, Gorman, Butterfield, Beckman, Friedlander and Heuck were in constant touch with each other. There were some disagreements, considerable pressure on Butterfield to balance that from the Democratic organization until his appointments were completed, but an effective and harmonious coöperation was achieved nevertheless.

Heuck's term began early in March and the handling of his office turned out to have great influence on Charter fortunes, or at least so it seemed for a while. As county auditor he was also, under the Ohio law, the chief assessor of real and personal property, and in 1931 he was by law required to reappraise all real estate. The new intangible tax went into effect in 1931, so that he was relieved of the personal property assessment, but the preparation and handling of the returns under the new law was a tremendously more difficult task than before.

So far as real estate was concerned, most auditors in Ohio who were reëlected in 1930, and especially those in all other large counties, started to work on their task in November, for by law it was to be completed by July of 1931. The last appraisal in Hamilton County had taken place seven years before, and the auditor at that time took one year for the land and the next year for the buildings. He had greatly improved on the 1920 appraisal methods, which were a mess, and had taken some of the advice in the Upson Report, which was simultaneous with his land appraisal. But a conscientious 100 per cent appraisal and a proper equalization, as required by Heuck's oath and his legal duty, was literally impossible by July and probably impossible by December 1 when the tax bills were supposed to go out.

Heuck set out to inform himself about modern appraisal methods, consulting both the Manufacturers' and other appraising companies, Philip H. Cornick, and several other of the best known authorities on public appraisal for tax purposes and at his own expense visiting a number of recommended cities to see their systems in operation. He sought to have his predecessor appoint him a deputy without salary and to permit him to employ a few expert advisers on the county payroll in order to lay the groundwork before he took office, but the request was refused. Several meetings of the Citizens group were held both before and after March at which Heuck sought assistance on questions of policy, but the members of the group were not really close enough to the situation to be able to help much. He secured a committee of public-spirited citizens, including Dean Schneider of the university, who went over his plan of attack on his problem and at the same time he asked the Chamber of Commerce to

FUSION IN THE COUNTY

appoint a committee to assist him with comments on unit values when he arrived at that point.

The valuation date was the day before the second Monday in April, 1931, and it is generally conceded by the fair-minded that Cincinnati real estate values had been amazingly little affected by the depression up to that date.[1] The best retail property was still held for as much as $22,000 per front foot, and offers close to that figure were turned down. The Real Estate Board was asked to undertake the fixing of these unit values, downtown first and then to work out, and Heuck made the men selected his deputies. He retained, as he must under the law, the final fixing of the values himself. He enlisted a committee of the best builders in town to check the cubic-foot reproduction values of downtown buildings and costs for other types, and his special staff, selected after a civil service examination given by the university and trained by experts on its faculty, went to work to list every structure

---

[1] In March, 1933, a report prepared for the United States Interstate Commerce Commission by its district appraiser, Paul H. Burman, and on file at the Bureau of Valuation in Washington, had the following to say:

"The City of Cincinnati, Ohio, and environs never had what is termed a real estate boom. Values gradually increased during the thirteen and one-half years prior to June 30, 1929, terminating at a peak or high level during the summer of 1929. From this date to the middle of the year 1931, reliable sources estimate no fluctuation in the value of real estate, either upward or downward. Beginning in the summer of 1931, real estate values generally throughout metropolitan Cincinnati began to decline, the acceleration being more rapid during 1932 and continuing into the first quarter of 1933.

"A study of all factors affecting the value of Cincinnati real estate, together with outside influences resulting from general economic conditions, has resulted in the conclusion that generally, throughout the city, land values have declined 25% during the year, and one-half prior to January 1, 1933. Eighty per cent of this recession occurred within the year 1932; the remainder, or 20 per cent, is attributable to the year 1931."

These conclusions were based on Burman's experience in appraisal in Cincinnati over a period of fifteen years, and in addition upon the trend of rentals as reported by active real estate operators and upon the opinion of eight well-known realtors. He also used all types of available and relevant statistical compilations.

in the county. Incidentally, over $2,000,000 of buildings were found not to be on the tax duplicate at all.

Some of the old records back of 1924 were missing from the auditor's files or were quite incomplete, and many mistakes were found on those that were there. Of course, Heuck's new men made a good many mistakes themselves. In their enthusiasm they listed ancient barns and outhouses, thus placing values that caused the owners to push them over for old lumber as soon as they found it out. But the fact remains that this was the first absolutely complete and conscientious equalization of property in this county.

As Heuck went into office the Bureau of Governmental Research made a study of the "Procedure for Billing, Collection and Settlement of Taxes." This applied to both treasurer and auditor's offices and recommended the printing by the auditor of the tax duplicate from addressograph plates, which could then be sent to the treasurer for the printing of the tax bills. If the plate was correct, no mistakes could be made, but the initial task of transferring to plates the necessary information for 250,000 pieces of property was overwhelming. The system was to be keyed to tabulating machines that could check and total land and buildings separately and by subdivisions. It was a tremendous improvement, likely to save $50,000 a year in the two offices, to say nothing of insuring accuracy, and it is still unique in any governmental agency handling tax billing and collecting.

But the question of policy—whether to install this system during a reappraisal—was serious and Heuck probably made a mistake in attempting it. There can be no doubt that it complicated tremendously his problem of office administration, for his first year with that problem was difficult enough anyway. As it was he left the multitudinous duties of his office, aside from these two, to the experienced staff of his predecessor, only eliminating a few especially obnoxious individual politicos, and concentrated with his new employees on his biggest task.

The Organization and the Downtown Property Owners were, of course, able to keep pretty close track of what went on in Heuck's office. The Property Owners were much disturbed by the arrival at last of the real estate collapse that had begun elsewhere considerably sooner, and they realized also that the equalization was adding greatly to the valuation of downtown property in comparison with other types of real estate. Their alarm was reflected among the real estate men, but the opinions of the latter were recorded under oath and they could hardly avoid standing to their guns. The experts on building costs reduced their opinions considerably as to what costs had been in April, 1931, for they found that they did not know until June or July what April costs actually had been, on account of the numerous bootleg building contracts. The final net result seemed likely to be an increase of about 5 per cent in the total duplicate of real estate, including new and omitted buildings, the increase downtown and in a few other neighborhoods being offset by general reductions elsewhere. The tax rate promised to be down 10 per cent, so that the prospect was for lower taxes for more people than would have to pay increases.

Not much of all this was known to the public as the city campaign got under way after Labor Day, but the auditor had to give the Budget Commission a tentative figure to permit it to fix the various tax rates. When he announced an estimate of 5 per cent increase, the Property Owners and the Organization let out roars of protest and the battle was on. At this stage, Heuck was still doubtful of his office being physically able to get out the tax bills by December 20, when under the law they were due and payable. If he could have sent out the bills with the announcement of the 5 per cent increase there would have been little political danger to the Charter, but he could only give the total. Knowing all this, the Organization began to demand that individual taxpayers be allowed to see the tentative figures of the valuations of their own properties. Heuck was appalled, not only because the figures were still at every conceivable stage of incompleteness and mostly unchecked, but at the clerical task of furnishing them and the effect on his office system of having to handle such records for thousands of inquisitive owners. Naturally he refused. This time the Organization forced the legal action, by demanding disclosure of public records, and their speakers began giving horrible examples of unjust and outrageous increases. Most of them were shown on investigation to be misleading and some definitely false, but it was always too late to catch up with the stories. The Attorney-General, in one of the quickest lengthy opinions on record, held the records public, and poor Heuck had to struggle as best he could to give service to the anxious crowds.

The Charter leaders were frantic and the recriminations in private between some of them and those more distinctly representative of the Citizens group continued for some time after the election was over. Apparently the movement in the city was facing defeat on an issue that had no relation to the city at all, and the fact that all the storm was created by Heuck's conscientious and able devotion to duty was not much of a solace. I have referred to the Joint Bond Program of the city, county and schools and the calculation of future tax rates by the Bureau of Governmental Research upon which the five-year plan was based. The tax rates, of course, had to be calculated with the tax duplicate in mind, and so the bureau in 1929 and 1930 had forecast the tax duplicate for five years ahead, showing percentages of increase based on past experience.

On the basis of this prediction one of the Organization candidates charged Heuck with being a conspirator trying to keep up the tax duplicate in order to furnish the city with money for what he alleged were its tremendously increased expenditures. So at last, more or less by chance, the claim of extravagance and expenditure was lent some apparent support and the future of good government in Cincinnati seemed dark.

For it was good government. I have given some account of Charter accomplishments up to July, 1929, but a great deal of water went over the dam in two years. I have referred to the waterworks reorganization; it was most successful, involving the adoption of a billing system, just previously adopted by the local utility for gas and electric bills, and among other things made possible in 1931 a water rate reduction in 1931 that saved consumers $300,000 per annum. The city began furnishing water meters at a saving of 50 per cent to consumers. The taste of phenol, long suffered in winter because of industrial waste from upriver, was finally conquered. In the old days inspections by way of fire prevention had averaged about 60,000; they reached 170,000 in 1930 and the results showed, for 1930 fire losses in the city were the lowest in cities of 450,000 or over, being $1.73 per capita as compared with $4.48 in Chicago, for instance. The work of the health department and the private social agencies produced in the same year the lowest infant, maternity and tuberculosis mortality in the city's history. After long battles in court, the building of incinerators had been held legal and on June 1, 1931, three of them were opened; the city took over the disposal of garbage, now collected at the rear house line and burned up by the dry waste. The whole change was already proving a great success and the predictions of neighborhood nuisances were speedily proved groundless.

Recreation and parks were under separate boards, but financed by the city, and they, too, were serving more and more of the community with more adequate facilities. A Traffic Safety Council studied every accident and gradually but steadily worked out improvements that reduced the number of fatalities.

Dykstra had changed the administrative set-up considerably. Sherrill had three executive secretaries, but no real department heads; by the end of a year Dykstra had taken Blandford from the bureau to be safety director and Root from the engineering staff of the Cincinnati Union Terminal to direct public works. They were held completely responsible for their departments, as were Ellis in the law department and Gilman in the utilities department.

The greatest progress came in the police under Blandford's leadership. A regional police study was made at the end of 1930 by the bureau for the new Regional Crime Committee. This was a group of private citizens in the two northern Kentucky counties and the four southwestern Ohio counties. The study recommended better coordination of the 147 police agencies in the area by interchange of information and intercommunication by teletype and radio. During the winter and spring all the officials were brought together in each county and a regional police association was formed. Meanwhile Blandford was working on radio and in June, 1931, opened the police broadcasting station. This he combined with the old First District police station as "Station X." The success was immediate. The radio was made available to the other police forces with receiving sets, and the Regional Crime Committee put on steady pressure that in two years had thirty cities and counties so equipped. Not only were stolen autos and prowling burglars spectacularly caught in Cincinnati, but a call from Covington,

Kentucky, for instance, reporting a stolen car, might be broadcast, picked up in Fort Thomas, Kentucky, and the car thieves captured within fifteen minutes. The rate on stolen cars was literally cut in two within a few months. The public was rapidly educated to call Station X as soon as suspicious circumstances of any kind were noticed.

More important than these results was the effect on police morale and discipline. Foot patrol was reduced to a minimum and the city districted for auto patrol. Replies to a broadcast were always within two or three minutes, and orders to go to a particular spot could be executed even more quickly. Though officers were not as noticeable downtown, two scout cars with tear gas, machine- and riot-guns, etc., and four men each were constantly cruising, and even more rapidly available. The officers had to be on the job, and the keen officer had far greater chance to show his ability.

This influence extended across the river into Kentucky and to the neighboring communities. The radio was available to them without charge and they were gladly permitted to use it as a recall system for their own men. When I was prosecutor we could hardly count on the Kentucky cities to make an arrest at our request, but now cooperation could hardly be avoided. Spats between Cincinnati and Hamilton (Ohio) police had been frequent; now they worked together. Comparative insurance rates clearly showed the absence of auto theft rings or racketeering in other fields.

One of the greatest steps forward was the inauguration on August 1, 1931, of the municipal retirement system. It was complicated somewhat by the situation of the fire and police pension funds already referred to. A study of the condition of these funds was made by the bureau through an actuary, but the respective boards simply refused to believe the report, and few of the police or firemen went into the municipal system. All recruits thereafter were required to do so, however.

One of the most significant evidences of what five years had done to Cincinnati could be seen in the population figures. The charge that the influence of the old Organization throttled the city had always been poohpoohed by its supporters, but the official estimate for 1925 showed only a 2 per cent increase since 1920, or a total of 409,000, while the census of 1930 was 451,000, an increase of over 12 per cent in five years.

With all this and in spite of its adequate care for increasing unemployment, the city was absolutely solvent and paid as it went. The net bonded indebtedness was nearly $2,000,000 less than on January 1, 1926, although nearly a million a year of the old current expense borrowing was being paid off. As revenues decreased, expenditures were cut, but so far as possible without laying off men or cutting salaries.

But what could this story eloquently told by Russell Wilson and the others do against the cry of a conspiracy to increase the tax duplicate? "We told everybody before election in 1924 what their valuation was to be," shouted the Organization. "You're trying to conceal it until afterward!" And no one remembered to point out that this disclosure seven years before had applied to land only, and that in 1925, when the first city election was on, the auditor was careful not to publish his figures or give them out until after election. In 1926 there was serious doubt whether he would be endorsed in that contested primary because of the reaction feared from taxpayers.

The result of the election was another example of that eternal problem in politics, "What arguments really affect the vote?" For while the Charter group lost one of their six places in council and had now only a bare majority of five to four, it was not really so much a change in

FUSION IN THE COUNTY 211

votes by arguments presented by speakers that produced the result, as two other circumstances.

In the first place, Stanley Matthews, the Democrat, with Rose the only remaining member of the original council, a fine man and a fine vote-getter, had retired from council to go back on the Common Pleas bench. His successor, Arthur Espy, just as able, was not a vote-getter. John Druffel, the second Democrat, had shown increasing popular strength. As a result the even division of the Democratic vote was now impossible. In addition, the dissatisfaction of the jobhunting part of the Democratic party was flaring up, and they made the labor group their tool, probably with the assistance of the Republican regulars. This resulted in a Labor ticket of nine, mostly from the building trades, and it drew off over 7,000 votes. The first-choice votes for the three Charter Democrats were over 12,000 less than in 1929, or only 18,000-odd, while the Republican Charterites held their strength. The inevitable result was the defeat of Espy, and to those "in the know" the defection of these less civic-minded Democrats from the Charter cause was a serious problem for the future.

In the second place, Hall, the colored man, was at last endorsed by the Organization. This unquestionably added to his strength. The Charter Committee in its approach to the colored voters decided quite properly to ask for second choice votes without opposing Hall in any way, and his total of first choices was 11,160. The quota was only 12,228. Hall picked up 550 or just over half what he needed when Russell Wilson's tremendous record surplus of 18,100 votes was distributed, but from then on he gained very slowly, so slowly that an increase of 1,000 in the quota might have beaten him. He was the first Republican elected after four Charterites were in. Except for the substitution of Hall for Espy, the council membership was unchanged and the charter had two more years of life. In some ways the most disturbing thing about the campaign was that for the first time the Organization had made no blunder in its campaign tactics.

One other issue was involved in this election. Nicholas Longworth had died suddenly and left a vacancy in the First District, the eastern half of Hamilton County. Robert Taft, as chairman of the Republican Executive Committee, had addressed the Citizens Republicans a letter through Captain Heintz, asking on what basis they would consider coöperation for the election of a successor, as well as for future elections in the county. The Republican members of the now combined Citizens Committee promptly met and there was some sentiment, especially from Seasongood, for a belligerent answer. I felt it was a real opportunity to lay down conditions for coöperation, as stringent as might be desired by the majority of us. The old crowd must then take the responsibility for rejecting them. I prepared a draft calling for the Organization to stay out of city elections entirely and in 1932 to endorse for reëlection the three Democrats in county offices if their records in office should justify it. In addition, the merit system was to be established for the county. This was agreed to in principle by the Citizens meeting, but at the final meeting when I could not be present the fiery view prevailed and an answer in that tone was sent.

Nevertheless, the effort continued to find a Republican candidate for Congress satisfactory to both factions, and after a fight in the County Central Committee, John B. Hollister was selected to run in November, 1931. He had been serving on the Board of Education during the first three city campaigns and that position had prevented his taking sides and antagonizing either group. All the prominent Republicans on the Charter side agreed to go on his

FUSION IN THE COUNTY

committee and worked for his election. His majority was three times that of Longworth the year before.

After January 1, Russell Wilson, like his predecessor an effective and decorative mayor, was reëlected to that office, but a real problem was presented by the prospect that a member of the Charter majority might die or resign and leave a deadlock behind. However, the threat of the majority was the election of a Charter representative if one of the minority should be similarly removed, and as a gentlemanly compromise it was agreed that in either event the choice of the group affected should be voted for by the others.

The handling of relief was fast becoming a most serious problem. In 1928 there were about 500 families on the relief roll of the private charities; by January, 1932, this had increased to a monthly average of over 23,000, and the total list of families on the rolls at one time or another was probably 30,000. This meant, of course, well over 100,000 people, men, women and children, or nearly one-quarter of the population. The original division of the work—transient men to the city and families to the Community Chest—could be kept up only by furnishing the chest with public money. At first, for the last half of 1931, this came from the city, and the people voted half a million dollars for it at the November election. But in December the State Tax Commission had reduced the land values 10 per cent under pressure from the Downtown Property Owners, and Heuck took 10 per cent off the buildings in the spring, while more reductions were in prospect. That meant that the city bond limitation had to be considered and, besides, the county could handle the whole matter better. The contact was close, Hoehler being welfare director in both units, and as the state began to add direct relief by special utilities taxes the county became the chosen unit of distribution.

At first the attempt was made to distribute the relief in kind through grocery orders. But as the load increased, and the allowance to each family perforce became less, it speedily became evident that something had to be done, and the only expedient possible was direct buying and distribution through a warehouse system. This, of course, is not the ideal method and is much disliked by case workers, especially as it creates great friction with local retailers. But the certainty of saving $30,000 to $60,000 a month could not be overlooked, and in spite of possible political comebacks the county went ahead, using a great deal of expert volunteer assistance. Everything was still on a temporary basis, for government had not yet acknowledged its obligation as a permanent matter to care for unemployment. But the much castigated dole was in fact with us and had been, under different names, for some time.

CHAPTER FIFTEEN

THE PLOT THICKENS—1932 AND 1933

As 1932 began with the presidential race in prospect, the combined Citizens group faced some difficult problems. Could they succeed in a presidential year? It was hard to tell, but again they could not quit. The 1931 incident involving the reply to Robert Taft's letter about the congressional race, seemed to have ended the possibility of the return of the Independents to the Republican fold. On the Democratic side the disaffection had increased, especially among those who felt it was a Democratic year in which they could elect an entire county ticket. This group threatened to run a slate in the primary (now combined with the presidential primary in May) against the proposed temporary slate, and threatened to prosecute under the Corrupt Practices Act if anyone ran in the primary under a promise to withdraw. In spite of this the Citizens went ahead and appointed the nominating committee. There was more difficulty in arriving at a division of the offices, nine being involved. Ach and Heuck's terms were four years and Friedlander was forbidden by law from running again. Butterfield and Beckman and Kearns were candidates for reëlection, but Gorman preferred to run for judge. That meant six places to fill, including two commissioners and two hard races for clerk and surveyor. The result was that among the new candidates the Democrats were assigned the two commissioners and the clerk, and the Republicans the prosecutor, surveyor and treasurer. It meant a majority of

Democrats on the ticket, but the two holdovers were Republicans and the commissioners are in a sense one office.

The finding of candidates was the most difficult job of any year in the city or county and, while the caliber of the final ticket was high, it was not strong, politically speaking. By this time the taxpayers had found their valuations not at all the outrage they had been led to expect in the city campaign, but the prospect of struggling to be heard over the roar of the presidential campaign, to say nothing of financing the fight, was not one to overjoy any of us.

On the other hand, the Citizens record in the county was outstanding. The treasurer had continued with the collection of delinquent personal property taxes even after the new intangible law, and the total ran over $600,000. The effect on the taxpayers was in great contrast to the effect of the tax policy in nearly all the other important Ohio counties, for the percentage of current delinquency even in payment of real estate taxes was very low, under 8 per cent, while other places in the state ran 30 to 60 per cent delinquent. The uncompromising attitude in our county brought a splendid return under the intangible tax, actually more in money than the old personal property tax. Then to the horror of Cincinnatians, it was learned that practically all other counties had small returns and the law compelled the payment of $1,600,000 of our collections to these delinquent communities. But Gorman, our prosecutor, enjoined the payment and succeeded in having the distributive feature of the law held unconstitutional by the Supreme Court of Ohio.

The recorder, sheriff, coroner and auditor have already been referred to, and Mr. Ach and Mr. Urban had brought order out of chaos in the county budget and administration. The two latter, with Gorman, had been pressing constantly to secure an independent civil service for the county against the inertia or worse of the state Civil Service Commission, and the hindrance of the Attorney-General, but they had finally succeeded in that also. The whole accounting system of the county was revised so that a complete financial statement—which took much of the auditor's office two weeks' time in March, 1931, to prepare—could be got up daily if necessary a year later. A complete study was made by the bureau of the management, operation and maintenance of the courthouse, long the object of criticism in comparison with the city hall, and the recommendations were adopted with considerable saving in money and efficiency. A personnel study was made of all county employees, though information was secured with difficulty from Organization sympathizers, who admitted no civil service jurisdiction, and a plan was prepared for classification under the new civil service examiner.

One of the most important steps was in joint purchasing for the city, county and schools. It was first tried in 1931 when specifications for coal were agreed on between the three subdivisions and the same time fixed for the opening of bids. The saving was $100,000 under the total for the three the year before, and not over half was due to the reduction in the price of coal. This led to a $25,000 grant from the Spelman Fund to a committee consisting of the city manager, the president of the Board of County Commissioners, and the president of the School Board for studies looking to further voluntary coördination, and the grant has been renewed for a second year.

None of this work was spectacular, and the county fight proved just as difficult as had been anticipated. Once again the Organization showed intelligence in its campaign and made no serious blunder. In 1931 in the city fight they attacked the Citizens in the county. Now in 1932 they talked principally of city expense, and the

Citizens found it difficult to continue as attacker. We could no longer talk of Hynicka and gang politics, for Hynicka was dead and Schneller remained in the background. Skinner, the candidate for surveyor, made a splendid campaign on the expense of his rival's administration, but he was hardly known at all and Gast had a long and on the whole favorable record with the public. Besides, the Democratic candidate for surveyor nominated in the primary refused to withdraw, perhaps at Republican urgings, and it left three candidates in the field. Our old friend Swing appeared on the Organization ticket this time, running for county commissioner, and he and his running mate promised to do away with the wholesale buying and the warehouse system of distribution of relief supplies, which made a deep appeal to the unthinking. There were constant recriminations from the regulars, of course, for injuring the Republican chances nationally and in the state.

The election resulted in the defeat of one of the Citizens candidates for commissioner but Geoghehan was elected and constituted a majority of the board with Ach. The prosecutor's office was lost, and the extra Democrat running for surveyor caused Skinner's defeat. But the other offices were retained, and Peter McCarthy was elected clerk of courts in a close fight decided only after a contest.

The effect on state and national votes is difficult to tell. Both Republican Congressmen won by normal majorities, Hollister doing much better than Longworth had done two years before, and all Republican state candidates carried the county except Governor and Lieutenant-Governor. Bettman only just lost the county for the Senate and he and the Republican candidate for Governor ran ahead of Hoover. Hoover's vote can hardly be blamed on the Citizens. About the only charge that can justly be made is that the local fight interfered seriously with campaign contributions to the Republican party.

The last political event of this story has to do with civil service and the clerk's office. A little background is necessary to give the full picture. The Civil Service Commission of Ohio is made up of two members, a Democrat and a Republican, who deadlock in case of a dispute, and for whose work the General Assembly has never made an adequate appropriation. Cities have a separate commission of three, but county positions are under the state commission and in the past it has given examinations for only a handful of positions in a few counties. The statute exempts "deputies" from the classified service, and so every clerk or messenger is appointed a deputy in Ohio counties, especially in all positions having to do with the courts.

Every candidate on the Citizens ticket had pledged himself to the merit system in accordance with the Ohio laws, and during the campaign the matter had been fully discussed at executive sessions of the group. In December McCarthy met with Heintz and Headley and asked them what persons they wished appointed. They assured him they were not in the position of asking for any jobs, with one single exception, a person who was not himself an applicant. McCarthy showed them a list of twelve or thirteen names furnished him by the heads of the Citizens men and women's organizations. Heintz and Headley said those names were not presented for political favors, but were known applicants about whom favorable comment was given. Nothing in the conversation indicated the extent to which McCarthy was expecting to make removals, but there had been general agreement that the bitter partisanship at the hands of some of the clerk's force, especially in the municipal court, called for immediate action to remove the objectionable ones, numbering perhaps fifteen or twenty at the most.

Without further notice there appeared in the afternoon papers about December 30 the announcement that 63 out of 81 places in the clerk's office would be filled by the list that followed. Of these, nine might be called Republicans, while the balance were organization Democrats. No mention was made of civil service or of anything in the nature of examinations. The storm from the women and the independent members of the Citizens group, both Republicans and Democrats, has not been stilled at this writing. McCarthy, in defense of his position, claimed that such action in "turning the rascals out" had been recommended by so important a member of the Citizens group as Seasongood.

But McCarthy followed this by refusing to commit himself as to which positions of the 81 he would submit to examinations and, in spite of certain definite private commitments, ended by refusing publicly to put any position under Civil Service, claiming they were all deputies.

So far as the Democratic organization is concerned, it had succeeded in 1932 in electing a majority of the legislative delegation to the House and Senate in Columbus, but when the Charter group sought to have introduced in the 1933 session a bill repealing that Schuessler Act ("We want the jobs!") which took the positions under McCarthy in the municipal court out of civil service, not one of that delegation could be found willing to introduce the repealer.

So far as McCarthy is concerned, the alternative was placed before him of either announcing examinations and designating a list of positions subject to examination in accordance with his pledge, or receiving a denunciation by the Citizens group headed by Heintz and Seasongood. He then decided to do what he would have done long before except for vicious advice given him from some source. He agreed to put his typists under civil service, and asked the bureau to make a study of his office, on the basis of which he could decide what other positions should be classified.

This was belated obedience to a principle to which he was pledged—a pledge believed by the public to have been given sincerely, and one to be carried out whole-heartedly and promptly. Whether this action can outweigh the harm already done among Charter and Citizens supporters is a question. It will undoubtedly alienate some votes of Republicans already annoyed by what they feel is Democratic cockiness. On the other hand, Roosevelt is very popular in Cincinnati and the tag of "Democratic" is not so distasteful in these days of the New Deal as it was a few years back.

There were other issues in the campaign this fall. There is always the cry that out-of-town contractors are favored, that supplies and materials are bought from out-of-town firms and that out-of-town individuals are chosen for city positions in preference to Cincinnati residents.

The laws of Ohio are clear that in public bidding the lowest and best bidder (and sometimes the lowest) must be awarded the contract. When this charge about contracts was made in the summer of 1931 before the last election, Mr. Dykstra answered it completely. He showed that of all money spent by the city on contract work and materials from January 1, 1930, to August 1, 1931, a total in the period of $6,359,008.21, only 6 per cent, or $416,046.59 was awarded to outside bidders, and $222,-110.00 of that was two large jobs, upon which the winners agreed to use Cincinnati labor and materials. The current percentage is even lower.

So far as materials are concerned, Cincinnati is a manufacturing center and it exports to other communities a large part of its output. It would seem a little short-sighted if it started a practice that would mean shutting other communities to its salesmen. Such a general policy all over the United States could hardly benefit Cincinnati business men or Cincinnati workmen.

So far as employees are concerned, it might be pointed out that the Organization county commissioners brought here from Toledo the county sanitary engineer (whose contract was rushed through in 1926 for fear the Citizens might get in) and also his successor. The present county probation officer appointed by the judges of the Court of Common Pleas no one of whom belongs to the independent group was a resident of Cleveland when he took the examination. As a matter of fact, I recommended this last appointment when I was prosecutor, so that I am not complaining of it at all. But it makes the Organization seem a little inconsistent.

In addition, they exaggerate the number of these non-resident appointments to meet their campaign needs. John Blandford had been in Cincinnati six years when he was appointed safety director. How long do you have to live in a place to cease being a nonresident? J. C. Root, the public works director, was seized on as coming in this class until it turned out he was a graduate of the University of Cincinnati and a former employee of the city under the Organization itself. The director of recreation was appointed as a nonresident, and recently when a well-known social worker here married an outstanding member of his own profession from the East, and brought her to Cincinnati to live, she was appointed director of case work for the welfare department. In both instances a careful search was made for the right person locally and the search was unsuccessful. The total number of such appointments is less than half a dozen on the city payroll of 4,400, and all employees are required to live in the city.

The whole argument is a good example of "economic municipalism," if I may coin the phrase. When the Ohio Legislature tries to require all public agencies to buy Ohio coal only (instead of the West Virginia product which we use in Cincinnati) the same citizens raise shouts of anger and seem to see no inconsistency in their attitude. How could our population increase as fast as our Chambers of Commerce wish if we waited for the birth rate to fix it and welcomed no "outsiders"?

A further argument and perhaps the most important has to do with expense. Here is the story.[1]

At the meeting of council on July 12, 1933, the budget for 1934 was presented for approval of the city manager and the Finance Committee of council. On this occasion Councilman Joseph H. Woeste, in a speech carefully prepared for him, stated the stock argument of the Organization on the subject of excessive city expense and his statement offers as good a text as any for the analysis of city expenditures since 1925 to see exactly what has happened under the charter. The complete figures of the bureau are printed as an appendix. These figures were carefully compiled by the bureau for the Cincinnatus Association from the reports of the city auditor as given to the Ohio State Bureau of Accounting. They differ a little from the published reports of the city auditor because there is a variation in practice as to whether the amounts accrued under contracts on December 31 are to be included, and if not, whether vouchers issued, but not cashed, shall be added. Furthermore, the city accounting system was changed, effective June 1, 1928, and that has been considered by the bureau so as to make the figures presented absolutely comparable. I have not bothered to

[1] Skip to page 229 if you don't like figures, however exciting.

include the reconciliation which the bureau made in its complete study.

For comparative purposes I give Judge Woeste's table:

	Total	Waterworks Expenses Included	University Expenses Included[1]	Net Expenditures Other Than Waterworks and University[2]	Payroll Other Than University
1925	$7,902.231.32	$1,152,286.07	$1,245,009.67	$5,504,934.98[3]	$4,197,228.05
1926	9,590,703.93	1,095,091.75	1,424,557.07	7,071,055.11	5,195,514.72
1927	10,295,472.13	1,129,308.64	1,162,111.56	8,004,051.93	5,681,910.31
1928	11,520,333.69	2,416,134.45	588,207.20	8,515,992.04	6,018,278.55
1929	12,022,790.53	2,780,324.41	597,427.18	8,636,058.94	6,248,737.13
1930	12,427,108.82	2,892,755.24	603,575.70	8,930,777.88	6,317,518.33
1931	12,328,173.02[4]	2,671,256.19	612,115.81	9,044,701.02[4]	6,541,612.85
1932	11,185,637.95[4]	2,172,986.69	547,011.16	8,465,710.10[4]	6,322,827.42
1933 (July Estimate)	11,128,695.00	2,151,555.00	495,000.00	8,482,140.00	....
1933 (Appr. Ord.)	10,234,724.00	2,105,684.00	489,264.00	7,639,776.00	5,786,344.00
1934 (July Estimate)	10,823,268.00	1,950,963.00	440,000.00	8,432,305.00	6,298,952.00

[1] Prior to 1928 the entire university expense was included in the auditor's reports. In 1928, and thereafter, only the university tax receipts were included.
[2] These expenditures do not include expenditures from the proceeds of the sale of bonds or from assessments.
[3] 1925—Does not include hospital maintenance, operated that year by the county (expense estimated $500,000).
[4] Figures for 1931 and 1932 exclude all but $100,000 of the expense of the Division of Public Welfare, representing poor relief expenditures since transferred to the county and state.

When I saw it I noticed that the waterworks expense seemed to have doubled in 1928. That struck me as peculiar and after a little research I discovered that he had blindly taken the auditor's totals without noticing, or at least without telling his public, that he was including from $1,200,000 to $1,700,000 of sinking fund and interest on bonds and purchases of property, all capital expense.

For further comparison I give another table whose exact authorship is not clear, but which was made up apparently for use in the 1933 campaign by the Organization.

THE PLOT THICKENS—1932 AND 1933

The Cost of Cincinnati's Government

Year	Total Expenditures	Salaries
1925	$ 6,862,862.69	$4,197,228.05
1926	8,381,766.47	5,193,514.72
1927	9,560,764.30	5,681,910.31
1928	11,520,333.69	6,018,278.55
1929	12,022,790.53	6,248,737.13
1930	12,427,108.82	6,317,518.33
1931	12,747,071.23	6,541,612.83
1932	11,533,992.22	6,322,827.42

Increase in Total Expenditures, 1925-1931, was 85.7 per cent
Decrease in Total Expenditures, 1931-1932, was 9.5 per cent

Increase in salaries, 1925-1931, was.......... 55.8 per cent
Decrease in salaries, 1931-1932, was......... 3.3 per cent

Authentic figures for your information issued by Research and Publicity Commission, Republican Party

It will be seen that the figures for 1928, 1929 and 1930 total expenditures are the same in both, but the first three years are each less by about $1,000,000. The last two years evidently include all welfare expense, instead of reducing it to a round $100,000, as Judge Woeste did. The figures on payroll are the same in each. This campaign card is a good sample of how to use figures when you want to get a substantial percentage of increase.

What are the facts? For purposes of comparison I shall use 1932, the last full year of experience. Judge Woeste used the budget for 1934 which is quite irrelevant for two reasons: It was prepared in July only under requirement of state law and is supplanted by the budget adopted when the tax rate is fixed in October; and that budget must be increased on the expenditure side to take care of prospective losses in collection of real estate taxes, for which neither the state law nor the charter permits any allowance at all in the budget.

The increase in total operating expenditures for 1932 over 1925 is $3,192,234.95. Certain parts of this increase occur from funds created by other than direct taxes. For instance, the waterworks is a self-supporting city-owned public utility, whose income can be used for nothing else, and it spent about $118,400 more. Improvement and repair of streets is paid for in part from gasoline tax and motor license trust funds available for nothing else. The increase in these expenditures was $279,500. That leaves, in round numbers, an increase of $2,794,000 in which the taxpayer is interested.

There are certain mandatory levies fixed by the city charter. Judge Woeste separated one of these in his table, expense of the university, but he failed to separate another, also quite out of the control of council, the expense of the Recreation Commission. The first has increased $57,000 and the second $144,500, or a total of $201,500. That leaves about $2,590,000 within the control of council.

In 1925 the General Hospital was operated and paid for by the county. In that year the Organization Republican county commissioners spent $650,000 (not $500,000 as Judge Woeste allows in his table), and the effect of the depression has made absolutely essential an increase of $120,000. In addition, the welfare department in 1932, before the county assumed the burden of unemployment relief, expended $420,000 more than the skeleton organization of 1925. So that the increase which can be considered as occurring in normal controllable expenditures shrinks to $1,400,000, or only about 23 per cent over 1925, while the population increased 12 per cent.

I append a table showing where this increase took place, dividing the items between new activities and expanded service.

1932 vs. 1925

New Activities
Retirement Fund ....$	95,000	
Traffic Lights	50,650	
Workhouse (net)	46,450	
Airport	17,400	
Miscellaneous	5,300	
		$ 214,800

Expanded Service
Administrative

Manager-Public Works-Public Safety .....$	7,200	
Purchasing	13,700	
Law	22,000	
Civil Service	11,000	
Planning	16,700	
Property Maintenance	38,200	
Municipal Court, Clerk, etc. (not administered by the city).....	54,000	
Police	299,000	
Police Relief	115,500	
Fire	148,000	
Fire Pensions	61,500	
Building Dept.	14,500	
Health	88,000	
Highways and Sewers	102,300	
Street Cleaning, Sprinkling, Refuse and Garbage Collection......	12,000	
Street Lights	104,600	
Parks	99,500	
Utilities	20,600	
Miscellaneous	33,900	
	$1,262,200	
Less savings	63,600	
		$1,198,600
		$1,413,400

I could give the same kind of table to explain 1926, but it seems unnecessary. The comparison with 1927 can be brief.

The total increase over 1927 is $609,516.17. Of this $263,600 is in expenditures from gasoline tax and motor license funds, and $202,900 is in the waterworks (although water rates were down $300,000 per year). The mandatory levies for the university and the Recreation Commission add net $24,000, while the hospital needs $30,000 more and the welfare department $420,000 more because of unemployment.

That leaves a real decrease in normal controllable expenditures in 1932 below the 1927 level of $331,000, which Schneller, Daly and Lackmann in 1927 authorized, although in 1932 there was a retirement fund for city employees ($95,000) and police expense had gone up $130,000, health work $44,000 and street lighting charges $65,000.

I have been telling about 1932 but figures are given by Judge Woeste for the 1933 appropriation ordinance that show a decrease this year from 1932 levels of $826,000. Without stopping to analyze his figures, I would add that the actual expenditures according to Mr. Dykstra and Mr. Rose's predictions will be $200,000 under the appropriation, making a saving in expense of over one million dollars to the taxpayer. The prediction of the same gentlemen is that less will be spent in 1934.

One final comparison indicates that the tax rate for next year will be 21.96 mills. The rate in 1926 was 21.16, an increase next year of about $6/10$ per cent. Of course, the taxpayer must also know what the valuations are in order to realize whether he will really pay more. The city real estate tax duplicate of 1925 (upon which the 1926 rate was paid) was $733,263,720, while the present duplicate is $662,409,684, a decrease of nearly 10 per

THE PLOT THICKENS—1932 AND 1933

cent, which means that real estate taxes are down about 10 per cent from those paid in December, 1925, and June, 1926. If tangible personal and public utility property is added the reduction is 20 per cent.

Lastly, I would recall that the net bonded indebtedness of the city has decreased since January, 1926, by over $4,500,000, and that over $6,000,000 of the Organization's deficit bonds have been paid off in that process.

About all that can be added about these comparisons is that no Organization speaker has commented on any individual item of expenditure except salaries of executive officers. To a degree they criticize the entire salary scale and the policy of not reducing personnel. Personnel was reduced by $3\frac{1}{2}$ per cent in 1932 by not filling vacancies. Salaries were cut in 1933 also, from 5 per cent for lower brackets to nearly 20 per cent for the highest.

The most important fact in Cincinnati's financial situation is its solvency. It has not run a deficit for any year and the surplus now predicted for the end of the year is $700,000 (on account of unexpected receipts in part). A year and a half ago Milwaukee was boasting of its surplus of $4,000,000 in bank. This turned out to be unexpended bond funds and now it not only has a deficit and is failing to pay its employees, but indictments are pending against its financial officers and a recall against its mayor. One or two other cities have received publicity occasionally on the way they have weathered the depression, but now that 1933 is nearly over and the upturn has come, I think I am safe in saying that Cincinnati is the only one of any size not facing bankruptcy or at best a serious deficit.

It is true that we have a fine conscientious citizenry, but our percentage of unemployment is higher than the average and our increase of employment with improving business is lagging behind most Ohio cities. The main difference between Cincinnati and other cities is that our citizens have confidence in their public officials and know that none of their taxes go into any politician's pocket for political services. Cincinnati bonds have always commanded a premium, but many cities with similar past records cannot now sell bonds at any price, while ours are still under a 4 per cent basis. Good government is not only possible; it pays.

Good government as in the Hunt administration has had a substantial effect on its opponents. Not only has the Organization developed far greater strength than it had in 1925 or 1926, but the vicious elements have been shoved out in many cases. Some say it is a case of "When the Devil is sick, the Devil a monk would be," but the change has given an opportunity for the decent element to secure a control they have not had since John Holmes died, and they can probably hold it even against the restless element that still remains.

COUNTY GOVERNMENT

The Charter movement in the city and the Citizens movement in the county brought to our citizens a far more intelligent understanding of government in general. Because of the obvious comparison, they soon began to realize how complicated, unwieldy and ineffective the form of county government was. For this reason they began to interest themselves in a movement to improve that form. Curiously enough, it had been C. A. Dykstra, our present city manager, who ten years or more ago, when he was executive of the Cleveland Civic League, brought to Columbus the first proposed constitutional amendment and submitted it to the legislature. Then followed a series of disappointments, for session after session either pigeonholed the proposal entirely or so manhandled it that none of its advocates wanted it and it was dropped.

After the Citizens fights of 1926 and 1928 it was brought home to them how difficult it was to get for such technical positions as surveyor or clerk candidates who also were good campaigners. When in 1930 the combination was made with the Democrats, the question of patronage was the most serious danger in the minds of the Republican part of the group. Thus when the State Chamber of Commerce called a meeting on the subject of county government I was interested enough to go and was made a member of a new committee to work on the problem.

We drafted a constitutional amendment and it was introduced into the 1931 Assembly by a member of our committee, Senator Greenlund, of Cleveland. Through his efforts and my brother's it was finally passed without much change, but the House killed it through the efforts of the small municipalities contiguous to large cities, especially our own Norwood.

With this final failure we were all agreed that our only prospect of success was to initiate the amendment. That required that we secure 195,671 signatures, which was 10 per cent of the vote for Governor in 1930. In addition we had to secure in each of half the counties (44) 5 per cent of the 1930 vote in that county. We knew that the League of Women Voters was much interested and we hoped to find volunteer circulators, but we still had to print the petitions and instructions, and to prepare enough publicity to make the work of the circulators less difficult. Where the finances were to come from we had no idea.

The so-called County Home Rule Amendment repeals the obstructing provisions of the constitution and gives the legislature power to fix the form of county government with alternatives for different types of community, urban, rural, metropolitan, etc. It also gives the legislature power to arrange the method by which municipalities and townships can transfer individual functions to the county. This would permit some most desirable experimentation in the redistribution of local governmental powers, according to convenience and efficiency rather than tradition.

But long experience with the legislature led the whole committee to distrust it completely and we added two long sections giving to counties nearly the same kind of home rule possessed by municipalities in Ohio. That is to say, a county under this amendment can adopt its own form of government even if the legislature fails to act under the powers given it.

Cleveland was especially interested in the possibility of some kind of metropolitan or borough government and a final provision permitted a county charter to set up such a government if a majority of municipalities and townships in the county voted favorably, in addition to a majority in the largest city and a majority outside.

We had hoped to submit the amendment in November, 1932, but, while we had the draft ready early in the year, our best efforts did not produce enough signatures by August and we decided we must wait a year. By paying circulators for the last 40,000 or 50,000 signatures we succeeded in filing on the day before election day, 1932, about 213,000 signatures on our petitions. That meant that we still were counted according to the 1930 vote and not by the greatly increased vote of the presidential year.

The next hurdle was the checking by 82 election boards, for we had signatures from all but six of the smaller counties. We knew they would generally be unfriendly, but with so little money to spend themselves because of depression, we hoped for fairly good results. The most difficult requirement to meet was that signers in cities over 16,000 in population must be registered. Most of the early returns gave us a small percentage of loss, but Cleveland's deduction went over 20 per cent and Hamilton (Cincinnati), where the Democratic organization was really as unsympathetic as the Republican, threw out 29,000 out of 31,000 names. Of course, we filed a protest that went into court and then, fortunately for us, a direct action in the Supreme Court disposed of the most technical objection and restored nearly 20,000 of the Hamilton County names. We filed enough additional signatures secured this summer to make sure now that the amendment will be voted on November 7, and a last minute attempt to keep it off the ballot was rejected by the Supreme Court of Ohio.

If this can be adopted, it will make it possible for the people to devise and achieve a simple and centralized form of government in the county and will get rid of all such problems as patronage or separate purchasing for a single office. Furthermore, it will give us a chance to find out by what subdivisions public hospitals, public welfare, police or any other functions can best be handled.

Most important of all it will give a chance for more activity, more citizen education, more goals for an amateur organization to aim for and better tools for it to work with.

CHAPTER SIXTEEN

BY WAY OF CONCLUSION

THE question is whether this movement can last. It has certain elements of weakness. From the very beginning, every move of the administration involved the alienation of some few or large numbers of voters because the particular step taken, wise as it might be, stepped on their private toes. I recall one prominent manufacturer, for instance, who supported the Charter ticket in 1925, whose car was tagged for a violation of the parking laws and who found it impossible to "fix" the tag. He had to pay $2. From that day to this he has appeared on the Organization side. Another thing, such as the building of the incinerator for the incineration of garbage, roused, or was used by the Organization to rouse, large numbers of voters living in the vicinity. Instances could be multiplied. Any strong, fair-minded, straightforward administration is bound to cause dissatisfaction to some few in the community. That dissatisfaction has grown, as it is bound to grow, in the course of the seven and a half years since the first of January, 1926.

Can this movement last? We are undertaking this year the most thorough organization we have ever had. Rather contrary to my own expectations, we are not meeting the amount of criticism I had expected to find in a careful canvass of the entire city. The criticism did exist far beyond the extent to which the present councilmen at the city hall were willing to admit, and yet the close contact with the man in the street indicates a gen-

BY WAY OF CONCLUSION

eral support of the kind of government that has been given the city for the last seven years. With an improved organization, the City Charter Committee may hope to produce at least as many votes as they did in 1931, and possibly more.

What bearing has this on the possible future in politics of other cities in the United States? It has just this. No independent movement in any community can succeed unless it carries with it the leadership, or some leadership, important leadership, of the dominant political party. Cincinnati is Republican. The leadership of an independent movement here never succeeded until it became Republican. New York is Democratic. No movement for good government in New York can ever succeed except under leadership principally Democratic. Furthermore, our experience would indicate that such a movement can never be successful unless it develops an independent amateur organization, devoted to the service of local ideals and determined to secure good government and the merit system in public service.

The city manager, small council, proportional representation system has been voted out of Cleveland. Why? For one reason, because it was never realized by those who were responsible for that charter in Cleveland that it could have no hope of permanent success unless an independent political organization was created to elect councilmen and to support them after their election. The Republican and Democratic organizations arrived at an agreement in Cleveland and distributed jobs as they always had before. The city manager scheme without proportional representation failed in Kansas City, because there, too, there was no gathering of independent groups behind a ticket and no support of that ticket after its election. The experiment in Cincinnati is unique, because there has been developed something in the nature of an independent municipal political party, having no selfish purpose.

By the development of such a party, it has proven possible to utilize the service of women in politics. Neither Republican nor Democratic party in Cincinnati, or elsewhere, has made of women anything but scenery in politics. After the primary of 1926 it was attempted to take over the women's organization into the Republican men's organization. The idea that women could style themselves precinct executives or ward captains was so repugnant to the Republican precinct executives and ward captains that from the very beginning the attempted combination was a complete failure and has never been worked since in the organization. The women will work for such an independent political party as the City Charter Committee or the Citizens Committee of Hamilton County, and will devote to it large amounts of time between elections, when men cannot be induced to do much of anything. They will persist; they will secure support; they will get out the vote.

The idea of a third party is not new so far as national politics is concerned, but in city affairs a permanent organization is unique to Cincinnati. Although no third party has ever succeeded nationally, hope springs eternal, and certain types of amateur politicians derive new encouragement in these days from the disappearance of the Liberals and the rise of the Labor party in England. Although many of this group are men who should be convinced of the soundness of the scientific method, they go forward without the slightest notice of the most apparent fact in national politics—that the permanence of the two national parties is grounded not in their policies or platforms, but in local patronage machines. The only thing in England having any similar effect was Lloyd George's financial war chest, which has greatly prolonged

BY WAY OF CONCLUSION

the life of the Liberal party. These high-minded American reformers will charge the citadels of Washington in vain so long as Tammany in New York, Vare in Philadelphia, and Long in Louisiana cut across their line of communications with the people who vote.

This Cincinnati experiment has demonstrated the place of faith in politics as well as in other walks of life. There is one characteristic of Lincoln which is most impressive. It was his deepest conviction, which endured through the darkest periods of the Civil War, that the right ultimately would prevail. There is in this movement in Cincinnati the type of religious conviction which is not fanatical; which is not even ecstatic; which is hard-headed, and yet idealistic; a conviction, a faith that local good government is a possibility. When we attacked the old administration, we were said to be "knocking" our town. When we said that we expected to put in an economical, efficient, honest government, many were the business men who said it could not be done. And, with that feeling, they hedged. They refused to come out. In some cases they contributed to both sides. They never committed themselves in such a way that they could not withdraw if the public should change its mind.

But the faith of the few men who started this movement has been amply justified. The giant may loom large; he may seem overwhelming. The inertia of people is even more discouraging. And yet this group of Davids, for all their weakness, were able to overcome Goliath of the Machine, and to establish in Cincinnati and in Hamilton County good government conducted by honest men, with most of the same tools, most of the same employees and the same electorate with which the job had been done so badly by their predecessors. They proved that good government in American cities of substantial size is a possibility.

APPENDIX A

HISTORY OF RECOMMENDATIONS OF THE UPSON REPORT

FOR INCREASE IN REVENUE OR DECREASE IN EXPENSE
WITHOUT ADDITIONAL LEGISLATION

1. Increased allowances by the County Budget Commission for the City.

    This was secured in August and September of 1925 by the efforts of Mr. Bentley and the author, as President of the Cincinnatus Association, and was made possible through the modification of the State tax laws carried through the Legislature by Mr. Robert A. Taft. This legislation also permitted a city to adopt its own tax limitation freed of the County altogether and the revision of the Charter in 1926 took advantage of this power.

2. Removal of all levies by the county for sinking fund purposes within the ten mill limitation until the surplus of $1,750,000 now in the county sinking fund is exhausted. This will make available to the City for operating revenue over $240,000 per annum for the next six years.

    The County promptly removed the levy *without* the ten mill limitation as well as that within, thus giving the city the additional revenue for the one year, but using up the surplus all at once, instead of spreading it.

3. Submission of special tax levy of 2.45 mills for the vote of the people.

    This was done, but in spite of the endorsement by the Upson Survey committee, it was decisively voted down.

APPENDIX A

4. Continue the reappraisement of land and improvements and establish a permanent division in the office of the County Auditor for annual appraisals.

    The appraisal was completed as required by law.

5. Reorganization of the activities of county charities, especially the Soldiers' Burial Committee and Soldiers' and Sailors' Relief Committee.

    This was accomplished in 1931 when the Citizens Committee succeeded in electing Mr. Samuel Ach County Commissioner; he with Mr. Charles Urban, a second Commissioner for whose appointment the Citizens Committee had been largely responsible in 1928, made Mr. Fred K. Hoehler, the city Welfare Director, a de facto County Welfare Director, and by the control of the purse strings forced the acceptance of his authority even by independent officers.

6. Have the city avail itself of county aid in the reconstruction of the Eighth Street Viaduct and through highways.

    The county built the Eighth Street Viaduct three years later and has contributed substantially to the construction of many through highways within the city limits since 1924, something unheard of before that.

7. Have the county assume the operating cost of the General Hospital.

    Before the extra levy was again defeated in November, 1924, the county agreed to take over the financing of the Hospital for the year 1925. A recent study of the Bureau of Governmental Research recommends that it do so permanently. Further studies are being made, and the result will eventually be brought about.

8. Increase revenue from the Hospital by collecting from patients who can afford to pay.

    Carried out both under the city and county until the present depression reduced collections to a minimum.

9. Use of photographic printing in the (County) Recorder's office.

    After the Citizens Committee succeeded in electing Robert Heuck to that office and after he had worked strenuously for several years against the underground influence of Fred Schneller, Chairman of the Republican Central Committee, he finally secured legislative authority for this. It is now in effect and has cut the cost of the office more than in half.

10. Full and better enforcement of the occupational and other taxes.

    This was done in the City as soon as the Charter Administration came in and in the county as soon as Mr. Samuel Ach took office as County Treasurer.

11. Reduction in the personnel and pay of county employees, including inter-transfer of employees in the offices of County Auditor and County Treasurer.

    Reductions have been brought about in the offices controlled by the Citizens Committee in accordance with a classification study prepared by the Bureau of Governmental Research, with the exception of the office of the County Clerk as filled at the last election, in spite of Mr. McCarthy's pledge on Civil Service. It is believed that this matter will be corrected before this book appears. The inter-transfer of employees could not be worked out as long as Mr. Hess was Auditor, because he said it was impossible, and is now unnecessary by reason of the introduction of mechanical equipment.

12. Make greater use of the increased power of assessment for public improvements on property benefited.

    This has been done in the city, but in the county so many roads had been built without it that the change in policy would have been unfair to the owners on new roads.

13. Reduce the expense of maintenance of county buildings.

    No attention was paid to this until the Citizens Committee elected a majority of the Commissioners in 1930; the recommendation is now being carried under a competent superintendent of maintenance who stood at the top in a civil service examination.

APPENDIX A

14. Changes in the method of billing and collecting taxes and mailing tax bills to all taxpayers.

    No attention was paid to this until Mr. Ach became Treasurer of the County. He at once installed typewritten bills and largely increased the use of the mails. When the Citizens Committee elected Heuck Auditor in 1930, he and Edgar Friedlander, Citizens County Treasurer, after a study by the Bureau, installed a joint addressograph system that prints the tax duplicate in the Auditor's office, and then prints the tax bills from the same plates for the Treasurer. It is geared into a tabulating machine that gives sub-totals and totals and provides a constant accounting check.

15. Agreement with the Sheriff for the maintenance of prisoners from county funds.

    No attention was paid to this until a change in the state law. Even after that the Organization Sheriff continued to consider the contract with the Federal Government for their prisoners as part of his perquisites. It was not carried out in full until the election of Asa Butterfield by the Citizens in 1930.

16. Use of registered mail for serving process in city and county courts.

    This has not been carried out by any of the courts, or even attempted.

17. Employment of a supervising architect by the Board of Education.

    This has not been carried out.

18. Have Board of Education take over the Boys' and Girls' Opportunity Farms.

    This was done as soon as the Charter Administration came in January, 1926.

19. Reduction in personnel in the offices of the City Clerk and the Board of Elections.

    This was done in the office of the City Clerk as soon as the Charter administration came in, but the Board of Elections in control of the two political organizations has not reduced its expense to speak of.

20. Combine the welfare activities of the City and County.
    As described above under 5, this has been done in effect, though without statutory authority.

FOR INCREASED EFFICIENCY OR ECONOMY

1. Transfer the details of administration of the County Sinking Fund to the City's Sinking Fund Trustees.
   This has not been attempted.
2. Retain all moneys received from the State for automobile licenses in a separate fund to be used only for street repairs.
   This was done at once in 1924, and has been continued. There have been several disputes however between the Charter administration and the State officials as to whether any equipment or overhead may be included in expenditures for Street Repair and Maintenance.
3. Open the budgets to public inspection before adoption.
   This has always been done since the Charter administration came in, and this year in particular certain interested civic and property-owner organizations have on invitation sat through the whole budget process in the city, county and schools.
4. Reëstablish civil service in city employment.
   This was done as soon as the Charter administration came in and secured control of the city civil service commission.
5. Make preparations now for a new contract for garbage disposal.
   Nothing was done until the Charter administration came in, when studies were begun at once. The contract had to be renewed, but for a brief period only. The city then built three incinerators and burns all garbage and most waste.
6. Consider revision of water rates.
   This was done by the Charter administration within the last three years.

APPENDIX A

7. Change the method of renting stalls in public markets by raising the rents and abolishing subletting.

    This was done as soon as the Charter Administration came in.

8. Secure greater expedition in the granting of building permits.

    The procedure was revised as soon as the Charter administration came in.

9. Carry out recommendations in report as to City Engineering Department.

    These included criticism of the amount of detail handled by the Engineer and the organization of his office; criticism of the specifications and the excessive use of granite in streets, and of the specifications as to sewers. All these matters have been corrected.

10. Provide for a Bureau of Municipal Research.

    This was done immediately under the leadership of George Warrington, and the work of the Bureau has been unique and outstanding in its scope and the extent to which its recommendations in city schools and county have been carried out.

11. Extend the activities of the County Purchasing Department to cover all county purchases.

    This was done as soon as the Citizens Committee secured control of the County Commissioners' office. The last item to come under the department was so-called emergency purchases by the County Surveyor, the only office at no time won by the Citizens Committee.

The following recommendations are dependent upon the City receiving more money from taxation:

1. Carry out the suggestions in the reports as to the Police and Fire Departments and Pension Funds.

    As to Police the outstanding recommendations have been carried out under the Charter Administration, as, for instance, more automobile patrols, a signal or recall system (supplied by the radio), a new record system, improvement of the detective bureau (now under way).

The defects in the fire department were only those due to reduced finances, and have been remedied. As to pensions, an actuarial study was recommended which was carried out by the Charter Administration with the result which the report predicted, an absolutely unsound condition of both funds. The city then established a general pension system for all employees, optional for those then retired from the Police and Fire Department, and compulsory for all new recruits. The retired men have injected the whole matter into politics.

2. Improve Health and Welfare Departments.

    This was done as soon as more funds were available.

3. Increase appropriations for the maintenance of the Parks.

    This was done as soon as more funds were available.

4. Increase appropriations for the street cleaning department.

    This was done as soon as more funds were available.

5. Restore the streets to proper condition.

    This was one of Colonel Sherrill's greatest accomplishments.

STATE LEGISLATION

The following recommendations will require additional legislation by the State and City.

1. City-County consolidation. This will require constitutional amendment.

    An initiated amendment to the Ohio Constitution which will permit this if desirable, is to be voted upon in November, after failure for many years to secure its submission by the legislature.

2. Changes in tax laws so as to provide greater revenue for the city.

    This was brought about in 1925 through the efforts of Robert A. Taft.

3. Change in law which gives County Budget Commission authority over city budget.

APPENDIX A

This was also secured through Mr. Taft's legislative program and incorporated in the City Charter in 1926.
4. Change in law that would give City and Board of Education representation on Budget Commission.
   One of these is no longer necessary. The other has not been secured.
5. Change in law to provide for quadrennial registration of voters in cities.
   Permanent registration was secured in 1930.
6. Change in law to place county Sheriff on salary basis.
   This was accomplished not long after.

CHARTER AMENDMENT

1. Small Council.
   Secured November, 1924.
2. Minor changes in city's budget procedure.
   Secured under Charter administration.
3. Abolish city primary elections and provide for nomination by petition.
   Secured legislature 1925.

It is interesting to note that in October, 1924, the Survey Committee met and passed a resolution expressing strong dissatisfaction with the attention paid to its recommendations up to that time. Mr. Hynicka thereupon called the heads of departments of the city and county government together and went over all the above. In a number of instances heads of departments objected strenuously or indicated they would if they got a chance to speak. Mr. Hynicka in many instances refused to allow objection, and instructed officials that they must take some of the steps and must make full investigation of the others. Results were scarce.

APPENDIX B

CINCINNATI BUREAU OF GOVERNMENTAL RESEARCH

REPORT NO.

1. A Retirement System for Municipal Employees—Preliminary Financial Analysis.
2. Comments and Recommendations on the Proposed Draft of the Amendment to the Charter of the City of Cincinnati.
3. Proposed Procedure for Preparation of Improvement Program and Plan of Financing.
4. Municipal Payroll Procedure—Analysis of Present System and Recommendations for Revision.
5. Police Department—Administrative Records and Personnel.
6. A Municipal Journal—Content and Procedure.
7. The Administrative Code.
8. An Improved Efficiency Rating System for Cincinnati.
9. The Joint Improvement Program—Analysis for 1927.
10. A Record System for the Cincinnati Police Department.
11. A System of Recording and Reporting Financial Transactions for the City of Cincinnati.
12. Hamilton County, Office of the County Recorder—A Survey with Recommendations.
13. Cincinnati Department of Waterworks—Report on Billing Division of Bureau of Collections.
14. Proposed Manual of Legislative Procedure for the City of Cincinnati—Proposed Permanent Improvement Procedure for Highways and Sewer Improvements.
15. Joint Bond Program, County—School District—City of Cincinnati—Annual Financial Analysis, 1929.
16. The Regulation of Minor Highway Privileges in Cincinnati.

APPENDIX B

REPORT NO.

17. The Sinking Fund of the County of Hamilton.
18. Cost Accounting Procedure, Division of Municipal Garage—Department of Service—Bureau of City Works, City of Cincinnati.
19. An Analysis of 11,180 Misdemeanor Cases (for the Cincinnatus Association).
20. Cost Accounting Procedure, Department of Sewers, City of Cincinnati.
21. Preliminary Financial Analysis as basis for Joint Bond Program, 1930, County of Butler—School District—and City of Hamilton.
22. Joint Bond Program, County—School District—and City of Cincinnati Annual Financial Analysis, 1930.
23. Retirement System for General Employees of City of Cincinnati.
24. Report on Actuarial Investigation of Police Relief Fund of City of Cincinnati.
25. Report on Actuarial Investigation of Firemen's Pension Fund of City of Cincinnati.
26. Regional Police Survey—For Southwestern Ohio and Northern Kentucky, 1930 (for the Regional Crime Committee).
27. Cincinnati Board of Education—Administrative Office Study.
28. Board of County Commissioners—Office Layout Study—Hamilton County, Ohio.
29. Minute Records of Board of County Commissioners—Hamilton County, Ohio.
30. Procedure for Billing, Collection and Settlement of Taxes—Hamilton County.
31. Report on a Proposed Retirement Plan for Employees of the City of Cincinnati.
32. Proposed Ordinance to Establish a Retirement System for City Employees.
33. Report on a Survey of the Accounting System of Hamilton County, Ohio.

34. Outline of System of Accounting Suggested for Hamilton County, Ohio.
35. Survey of the Management, Operation and Maintenance of the Hamilton County Courthouse.
36. Report on Organization and Administration of the Sanitary Engineering Department of Hamilton County.
37. Survey of Personnel in Hamilton County Government Service with a Proposed Plan for Classification and Compensation to be Administered Under Civil Service.
38. Survey and Report on the Purchasing Procedure of Hamilton County, Ohio.
39. A Survey of the Organization and Operation of the Tax-Supported Hospitals in the County of Hamilton and City of Cincinnati.
40. Survey and Report on the Budget Procedure for County of Hamilton, Ohio.
41. A Survey of the Office of the Clerk of Council, Cincinnati, Ohio.
42. Bail Administration in the Cincinnati Region—Survey of Bail Practices (for the Regional Crime Committee).
43. A Survey Defining the Boundaries of the Cincinnati Region.
44. An Analysis of the Sinking Fund of the County of Hamilton, Ohio.
45. The Development of Coördinated Purchasing by the Principal Governmental Units in Hamilton County, Ohio.
46. An Analysis of the Sinking Fund for the School District of the City of Cincinnati.
47. An Analysis of the Sinking Fund for the City of Cincinnati.
48. A Survey and Report of the Organization for Welfare Relief Administration in Hamilton County, Ohio.
49. An Analysis of the Tax Duplicates for the City of Cincinnati, County of Hamilton and School District of the City of Cincinnati.

APPENDIX C

BIBLIOGRAPHY ON THE GOVERNMENT OF CINCINNATI AND THE CITY CHARTER MOVEMENT

"The Government of Cincinnati and Hamilton County," The Upson Report, 1924.

"Why Cincinnati Voted for Proportional Representation and a City Manager." Henry Bentley, National Municipal Review, Vol. XIV, No. 2, February, 1925.

"Cincinnati's Right About Face in Government." Henry Bentley, National Municipal Review, Vol. XV, No. 8, August, 1926.

"Municipal Progress in Cincinnati." Col. C. O. Sherrill, Public Management, October, 1928.

"What Proportional Representation Has Done for Cincinnati." Henry Bentley, National Municipal Review, Vol. XVIII, No. 2, February, 1929.

"Our American Mayors—Murray Seasongood of Cincinnati," by Russell Wilson, National Municipal Review, Vol. XVIII, No. 2, February, 1929.

"The First Proportional Representation Election in Cincinnati." Proportional Representation Review, January, 1926. Address, 34th Street and Second Avenue, New York City.

"The Practical Workings of Proportional Representation in the United States and Canada." Joseph P. Harris, National Municipal Review, Vol. XIX, No. 5, May, 1930.

"An Analysis of Cincinnati's Proportional Representation Elections," Robert P. Goldman, American Political Science Review, Vol. XXIV, No. 3, August, 1930.

"Four Years of Progress in Cincinnati." Charles P. Taft,

II, Public Management, Vol. XIX, No. 5, Page 324, May, 1930.

"The City Manager." Leonard D. White. Published by the University of Chicago Press.

"Municipal Activities"—Reports of City Manager of Cincinnati issued in 1926, 1927, 1928, 1929, 1930, 1931 and 1932.

"How Political Gangs Work." Murray Seasongood, Harvard Graduates' Magazine, March, 1930.

"When Citizens Unite." Henry Bentley, Survey Graphic, October, 1931.

"Cincinnati Shows the Way." Russell Wilson, Review of Reviews, May, 1932.

"A City on a Budget." C. A. Dykstra, Forum, August, 1932.

"Maintaining Sustained Citizen Interest in Government." Henry Bentley, Public Management, December, 1932.

For articles on Administration of Cincinnati's Government since January 1, 1926, see file of National Municipal Review, 309 E. 34th Street, New York City; American City, 443 Fourth Avenue, New York City, and Public Management, 923 E. 60th Street, Chicago, Illinois.

"Local Government in the United States," by Murray Seasongood, Harvard University Press, May, 1933. How Cincinnati was changed from the "worst" governed city to the "best" governed city. (Book) 145 pp.

"When Youth Takes the Reins in Politics," by Jerome Beatty, American Magazine, June, 1933.

APPENDIX D
RESULTS OF ELECTIONS

1925

Candidates	Official Count	Second Count (A)	Third Count (B)	Fourth Count (40)	Fifth Count (39)	Sixth Count (38)	Seventh Count (37)	Eighth Count (36)	Ninth Count (35)	10th Count (33)	11th Count (34)	12th Count (31)	13th Count (30)	14th Count (29)	15th Count (32)	16th Count (28)	17th Count (27)
1 Dixon (C)	21,699	11,974	11,974	....	11,974	11,974	11,974	11,974	11,974	11,974	11,974	11,974	11,974	11,974	11,974	11,974	11,974
2 Seasongood (C)	20,543	11,974	11,974	....	11,974	11,974	11,974	11,974	11,974	11,974	11,974	11,974	11,974	11,974	11,974	11,974	11,974
3 Schneller (R)	9,491	9,657	9,798	....	9,801	9,804	9,810	9,816	9,819	9,821	9,823	9,846	9,856	9,863	9,873	9,874	9,892
4 Field (C)	6,736	8,173	10,165	....	10,167	10,175	10,188	10,194	10,201	10,206	10,212	10,217	10,226	10,238	10,244	10,257	10,283
5 Rose (C)	6,418	7,312	9,495	....	9,495	9,498	9,502	9,506	9,529	9,534	9,560	9,571	9,587	9,602	9,613	9,623	9,648
6 Daly (R)	5,751	6,521	6,629	....	6,630	6,640	6,643	6,655	6,659	6,661	6,664	6,667	6,680	6,685	6,703	6,708	6,714
7 Lackmann (R)	5,629	5,656	5,700	....	5,701	5,701	5,702	5,702	5,707	5,732	5,739	5,749	5,760	5,770	5,773	5,791	5,820
8 Luchsinger (C)	5,600	6,241	6,766	....	6,771	6,774	6,776	6,780	6,786	6,797	6,806	6,810	6,818	6,825	6,845	6,873	6,906
9 Schmidt (R)	5,510	5,630	5,685	....	5,686	5,687	5,688	5,688	5,692	5,697	5,702	5,723	5,734	5,744	5,750	5,761	5,771
10 Gamble (C)	5,412	5,837	6,892	....	6,893	6,896	6,902	6,909	6,912	6,925	6,929	6,935	6,953	6,961	6,967	6,988	7,048
11 Matthews (C)	4,911	6,258	7,376	....	7,377	7,379	7,381	7,382	7,400	7,412	7,419	7,428	7,437	7,448	7,457	7,465	7,505
12 Kellogg (R)	3,504	3,571	3,607	....	3,611	3,612	3,614	3,618	3,619	3,622	3,624	3,625	3,628	3,629	3,633	3,642	3,654
13 Kummer (R)	3,419	3,493	3,516	....	3,518	3,518	3,521	3,524	3,526	3,547	3,549	3,552	3,556	3,561	3,564	3,577	3,612
14 Higgins (C)	3,381	6,273	6,514	....	6,517	6,522	6,524	6,526	6,529	6,529	6,540	6,541	6,542	6,546	6,548	6,551	6,563
15 Hicks (C)	1,705	1,950	2,396	....	2,398	2,400	2,403	2,406	2,410	2,419	2,420	2,422	2,425	2,430	2,445	2,452	2,470
16 Fielding (I)	1,199	1,213	1,240	....	1,241	1,242	1,248	1,266	1,266	1,267	1,268	1,272	1,273	1,275	1,277	1,278	1,279
17 Hunter (I)	1,110	1,115	1,129	....	1,135	1,136	1,136	1,142	1,142	1,142	1,142	1,146	1,146	1,147	1,147	1,158	1,160
18 Cox (I)	1,012	1,035	1,127	....	1,127	1,130	1,132	1,138	1,139	1,143	1,145	1,146	1,149	1,155	1,161	1,162	1,176
19 Roth (I)	889	1,204	1,319	....	1,319	1,326	1,327	1,330	1,332	1,334	1,357	1,359	1,360	1,367	1,371	1,373	1,382
20 Schuch (I)	850	864	894	....	894	894	894	894	895	891	902	903	914	919	924	925	
21 Price (I)	740	744	756	....	756	757	757	758	775	776	777	779	780	788	790	794	797
22 MacDonald (I)	698	725	729	....	742	742	742	743	747	750	751	753	754	756	757	773	777
23 Feldman (I)	503	536	576	....	580	580	603	605	607	608	609	610	614	635	648	661	666
24 Driemeyer (I)	484	517	544	....	545	546	547	551	557	558	559	560	562	565	567	567	570
25 Bridgeford (I)	434	437	455	....	455	459	459	467	467	467	467	473	479	517	519	519	
26 Davis (I)	352	405	429	....	430	431	432	437	438	438	439	442	447	453	461	464	467
27 Kramer (I)	296	311	360	....	363	363	364	364	364	365	366	376	377	379	386	392	....
28 Hitzman (I)	316	221	222	....	223	224	225	226	226	226	226	227	227	228	....	....	
29 Sevester (I)	161	174	198	....	198	199	199	200	201	201	202	202	202	....	....		
30 Siegler (I)	144	146	161	....	163	163	163	163	166	167	167	168	....	....			
31 Potter (I)	134	137	151	....	151	151	151	151	151	152	159	....	....				
32 Bloch (I)	131	135	166	....	166	178	179	186	186	186	186	194	204	221	....		
33 Krehbiel (I)	128	132	137	....	139	139	139	140	144	....	....						
34 Roebling (I)	120	125	140	....	140	140	140	140	145	148	....	....					
35 Niederhauser	118	125	133	....	133	133	135	137	....	....							
36 Underwood	105	111	131	....	131	131	133	....	....								
37 Ehrman	87	99	102	....	103	103	....										
38 Winter	56	74	77	....	77	....											
39 Houper	53	55	56	....													
40 Lietze	1	1	1	....													
Cumulative total of ineffective votes	....	....	....	1	6	9	23	36	45	57	76	94	109	119	138	155	178

1927

Candidates	Official Count	Second Count (A)	Third Count (B)	Fourth Count (C)	Fifth Count (25)	Sixth Count (24)	Seventh Count (23)	Eighth Count (22)	Ninth Count (21)	Tenth Count (20)
1 Seasongood (C)	24,121	12,429	12,429	12,429	12,429	12,429	12,429	12,429	12,429	12,429
2 Schneller (R)	19,949	19,949	12,429	12,429	12,429	12,429	12,429	12,429	12,429	12,429
3 Dixon (C)	19,141	19,141	19,141	12,429	12,429	12,429	12,429	12,429	12,429	12,429
4 Yeatman (I)	6,729	7,711	8,393	8,697	8,697	8,705	8,758	8,789	8,896	9,072
5 Eisen (C)	6,533	7,422	7,551	8,286	8,286	8,296	8,307	8,343	8,388	8,435
6 Matthews (C)	5,375	7,272	7,384	8,503	8,503	8,509	8,548	8,574	8,653	8,828
7 Field (C)	5,181	7,564	7,798	8,516	8,516	8,529	8,557	8,666	8,724	8,814
8 Lackmann (R)	4,900	5,028	5,932	5,980	5,980	5,991	6,021	6,048	6,141	6,283
9 Imbus (C)	4,029	4,631	4,693	6,039	6,039	6,043	6,084	6,100	6,154	6,209
10 Rose (C)	3,822	6,330	6,634	7,113	7,113	7,121	7,136	7,163	7,224	7,303
11 Hall (I)	3,409	3,457	3,893	3,910	3,910	4,047	4,051	4,069	4,090	4,097
12 Daly (R)	3,385	3,527	4,817	5,401	5,401	5,445	5,473	5,508	5,597	5,698
13 Hock (R)	2,999	3,067	3,286	3,410	3,410	3,420	3,454	3,476	3,587	3,634
14 Bradford (R)	2,684	2,800	3,254	3,299	3,299	3,305	3,321	3,380	3,403	3,431
15 Mees (C)	2,057	2,386	2,434	2,644	2,644	2,649	2,659	2,664	2,684	2,714
16 Bernard (I)	2,009	2,340	2,461	2,641	2,641	2,646	2,656	2,662	2,676	2,698
17 O'Hara (I)	1,937	1,974	2,201	2,342	2,342	2,344	2,356	2,361	2,400	2,457
18 Dickerson (C)	1,874	2,831	2,868	3,184	3,184	3,197	3,209	3,280	3,314	3,346
19 Mitchell (R)	1,190	1,318	3,282	3,474	3,474	3,482	3,495	3,562	3,597	3,675
20 Kellogg (I)	996	1,034	1,097	1,160	1,161	1,167	1,208	1,211	1,257	....
21 Handley (I)	843	880	942	989	989	992	1,010	1,014	....	....
22 Davis (R)	428	474	556	574	574	589	595	....	....	....
23 Harris (I)	426	440	458	479	479	483	....	....	....	....
24 Dalton (I)	269	291	353	358	358	....	....	....	....	....
25 Bentley	1	1	1	1	....	....	....	....	....	....
Votes Eliminated	....	....	....	....	1	358	483	595	1,014	1,257
Ineffective Ballots (Cumulative)	....	....	....	....	....	40	102	130	215	306

Vote

	18th Count	19th Count	20th Count	21st Count	22d Count	23d Count	24th Count	25th Count	26th Count	27th Count	28th Count	29th Count	30th Count	31st Count	32d Count	33d Count	Final Count	
	(26)	(25)	(24)	(23)	(22)	(21)	(20)	(17)	(18)	(19)	(16)	(15)	(13)	(12)	(9)	(14)	(10)	Candidates
	11,974	11,974	11,974	11,974	11,974	11,974	11,974	11,974	11,974	11,974	11,974	11,974	11,974	11,974	11,974	11,974	11,974	Dixon
	11,974	11,974	11,974	11,974	11,974	11,974	11,974	11,974	11,974	11,974	11,974	11,974	11,974	11,974	11,974	11,974	11,974	Seasongood
	9,920	9,926	9,938	9,951	9,982	9,995	10,025	10,099	10,123	10,221	10,488	10,547	10,793	11,224	11,974	11,974	11,974	Schneller
	10,337	10,370	10,479	10,577	10,624	10,654	10,716	10,760	11,378	11,532	11,642	11,974	11,974	11,974	11,974	11,974	11,974	Field
	9,682	9,891	9,961	9,991	10,109	10,231	10,685	10,725	10,847	11,031	11,107	11,471	11,577	11,854	11,974	11,974	11,974	Rose
	6,749	6,766	6,783	6,796	6,831	6,839	6,868	6,920	6,996	7,120	7,327	7,392	7,567	9,078	11,360	11,974	11,974	Daly
	5,828	5,849	5,871	5,974	6,038	6,073	6,107	6,124	6,147	6,188	6,223	6,295	8,306	9,013	10,930	11,161	11,974	Lackmann
	6,953	6,969	6,990	7,044	7,126	7,489	7,559	7,591	7,646	7,763	7,820	8,108	8,431	8,620	9,041	11,265	11,974	Luchsinger
	5,786	5,792	5,801	5,827	5,895	5,928	5,955	5,975	6,006	6,136	6,184	6,234	6,726	7,032	....	....	....	Schmidt
	7,079	7,095	7,165	7,302	7,351	7,403	7,453	7,497	7,677	7,748	7,954	8,746	8,802	9,061	9,467	11,084	....	Gamble
	7,529	7,541	7,589	7,616	7,737	7,785	7,833	7,861	7,926	8,152	8,237	8,576	8,701	8,971	9,505	11,974	11,974	Matthews
	3,666	3,673	3,686	3,695	3,713	3,719	3,725	3,811	3,835	3,851	3,956	4,043	4,182	....	....	....	....	Kellogg
	3,632	3,634	3,644	3,660	3,682	3,689	3,701	3,722	3,735	3,757	3,780	3,817	....	....	....	....	....	Kummer
	6,604	6,606	6,632	6,646	6,676	6,679	6,698	6,717	6,730	6,951	7,052	7,421	7,473	7,540	7,709	....	....	Higgins
	2,496	2,509	2,534	2,575	2,597	2,606	2,621	2,675	2,739	2,783	2,950	....	....	....	....	....	....	Hicks
	1,289	1,295	1,308	1,354	1,358	1,362	1,373	1,884	1,901	1,908	....	....	....	....	....	....	....	Fielding
	1,160	1,163	1,167	1,185	1,190	1,190	1,194	....	....	....	....	....	....	....	....	....	....	Hunter
	1,185	1,268	1,301	1,308	1,318	1,324	1,390	1,394	....	....	....	....	....	....	....	....	....	Cox
	1,390	1,399	1,406	1,414	1,441	1,458	1,478	1,486	1,508	....	....	....	....	....	....	....	....	Roth
	932	943	951	963	974	1,003	....	....	....	....	....	....	....	....	....	....	....	Schuch
	800	802	809	819	833	....	....	....	....	....	....	....	....	....	....	....	....	Price
	779	783	787	813	....	....	....	....	....	....	....	....	....	....	....	....	....	MacDonald
	695	701	746	....	....	....	....	....	....	....	....	....	....	....	....	....	....	Feldman
	588	597	....	....	....	....	....	....	....	....	....	....	....	....	....	....	....	Driemeyer
	520	....	....	....	....	....	....	....	....	....	....	....	....	....	....	....	....	Bridgeford
	....	....	....	....	....	....	....	....	....	....	....	....	....	....	....	....	....	Davis
	....	....	....	....	....	....	....	....	....	....	....	....	....	....	....	....	....	Kramer
	....	....	....	....	....	....	....	....	....	....	....	....	....	....	....	....	....	Hitzman
	....	....	....	....	....	....	....	....	....	....	....	....	....	....	....	....	....	Sevester
	....	....	....	....	....	....	....	....	....	....	....	....	....	....	....	....	....	Siegler
	....	....	....	....	....	....	....	....	....	....	....	....	....	....	....	....	....	Rotter
	....	....	....	....	....	....	....	....	....	....	....	....	....	....	....	....	....	Bloch
	....	....	....	....	....	....	....	....	....	....	....	....	....	....	....	....	....	Krehbiel
	....	....	....	....	....	....	....	....	....	....	....	....	....	....	....	....	....	Roebling
	....	....	....	....	....	....	....	....	....	....	....	....	....	....	....	....	....	Niederhauser
	....	....	....	....	....	....	....	....	....	....	....	....	....	....	....	....	....	Underwood
	....	....	....	....	....	....	....	....	....	....	....	....	....	....	....	....	....	Ehrman
	....	....	....	....	....	....	....	....	....	....	....	....	....	....	....	....	....	Winter
	....	....	....	....	....	....	....	....	....	....	....	....	....	....	....	....	....	Hooper
	....	....	....	....	....	....	....	....	....	....	....	....	....	....	....	....	....	Lietze
																		Cumulative total of
	190	210	229	272	305	355	401	541	588	641	1,062	1,158	1,250	1,415	1,844	....	....	ineffective ballots

Vote

Eleventh Count	12th Count	13th Count	14th Count	15th Count	16th Count	17th Count	18th Count	19th Count	Final Count	
(17)	(15)	(16)	(18)	(14)	(11)	(19)	(13)	(9)	(8)	Candidates
12,429	12,429	12,429	12,429	12,429	12,429	12,429	12,429	12,429	12,429	Seasongood
12,429	12,429	12,429	12,429	12,429	12,429	12,429	12,429	12,429	12,429	Schneller
12,429	12,429	12,429	12,429	12,429	12,429	12,429	12,429	12,429	12,429	Dixon
9,319	9,460	9,730	10,000	10,457	10,817	11,218	11,812	12,429	12,429	Yeatman
8,474	8,696	8,859	10,040	10,310	10,493	10,599	10,877	12,429	12,429	Eisen
8,948	9,343	9,815	10,231	10,406	10,623	10,892	11,326	12,429	12,429	Matthews
8,880	9,037	9,280	9,976	10,488	10,732	11,104	11,617	12,429	12,429	Field
6,374	6,446	6,557	6,605	6,992	7,165	8,082	9,086	9,590	....	Lackmann
6,322	6,589	7,026	7,227	7,364	7,472	7,612	8,053	....	....	Imbus
7,431	7,851	8,067	8,496	8,728	8,984	9,281	9,574	11,598	12,429	Rose
4,410	4,152	4,167	4,202	4,230	....	....	....	....	....	Hall
6,464	6,561	6,963	7,052	8,058	8,791	10,542	11,882	12,429	12,429	Daly
3,831	4,433	4,527	4,556	4,660	5,055	5,368	....	....	....	Hock
3,486	3,515	3,613	3,674	....	....	....	....	....	....	Bradford
2,772	....	....	....	....	....	....	....	....	....	Mees
2,841	2,895	....	....	....	....	....	....	....	....	Bernard
....	....	....	....	....	....	....	....	....	....	O'Hara
3,372	3,467	3,595	....	....	....	....	....	....	....	Dickerson
3,873	3,934	4,054	4,082	4,389	4,727	....	....	....	....	Mitchell
....	....	....	....	....	....	....	....	....	....	Kellogg
....	....	....	....	....	....	....	....	....	....	Handley
....	....	....	....	....	....	....	....	....	....	Davis
....	....	....	....	....	....	....	....	....	....	Harris
....	....	....	....	....	....	....	....	....	....	Dalton
....	....	....	....	....	....	....	....	....	....	Bentley
2,457	2,772	2,895	3,595	3,674	4,230	4,727	5,368	8,053	9,590	Votes Eliminated
										Ineffective Ballots
503	621	747	859	918	2,132	2,302	2,773	3,667	12,426	(Cumulative)

1929

Candidates	Official Count	Second Count (A)	Third Count (25)	Fourth Count (24)	Fifth Count (23)	Sixth Count (22)	Seventh Count (21)	Eighth Count (20)	Ninth Count (19)
1 Wilson (C)	22,112	13,877	13,877	13,877	13,877	13,877	13,877	13,877	13,877
2 Druffel (C)	10,622	11,117	11,117	11,121	11,124	11,152	11,190	11,210	11,410
3 Rose (C)	10,394	13,877	13,877	13,877	13,877	13,877	13,877	13,877	13,877
4 Matthews (C)	10,308	11,633	11,633	11,651	11,670	11,704	11,762	11,770	12,300
5 Imbus (C)	9,706	9,949	9,949	9,951	9,957	10,029	10,074	10,100	10,347
6 Woeste (R)	9,082	9,247	9,248	9,259	9,274	9,287	9,328	9,358	9,437
7 Yeatman (R)	8,668	8,883	8,695	8,891	8,912	8,926	8,951	8,972	9,067
8 Hall (I)	6,781	6,786	6,786	6,788	6,790	6,794	6,798	7,651	7,659
9 Patterson (R)	6,715	6,745	6,745	6,750	6,777	6,782	6,821	6,825	6,937
10 Daly (R)	5,999	6,052	6,052	6,056	6,061	6,071	6,114	6,173	6,218
11 Friedman (R)	5,683	5,724	5,724	5,726	5,728	5,741	5,747	5,777	5,798
12 Pollak (C)	5,357	6,430	6,431	6,437	6,458	6,469	6,501	6,516	6,975
13 Dornette (R)	4,899	4,961	4,961	4,963	4,971	4,974	4,985	5,008	5,036
14 Garrison (C)	4,824	5,226	5,227	5,230	5,254	5,241	5,250	5,260	5,427
15 Schulte (R)	3,944	3,988	3,988	3,996	4,007	4,019	4,033	4,039	4,077
16 Hauser (R)	3,270	3,319	3,319	3,320	3,323	3,340	3,347	3,353	3,380
17 Licht (C)	3,268	3,658	3,658	3,691	3,696	3,715	3,730	3,734	3,859
18 Rebman (R)	2,663	2,684	2,684	2,686	2,691	2,694	2,715	2,721	2,845
19 Murray (C)	2,162	2,282	2,282	2,287	2,292	2,299	2,349	2,356	....
20 Conrad (I)	1,179	1,185	1,185	1,187	1,188	1,190	1,194	....	....
21 McFarland (I)	472	476	476	478	485	490	....	....	....
22 Hummel (I)	296	302	302	305	306	....	....	....	....
23 Neuhaus (I)	188	191	191	198	....	....	....	....	....
24 Jollie (I)	164	164	164	....	....	....	....	....	....
25 Written in	7	7	....	....	....	....	....	....	....
Votes eliminated	....	....	7	164	198	306	490	1,194	2,356
Ineffective (cumulative)	....	....	2	38	65	93	139	186	236

1931

Candidates	Official Count	Second Count (A)	Third Count (29)	Fourth Count (28)	Fifth Count (26)	Sixth Count (27)	Seventh Count (25)	Eighth Count (24)	Ninth Count (23)	Tenth Count (22)
1 Wilson (C)	30,328	12,228	12,228	12,228	12,228	12,228	12,228	12,228	12,228	12,228
2 Hall (R)	11,690	11,713	11,716	11,741	11,747	11,750	11,754	11,756	11,764
3 Druffel (C)	9,215	11,451	11,451	11,484	11,495	11,505	11,517	11,544	11,574	11,599
4 Yeatman (R)	6,581	7,267	7,267	7,268	7,273	7,285	7,303	7,380	7,424	7,495
5 Patterson (R)	6,530	6,765	6,765	6,772	6,777	6,784	6,825	6,901	6,912	6,942
6 Imbus (C)	6,359	7,202	7,203	7,211	7,234	7,238	7,250	7,276	7,296	7,329
7 Pollak (C)	5,952	8,719	8,723	8,727	8,739	8,766	8,799	8,835	8,862	8,900
8 DeCourcy (R)	5,458	5,566	5,566	5,590	5,601	5,611	5,628	5,669	5,716	5,738
9 Woeste (R)	5,420	5,875	5,875	5,881	5,889	5,908	5,933	6,097	6,120	6,223
10 Rose (C)	4,911	12,228	12,228	12,228	12,228	12,228	12,228	12,228	12,228	12,228
11 Adams (R)	3,881	4,043	4,043	4,047	4,050	4,054	4,065	4,112	4,131	4,166
12 Nippert (R)	3,712	3,900	3,900	3,902	3,922	3,929	3,937	3,985	4,002	4,020
13 Spiegel (R)	2,987	3,063	3,063	3,063	3,070	3,079	3,087	3,179	3,187	3,196
14 Espy (C)	2,743	3,400	3,400	3,402	3,406	3,412	3,419	3,444	3,454	3,464
15 Culkins (R)	2,177	2,263	2,263	2,271	2,286	2,286	2,290	2,301	2,342	2,354
16 Stilwell (C)	1,989	2,834	2,834	2,837	2,838	2,849	2,858	2,832	2,895	2,911
17 Dempsey (I)	1,905	2,004	2,004	2,027	2,035	2,044	2,054	2,074	2,101	2,118
18 Allgaier (C)	1,766	2,556	2,556	2,559	2,563	2,565	2,572	2,586	2,601	2,634
19 Fitzpatrick (L)	1,659	1,698	1,698	1,787	1,847	1,883	1,990	2,014	2,257	2,666
20 Colman (L)	1,396	1,429	1,429	1,476	1,510	1,547	1,623	1,639	1,891	2,405
21 Murray (C)	1,308	1,600	1,600	1,604	1,622	1,629	1,636	1,644	1,665	1,676
22 Von Hagen (L)	874	900	900	905	921	1,006	1,279	1,346	1,451	....
23 Cordes (L)	851	882	882	911	932	950	995	1,011	....	....
24 Schneider (I)	830	863	863	865	870	909	944	....	....	....
25 Obermeyer (L)	656	674	674	686	750	786	....	....	....	....
26 Friedrich (L)	389	397	397	401	...	...	...	....	....	....
27 Rice (L)	364	402	402	417	426	...	...	....	....	....
28 Dardes (L)	340	349	349	...	...	...	...	....	....	....
29 Written in	7	7	...	...	...	...	...	....	....	....
Total transfer	...	...	7	349	401	426	786	944	1,011	1,451
Ineffective (cumulative)	...	...	2	13	25	50	68	149	185	222

Vote

	10th Count	11th Count	12th Count	13th Count	14th Count	15th Count	16th Count	17th Count	Final Count	Candidates
	(18)	(16)	(17)	(15)	(14)	(13)	(11)	(8)	(10)	
	13,877	13,877	13,877	13,877	13,877	13,877	13,877	13,877	13,877	Wilson
	11,462	11,538	11,849	11,956	12,728	12,985	13,175	13,358	13,877	Druffel
	13,877	13,877	13,877	13,877	13,877	13,877	13,877	13,877	13,877	Rose
	12,459	12,665	13,877	13,877	13,877	13,877	13,877	13,877	13,877	Matthews
	10,430	10,585	11,017	11,125	12,439	12,648	12,944	13,435	13,877	Imbus
	9,984	10,382	10,470	12,136	12,282	13,010	13,877	13,877	13,877	Woeste
	9,401	9,925	10,120	10,935	11,417	12,936	13,877	13,877	13,877	Yeatman
	7,694	7,724	7,734	7,751	7,812	7,858	8,099	....	....	Hall
	7,167	7,650	7,740	8,482	8,616	10,194	12,022	12,725	13,877	Patterson
	6,540	6,875	6,911	7,336	7,425	8,245	9,816	11,499	....	Daly
	5,897	6,178	6,216	6,527	6,573	7,282	....	....	....	Friedman
	7,032	7,131	8,023	8,162	10,740	11,088	12,093	12,722	13,877	Pollak
	5,140	5,596	5,687	6,084	6,371	....	....	....	....	Dornette
	5,448	5,490	5,971	6,032	....	....	....	....	....	Garrison
	4,633	4,855	4,897	....	....	....	....	....	....	Schulte
	3,503	....	....	....	....	....	....	....	....	Hauser
	3,890	3,981	....	....	....	....	....	....	....	Licht
	....	....	....	....	....	....	....	....	....	Rebman
	....	....	....	....	....	....	....	....	....	Murray
	....	....	....	....	....	....	....	....	....	Conrad
	....	....	....	....	....	....	....	....	....	McFarland
	....	....	....	....	....	....	....	....	....	Hummel
	....	....	....	....	....	....	....	....	....	Neuhaus
	....	....	....	....	....	....	....	....	....	Jollie
	....	....	....	....	....	....	....	....	....	Written in
	2,845	3,503	3,981	4,897	6,032	6,371	7,282	8,099	11,459	Ineffective (cumulative)
	329	434	497	606	729	886	1,229	4,450	....	Votes eliminated

Vote

	11th Count	12th Count	13th Count	14th Count	15th Count	16th Count	17th Count	18th Count	19th Count	20th Count	21st Count	Final Count	Candidates
	(21)	(17)	(15)	(20)	(18)	(13)	(16)	(12)	(19)	(14)	(11)	(8)	
	12,228	12,228	12,228	12,228	12,228	12,228	12,228	12,228	12,228	12,228	12,228	12,228	Wilson
	11,772	11,809	11,861	11,884	11,901	12,003	12,037	12,125	12,228	12,228	12,228	12,228	Hall
	11,779	12,228	12,228	12,228	12,228	12,228	12,228	12,228	12,228	12,228	12,228	12,228	Druffel
	7,550	7,623	7,952	7,994	8,101	8,636	8,801	9,657	9,937	10,334	12,188	12,228	Yeatman
	7,022	7,128	7,370	7,414	7,469	7,777	7,859	9,289	9,603	10,002	11,038	12,228	Patterson
	7,566	7,788	7,831	7,885	8,335	8,387	8,922	9,203	9,592	12,228	12,228	12,228	Imbus
	9,309	9,405	9,482	9,524	10,028	10,546	11,916	12,228	12,228	12,228	12,228	12,228	Pollak
	5,769	6,003	6,423	6,523	6,614	6,822	6,881	7,175	7,439	7,589	9,220	....	DeCourcy
	6,276	6,443	6,654	6,687	6,740	7,585	7,756	8,471	8,860	9,105	10,053	12,228	Woeste
	12,228	12,228	12,228	12,228	12,228	12,228	12,228	12,228	12,228	12,228	12,228	12,228	Rose
	4,194	4,262	4,814	4,845	4,905	5,237	5,332	5,794	5,986	6,136	....	....	Adams
	4,099	4,160	4,334	4,357	4,524	4,749	4,853	....	....	....	....	....	Nippert
	3,219	3,246	3,360	3,367	3,394	....	....	....	....	....	....	....	Spiegel
	3,567	3,691	3,750	3,794	4,638	4,678	5,497	5,712	5,872	....	....	....	Espy
	2,359	2,397	....	....	....	....	....	....	....	....	....	....	Culkins
	3,021	3,056	3,077	3,097	3,452	3,552	....	....	....	....	....	....	Stilwell
	2,155	....	....	....	....	....	....	....	....	....	....	....	Dempsey
	2,735	2,794	2,819	2,848	....	....	....	....	....	....	....	....	Allgaier
	2,726	2,928	2,960	4,913	4,971	5,005	5,041	5,103	....	....	....	....	Fitzpatrick
	2,448	2,539	2,555	....	....	....	....	....	....	....	....	....	Colman
	....	....	....	....	....	....	....	....	....	....	....	....	Murray
	....	....	....	....	....	....	....	....	....	....	....	....	Von Hagen
	....	....	....	....	....	....	....	....	....	....	....	....	Cordes
	....	....	....	....	....	....	....	....	....	....	....	....	Schneider
	....	....	....	....	....	....	....	....	....	....	....	....	Obermeyer
	....	....	....	....	....	....	....	....	....	....	....	....	Friedrich
	....	....	....	....	....	....	....	....	....	....	....	....	Rice
	....	....	....	....	....	....	....	....	....	....	....	....	Dardes
	....	....	....	....	....	....	....	....	....	....	....	....	Written in
	1,676	2,155	2,397	2,555	2,848	3,394	3,552	4,853	5,103	5,872	6,136	9,220	Total transfer
	256	322	355	462	522	617	699	837	3,849	5,744	6,411	12,226	Ineffective, cumulative

1933

Candidates	Official Count	Second Count	Third Count	Fourth Count	Fifth Count	Sixth Count	Seventh Count
R. Wilson (C)	....	....	....	....	....	....	....
Rose (C)	....	....	....	....	....	....	....
Pollak (C)	....	....	....	....	....	....	....
Von Unruh (C)	....	....	....	....	....	....	....
Early (C)	....	....	....	....	....	....	....
J. Wilson (C)	....	....	....	....	....	....	....
Imbus (C)	....	....	....	....	....	....	....
Dunlap (C)	....	....	....	....	....	....	....
Muhlhauser (C)	....	....	....	....	....	....	....
Woeste (R)	....	....	....	....	....	....	....
Patterson (R)	....	....	....	....	....	....	....
Hall (R)	....	....	....	....	....	....	....
Gradison (R)	....	....	....	....	....	....	....
Adams (R)	....	....	....	....	....	....	....
Dugan (R)	....	....	....	....	....	....	....
Campbell (R)	....	....	....	....	....	....	....
Behymer (R)	....	....	....	....	....	....	....
Stewart (R)	....	....	....	....	....	....	....
Weller (I)	....	....	....	....	....	....	....
Friedman (I)	....	....	....	....	....	....	....
Dorsey (I)	....	....	....	....	....	....	....
Murphy (I)	....	....	....	....	....	....	....
Written in	....	....	....	....	....	....	....
Total transfer	....	....	....	....	....	....	....
Ineffective (cumulative)	....	....	....	....	....	....	....

Vote

Eighth Count	Ninth Count	Tenth Count	11th Count	12th Count	13th Count	14th Count	15th Count	Final Count	Candidates
....	....	....	....	....	....	....	....	....	R. Wilson
....	....	....	....	....	....	....	....	....	Rose
....	....	....	....	....	....	....	....	....	Pollak
....	....	....	....	....	....	....	....	....	Von Unruh
....	....	....	....	....	....	....	....	....	Early
....	....	....	....	....	....	....	....	....	J. Wilson
....	....	....	....	....	....	....	....	....	Imbus
....	....	....	....	....	....	....	....	....	Dunlap
....	....	....	....	....	....	....	....	....	Muhlhauser
....	....	....	....	....	....	....	....	....	Woeste
....	....	....	....	....	....	....	....	....	Patterson
....	....	....	....	....	....	....	....	....	Hall
....	....	....	....	....	....	....	....	....	Gradison
....	....	....	....	....	....	....	....	....	Adams
....	....	....	....	....	....	....	....	....	Dugan
....	....	....	....	....	....	....	....	....	Campbell
....	....	....	....	....	....	....	....	....	Behymer
....	....	....	....	....	....	....	....	....	Stewart
....	....	....	....	....	....	....	....	....	Weller
....	....	....	....	....	....	....	....	....	Friedman
....	....	....	....	....	....	....	....	....	Dorsey
....	....	....	....	....	....	....	....	....	Murphy
....	....	....	....	....	....	....	....	....	Written in
....	....	....	....	....	....	....	....	....	Total transfer
....	....	....	....	....	....	....	....	....	Ineffective (cumulative)

APPE[N]

CITY OF CINCINNATI—GENERA[L]

REVENUES	1921	1922	1923	1924	1925
TAXES					
Real & Personal Property	$2,345,350.61	$4,049,021.42	$4,002,807.69	$4,397,733.15	$3,556,781.1[
Intangible Property	....	....	....	....	....
Occupation Tax	502,237.17	509,924.90	538,021.08	536,652.10	529,858.2[
Total Taxes	$2,847,587.78	$4,558,946.32	$4,540,828.77	$4,934,385.25	$4,086,639.4[
RIGHTS AND PRIVILEGES					
Licenses and Permits					
Taxicab	....	....	15,819.00	12,479.00	14,649.0[
Motor Bus	....	....	....	....	....
Other Vehicles	17,905.66	16,212.33	14,711.70	12,508.39	10,654.4[
Vendors and Curb Stands	34,853.30	32,436.70	38,759.97	40,001.61	36,948.5[
Quasi-Public Business	6,295.70	13,716.60	3,598.50	3,881.54	3,606.9[
Chauffeur	....	....	....	....	....
Plumbers' License & Examination	1,489.00	1,571.00	1,603.50	1,550.00	1,378.0[
Coal & Coke Weighers	....	....	....	....	....
Indoor Amusements	42,487.00	40,551.39	38,145.18	37,174.28	36,080.85
Outdoor Amusements	1,250.00	1,650.00	2,135.00	4,915.00	1,435.0[
Milk & Dairy	....	....	1,200.00	1,200.00	1,264.0[
Food Products	1,479.00	3,595.00	4,250.50	4,641.00	4,330.0[
Barber Shop & Beauty Parlor	....	....	....	....	....
Sewer Tap	7,345.00	8,055.00	6,915.00	6,830.00	6,430.0[
Building Department	68,260.76	88,337.75	101,721.40	96,109.46	113,762.61
Ferry	15.00	10.00	5.00	5.00	5.00
Miscellaneous	....	....	....	....	....
Total Licenses & Permits	$181,380.42	$206,135.77	$228,864.75	$221,295.28	$230,553.42
Franchises					
St. Ry. Share of Office Expense	....	23,598.09	....	....	612,500.00
St. Ry. Highway Privileges	6,000.00	6,000.00	6,000.00	6,000.00	6,000.00
U. G. & E. Co. Privileges	22,739.07	25,973.58	30,443.62	33,524.78	36,578.77
Viaduct Rentals	6,500.00	6,500.00	6,875.00	6,500.00	6,500.00
St. Ry. Share of Street Repair	....	....	....	....	....
Total Franchises	$35,239.07	$62,071.67	$43,318.62	$46,024.78	$661,578.77
Concessions					
Recreation Department	....	....	....	....	....
Park Board	1,034.00	1,007.00	1,003.00	....	....
Total Concessions	$1,034.00	$1,007.00	$1,003.00	....	....
Rents					
Docks & Wharves	6,067.55	6,280.49	5,949.51	9,628.77	9,486.68
Ground for Signal	1.00	1.00	1.00	1.00	1.00
Markets	12,114.10	19,988.50	16,541.88	16,350.78	16,380.63
Police & Fire Departments	1,504.59	1,699.75	943.50	1,072.00	917.59
Municipal Airport	....	....	....	....	....
Other Lands and Buildings	13,395.64	13,328.46	13,345.96	10,708.47	9,854.44
Total Rents	$33,082.88	$41,298.20	$36,781.85	$37,761.02	$36,640.34
Total Rights and Privileges	$250,736.37	$310,512.64	$309,968.22	$305,081.08	$928,772.53
SERVICES AND SALES					
Fees					
Birth & Death Certificates	961.50	1,049.50	1,035.00	1,108.50	1,229.00
Meter Tests	40.00	33.00	21.00	312.00	683.25
Miscellaneous Fees	....	....	....	....	....
Total Fees	$1,001.50	$1,082.50	$1,056.00	$1,420.50	$1,912.25

DIX E

FUND—INCOME BY YEARS

1926	1927	1928	1929	1930	1931	1932
$5,618,500.65	$5,869,300.51	$6,620,938.74	$6,179,757.74	$6,240,805.42	$6,819,077.42	$6,400,053.38
....	....	....	....	....	....	277,777.89
546,751.70	550,422.24	539,862.87	540,428.80	514,218.84	445,422.95	171,986.21
$6,165,252.35	$6,419,722.75	$7,160,801.61	$6,720,186.54	$6,755,024.26	$7,264,500.37	$6,849,817.48

16,450.00	13,595.00	16,049.00	12,981.95	10,966.00	9,675.00	9,853.00
33,478.97	17,966.51	9,882.35	10,486.32	10,047.34	25,230.12	9,295.82
8,819.05	6,868.50	5,744.16	4,714.92	1,522.16	2,574.58	1,816.13
35,420.16	44,156.37	45,297.76	43,419.16	43,684.46	42,579.50	39,482.58
4,254.50	3,802.40	3,793.00	4,650.80	4,357.00	4,100.80	4,293.20
....	....	....	1,039.00	2,038.00	1,421.00	1,628.00
1,264.50	1,207.50	1,878.00	1,421.00	1,537.00	1,719.00	1,402.50
....	....	....	345.00	335.00	395.00	740.00
35,769.01	37,364.10	33,589.60	35,194.20	34,382.20	33,350.50	30,327.50
2,935.00	1,960.00	1,850.00	1,925.00	1,960.00	1,285.00	2,405.00
2,763.00	6,547.00	7,028.00	6,531.00	6,263.00	7,726.25	7,263.00
7,035.50	11,778.00	19,203.00	12,439.00	12,751.00	12,690.00	12,636.00
....	....	....	....	1,752.00	1,899.00	2,080.00
6,215.00	9,150.00	6,405.00	3,945.00	2,425.00	1,350.00	675.00
127,233.07	141,767.57	134,627.60	115,055.44	106,801.76	85,067.94	51,540.80
5.00	5.00	....	....	....	....	....
....	4,583.34	....	....	....	....	9.75
$281,642.76	$300,751.29	$285,347.47	$254,147.79	$240,821.92	$231,063.69	$175,448.28

5,748.49	7,503.20	7,583.59	7,442.43	7,805.70	7,549.11	7,573.36
6,000.00	6,000.00	6,000.00	6,000.00	6,000.00	6,000.00	6,000.00
33,739.59	58,255.58	53,506.95	54,314.55	55,394.61	56,013.52	53,748.17
1,375.00	10,625.00	6,500.00	6,500.00	5,500.00	5,125.00	4,065.92
35,000.00	35,000.00	....	....	....	....	....
$81,863.08	$117,383.78	$73,590.54	$74,256.98	$74,700.31	$74,687.63	$71,387.45

....	844.25	....	....	....	3,215.00	2,701.00
2,530.50	2,741.00	2,304.51	2,276.97	4,627.32	4,679.42	5,848.78
$2,530.50	$3,585.25	$2,304.51	$2,276.97	$4,627.32	$7,894.42	$8,549.78

9,300.42	9,318.48	9,507.72	10,132.41	10,142.61	9,119.06	7,404.58
1.00	1.00	1.00	1.00	1.00	1.00	1.00
26,320.63	29,806.00	32,798.75	35,146.00	35,542.50	36,376.10	30,925.00
943.59	994.19	883.39	794.19	447.39	501.39	501.39
....	....	10.00	8,148.68	18,507.36	20,629.71	12,742.84
24,679.13	29,440.39	24,811.62	22,277.68	26,018.40	25,859.89	22,374.88
$61,244.77	$69,560.06	$68,012.48	$76,499.96	$90,659.26	$92,487.15	$73,949.69
$427,281.11	$491,280.38	$429,255.00	$407,181.70	$410,808.81	$406,132.89	$329,335.20

1,305.50	1,534.50	1,508.00	1,553.00	1,243.50	1,218.50	1,023.00
2,405.25	2,848.20	3,152.50	3,495.00	3,830.25	4,139.75	3,879.75
....	24.00	184.55	772.60	128.20	320.29	230.58
$3,710.75	$4,406.70	$4,845.05	$5,820.60	$5,201.95	$5,678.54	$5,133.33

	1921	1922	1923	1924	1925
Sale of Services and Commodities					
Hauling Ashes	2,618.00	1,584.00	1,765.50	2,807.75	2,142.2
Public Baths	10,608.10	4,906.30	2,638.75	1,764.70	2,723.0
Comfort Stations	3,569.46	3,377.23	3,311.39	3,370.21	3,225.0
Hospital—Pay Patients	99,034.18	99,403.52	39,977.56	45,463.90	3,751.5
Board & Maint. of Prisoners	....	....	....	....	....
Storage on Cars	....	....	....	....	....
City Bulletin	....	....	....	....	....
Services at Fires	....	....	....	....	....
Recreation Dept. Sales	....	....	....	....	6,025.2
Miscellaneous	18,020.32	13,625.02	37,592.77	17,546.68	9,766.9
Total Sale of Serv. & Com.	$133,850.06	$122,896.07	$85,285.97	$70,953.24	$27,634.1
Total Services and Sales	$134,851.56	$123,978.57	$86,341.97	$72,373.74	$29,546.3
Interest on Deposits	78,616.42	65,343.60	55,774.45	77,950.51	60,327.7
Fines and Forfeitures					
Municipal Court	80,140.10	135,844.62	246,097.51	354,295.89	349,474.1
Damages	....	....	....	....	....
Forfeitures	....	....	....	....	....
Penalties	972.86	2,144.19	1,584.56	1,026.03	1,229.6
Total Fines and Forfeitures	$81,112.96	$137,988.81	$247,682.07	$355,321.92	$350,703.7
GRANTS AND DONATIONS					
Grants and Subventions					
Cigarette Tax	16,927.28	17,149.13	17,206.64	8,466.09	8,744.89
Collateral Inheritance Tax	5,670.84	12,354.65	3,449.01	8,047.97	1,424.4
Direct Inheritance Tax	105,889.66	115,342.65	96,327.45	140,778.66	280,021.7
Liquor Tax	....	....	....	....	....
Pawn Broker's License	7,208.00	3,049.40	2,287.50	2,237.50	2,137.50
Automobile License Tax	247,273.10	199,887.48	202,778.67	214,758.52	....
Health Dept.—Subsidy from State	....	....	1,000.00	1,900.00	2,100.00
Total Grants & Subventions	$382,968.88	$347,783.31	$303,049.27	$376,188.74	$294,428.57
Donations and Gifts					
Dental, Venereal, T.B. & X-Ray Clinics	....	....	3,570.20	3,679.85	3,861.65
Unclaimed Money	....	....	....	....	17.37
Conscience Money	3.00	....	55.00	....	....
Donations of Salary—Employees	....	....	....	....	....
Other Donations	....	200.00	....	....	....
Total Donations & Gifts	$3.00	$200.00	$3,625.20	$3,679.85	$3,879.02
Total Grants & Donations	$382,971.88	$347,983.31	$326,674.47	$379,868.59	$298,307.59
Miscellaneous Revenues	....	....	....	....	....
Total Revenues	$3,775,876.97	$5,544,753.25	$5,567,269.95	$6,124,981.09	$5,754,297.49
Refund of Taxes and Expenditures of Former Years	....	....	8,658.35	4,351.34	1,831.01
Sale of Property	8,900.00	43,000.00	24,160.61	....	7,285.50
Excess Receipts of Revolving Funds	....	....	....	....	....
BORROWING					
Sale of Deficiency Bonds	2,873,000.00	....	250,054.70	....	....
Sale of Tax Anticipation Notes	....	....	....	....	....
Total Borrowing	$2,873,000.00	....	$250,054.70	....	....
Adjustment to Auditor's Report	504,278.48	....	....	....	....
TOTAL INCOME	$7,162,055.45	$5,587,753.25	$5,850,143.61	$6,129,332.43	$5,763,414.00

1926	1927	1928	1929	1930	1931	1932
2,565.00	250.00	....	3,391.67	4,116.67	3,799.99	3,799.92
2,802.05	2,017.45	1,722.10	1,549.50	1,282.35	2,490.95	2,381.90
3,256.57	3,706.11	4,122.35	3,770.03	4,928.25	3,319.15	2,087.10
109,237.85	104,172.04	121,213.85	149,015.07	127,530.41	86,538.93	98,659.69
....	....	2,336.70	29,143.45	48,850.80	50,234.80	30,189.80
....	....	....	5,432.95	4,912.00	4,122.90	3,756.25
....	3,583.77	11,122.41	4,625.02	21,352.60	16,291.21	14,167.75
....	....	....	200.00	4,749.36	2,437.50	2,617.50
....	....	6,709.16	54,323.29	57,190.86	49,555.52	35,669.17
12,143.29	42,312.33	30,387.91	18,452.36	14,775.11	18,277.88	12,114.57
$130,004.76	$156,041.70	$177,614.48	$269,903.34	$289,688.41	$237,068.83	$205,443.65
$133,715.51	$160,448.40	$182,459.53	$275,723.94	$294,890.36	$242,747.37	$210,576.98
68,478.77	89,665.31	88,743.50	106,589.35	94,066.56	55,690.16	25,348.54
422,838.51	438,795.38	383,355.02	329,552.29	316,515.32	287,948.67	249,076.98
41,990.43	3,283.55	23.31	9,412.69	47.59	473.66	271.63
....	....	2,245.50	....	100.00	....	....
1,038.50	196.86	9.40	....	....	....	....
$465,867.44	$442,275.79	$385,633.23	$338,964.98	$316,662.91	$288,422.33	$249,348.61
9,346.53	9,946.17	12,537.40	11,804.81	11,354.40	10,739.34	12,021.39
....	975.31	47.31	711.01	....	248.36	....
239,264.87	245,640.17	213,958.93	275,456.87	277,053.04	497,412.83	272,469.45
588.00	588.00	....	....	....	....	....
2,256.25	2,318.75	2,250.00	2,943.75	2,600.00	2,175.00	2,181.25
....	....	....	....	497.00	....	....
....	1,865.00	1,840.00	2,195.00	1,740.00	2,160.00	800.00
$251,455.65	$261,333.40	$230,633.64	$293,111.44	$293,244.44	$512,735.53	$287,472.39
....	3,234.05	4,931.55	7,285.25	7,361.50	4,981.45	3,513.00
391.72	776.64	347.63	4,957.46	....	274.20	334.72
37.00	19.00	....	1.00	2.00	....	....
....	....	....	....	....	....	16,152.27
....	....	....	1.43	....	....	1,918.63
$428.72	$4,029.69	$5,279.18	$12,245.14	$7,363.50	$5,255.65	$21,918.62
$251,884.37	$265,363.09	$235,912.82	$305,356.58	$300,607.94	$517,991.18	$309,391.01
....	....	....	....	....	2,091.11	....
$7,512,479.55	$7,868,755.72	$8,482,805.69	$8,154,003.09	$8,172,060.84	$8,777,575.41	$7,973,817.82
....	25,722.34	....	....	....	....	....
80,904.00	500.00	....	....	....	14,432.34	2,462.36
....	....	....	....	....	....	....
....	....	....	....	....	....	185,000.00
....	....	....	....	....	....	$185,000.00
....	....	....	....	....	....	....
$7,593,383.55	$7,894,978.06	$8,482,805.69	$8,154,003.09	$8,172,060.84	$8,792,007.75	$8,161,280.18

APPEN

CITY OF CINCINNATI: GENERAL FUND—EXP

	1921	1922	1923	1924	1925
Legislative					
Council	$42,872.31	$41,364.96	$40,605.84	$40,375.02	$40,914.79
Clerk of Council	39,526.80	37,878.20	34,068.92	36,634.12	37,885.23
Mayor	17,704.41	17,311.49	15,150.61	24,136.33	6,204.19
Estimating & Equalizing Bd.	....	....	....	465.00	240.00
Total Legislative	$100,103.52	$96,554.65	$89,825.37	$101,610.47	$85,244.21
Administrative					
Manager	....	....	....	....	....
Purchasing Dept.	20,716.94	20,267.36	17,237.92	18,914.36	17,168.89
Reproduction Dept.	....	....	....	....	....
Law Dept.	43,036.32	40,411.75	36,388.55	37,533.67	42,995.93
Zoning Bd. of Appeals	....	....	....	....	....
Civil Service Commission	19,475.83	18,356.24	15,574.00	17,719.06	18,959.23
Planning Commission	....	....	1,059.96	7,992.80	13,367.07
Regional Planning Comm.					
Maintenance of City Lands & Bldgs.	67,285.43	61,297.21	55,684.46	62,961.44	64,906.81
Judgments	....	25,000.00	24,615.32	24,984.98	26,632.51
State Examiner	3,475.77	7,738.96	8,983.58	10,015.78	9,461.63
Garage (Rotating Acct. Undistributed)	36,300.40	25,755.20	18,802.39	17,780.72	21,620.25
Retirement System	....	....	....	....	....
Elections	134,119.47	183,179.90	85,126.83	166,250.12	92,104.24
Workmen's Compensation—Undistributed	....	....	20,525.35	109,467.20	....
Total Adm.	$324,410.16	$382,006.62	$283,998.36	$473,620.13	$307,216.56
Expert Services					
Rate Investigations	....	....	9,802.47	338.35	145.50
New Accounting System	....	....	....	....	....
Pension Investigation	....	....	....	....	....
Total Expert Serv.	....	....	$9,802.47	$338.35	$145.50
Financial					
Treasurer	26,561.36	25,905.76	21,949.13	21,775.02	22,158.94
Auditor	56,967.54	54,367.75	50,410.32	51,660.14	56,035.60
County Auditor & Treasurer's Fees	28,552.74	38,864.46	27,709.25	40,055.25	33,569.74
Total Financial	$112,081.64	$119,137.97	$110,068.70	$113,490.41	$111,764.28
Judicial					
Municipal Court	26,923.22	25,033.80	20,300.31	20,022.22	25,153.12
Clerk of Municipal Court	51,861.97	51,876.12	50,951.43	53,787.77	51,909.44
Jury & Witness Fees	....	....	5,651.50	6,328.00	6,526.00
Court Costs	....	....	616.35	747.85	1,040.34
Total Judicial	$78,785.19	$76,909.92	$77,519.59	$80,885.84	$84,628.90
Public Safety Administration	$38,802.47	$27,183.02	$32,043.20	$27,522.94	$33,396.96
Police					
Police Dept.	1,217,467.35	1,151,397.29	960,044.22	1,011,948.49	1,023,398.84
Police Relief	139,533.72	130,784.32	156,642.91	196,851.25	197,080.55
Humane Society Agents	3,540.00	3,540.00	3,540.00	3,540.00	3,540.00
Weights, Measures & Scales	6,325.65	6,121.85	4,510.55	4,462.18	4,519.81
Total Police	$1,366,866.72	$1,291,843.46	$1,124,737.68	$1,216,801.92	$1,228,539.20

* Indicates that division of expenditures between functions has been estimated.

DIX F

ENDITURES AS CONTRACTED BY YEARS

1926	1927	1928	1929	1930	1931	1932
$46,407.76	$45,245.71	$44,560.00	$45,000.00	$45,000.00	$45,000.00	$44,100.00
39,328.68	33,029.21	46,451.38	46,789.23	48,609.81	44,697.49	30,341.69
3,819.91	4,003.22	5,431.39	4,384.07	3,515.26	3,432.64	3,244.08
....	1,080.00	1,965.00	2,855.00	2,280.00	1,170.00	75.00
$89,556.35	$83,358.14	$98,371.77	$99,028.30	$99,405.07	$94,300.13	$77,760.77
33,948.26	35,736.15	36,708.12 *	35,595.43 *	35,669.88 *	40,364.30	35,181.30
19,909.36	21,001.65	23,995.93	29,708.69	32,689.61	32,794.72	30,858.21
....	....	....	....	2,230.93	333.97	421.13
114,913.82	71,471.30	52,677.00	60,278.05	63,932.22	63,211.45	64,848.64
....	....	6,163.08	6,140.00	5,840.00	4,700.00	2,125.00
22,079.60	31,096.51	33,618.38	31,123.29	32,420.66	31,401.27	29,720.07
5,349.84	10,557.30	11,371.82	17,218.36	23,631.05	23,736.06	{ 3,470.00 / 18,729.24
120,996.21	88,657.40	118,677.51	107,573.95	79,521.84	91,977.20	101,221.38
....	139,394.42	25,000.00	....	8,080.60	17,033.30	9,869.81
2,750.20	9,481.90	12,243.92	9,378.19	10,029.13	9,717.46	12,858.13
50,346.39	53,716.53	165,335.35	— 22,434.52	17,481.17	— 1,072.70	4,561.77
....	....	....	....	....	4,980.57	94,993.50
163,097.63	73,266.96	197,579.50	92,587.77	77,758.44	49,917.16	77,294.55
48,444.04	52,732.69	....	49,311.58	....	....	10,731.38
$581,835.35	$587,112.81	$683,370.61	$416,480.79	$389,285.53	$369,094.76	$496,884.11
....	....	3,626.19	....	25,442.00	4,448.35	1,522.88
....	....	....	3,390.29	....	....	....
....	....	....	....	5,000.00	1,000.00	....
....	....	$3,626.19	$3,390.29	$30,442.00	$5,448.35	$1,522.88
24,092.19	26,836.33	48,258.54	39,610.17	39,957.54	37,646.25	33,172.38
69,272.59	67,753.93	51,460.03	37,043.73	30,462.82	31,507.58	31,659.68
43,878.26	45,186.69	43,712.77	42,551.27	40,436.96	41,286.08	44,559.44
$137,243.04	$139,776.95	$143,431.34	$119,205.17	$110,857.32	$110,439.91	$109,391.50
30,401.59	30,454.40	30,013.30	30,904.38	44,787.52	44,624.81	47,650.99
73,457.21	68,556.91	68,991.21	70,418.28	76,142.49	79,273.16	79,118.41
178.07	7,565.20	7,053.00	6,740.00	7,193.00	7,676.00	7,791.40
....	559.92	....	....	5,359.70	3,149.27	4,149.40
$104,036.87	$107,136.43	$106,057.51	$108,062.66	$133,482.71	$134,723.24	$138,710.20
$27,056.30	$23,478.43	$22,000.00 *	$21,000.00 *	$20,000.00 *	$18,202.02	$14,875.25
1,138,484.06	1,192,058.48	1,293,171.26	1,341,187.83	1,449,395.61	1,417,787.99	1,322,218.22
200,344.69	318,483.23	334,134.94	293,588.00	300,000.00	319,000.00	312,500.00
3,540.00	3,540.00	3,540.00	5,040.00 *	5,040.00	5,040.00 *	5,040.00
5,906.96	7,000.00 *	7,000.00 *	8,202.85	6,154.25	5,176.42	7,264.16
$1,348,275.71	$1,521,081.71	$1,637,846.20	$1,648,018.68	$1,760,589.86	$1,747,004.41	$1,647,022.38

	1921	1922	1923	1924	1925
Traffic Control—Traffic Lighting	....	....	....	....	....
Fire					
Fire Dept.	1,211,851.70	1,126,252.68	983,424.45	1,042,940.36	1,110,809.71
Firemen's Pensions	161,565.36	153,780.94	164,102.10	171,866.30	172,223.55
Total Fire Dept.	$1,373,417.06	$1,280,033.62	$1,152,526.55	$1,214,806.66	$1,283,033.26
Safety Engineering					
Dept. of Buildings	78,084.70	73,471.81	72,107.22	91,208.30	108,170.09
Bd. of Plumbers' Examiners	....	....	....	....	....
Bd. of Moving Picture Operators' Examiners	....	....	....	....	....
Total Safety Engineering	$78,084.70	$73,471.81	$72,107.22	$91,208.30	$108,170.09
Charities—Welfare Dept.	$20,732.65	$19,934.40	$19,796.51	$19,479.42	$20,249.43
Correction					
Workhouse	....	....	....	....	....
Support of Prisoners in County Jail	21,682.87	31,001.27	25,200.87	46,835.82	47,702.46
House of Refuge	54,307.21	—1,949.87	—565.64	—379.18	1,192.28
Boys' Farm	....	21,308.04	13,977.17	16,031.01	11,370.77
Girls' Farm	....	25,164.47	24,666.79	25,394.08	26,283.48
Total Correction	$75,990.08	$75,523.91	$63,279.19	$87,881.73	$86,548.99
Conservation of Health					
Health Dept.					
Administration	....	....	....	....	....
Sanitary Inspection	....	....	....	....	....
Medical Inspection	....	....	....	....	....
Food Inspection	....	....	....	....	....
Laboratories	....	....	....	....	....
Health Center	....	....	....	....	....
Vital Statistics	....	....	....	....	....
Nursing	....	....	....	....	....
Total Health Dept.	$161,804.78	$149,654.11	$129,406.34	$136,609.06	$155,771.30
Public Baths	$19,474.10	$5,165.35	$2,842.17	$2,833.44	$4,138.39
Total Conservation of Health	$181,278.88	$154,819.46	$132,248.51	$139,442.50	$159,909.69
Hospitals					
Hospital	576,963.06	519,513,95	530,307.39	566,571.46	48.83
Tuberculosis Sanitarium	202,001.13	191,513.86	—11,675.47	....	107.76
Infirmary	77,449.13	76,994.23	75,870.42	....	....
Total Hospitals	$856,413.32	$788,022.04	$594,502.34	$566,571.46	$156.59
Public Works Administration					
Public Works Administration	....	....	....	....	....
Public Service Administration	28,959.08	21,566.72	36,148.20	26,876.15	23,616.26
Total Public Works Adm.	$28,959.08	$21,566.72	$36,148.20	$26,876.15	$23,616.26
Highways					
Street Repair	320,639.87	108,917.53	98,348.34	423,131.19	87,677.84
Bridges and Viaducts	62,674.98	30,029.60	27,304.87	26,566.11	27,911.26
Sidewalks and Steps	....	....	....	....	....
Highway Engineering / Highway Maintenance Eng.	60,702.38	75,145.06	43,563.86	56,440.63	70,411.18
Total Highways	$444,017.23	$214,092.19	$169,217.07	$506,137.93	$186,000.28

* Indicates that division of expenditures between functions has been estimated.

	1926	1927	1928	1929	1930	1931	1932
					$52,516.98	$52,852.62	$50,640.57
	1,338,873.38 170,292.99	1,332,172.58 261,239.52	1,346,939.16 266,982.00	1,352,716.28 245,332.00	1,351,786.68 218,000.00	1,330,651.06 239,000.00	1,258,789.91 233,900.00
	$1,509,166.37	$1,593,412.10	$1,613,921.16	$1,598,048.28	$1,569,786.68	$1,569,651.06	$1,492,689.91
	133,941.45	153,133.78	143,614.21 15.00	147,348.37 490.00	152,731.93 480.00	145,831.44 505.00	122,723.45 395.00
	....	....	20.00	320.00	285.00	310.00	221.25
	$133,941.45	$153,133.78	$143,649.21	$148,158.37	$153,496.93	$146,646.44	$123,339.70
	$24,192.25	$21,474.34	$51,749.81 *	$66,032.35 *	$144,346.50 *	$613,609.80 *	$441,555.96
	....	97,914.88	154,390.29	175,881.83	149,076.06	175,535.72	133,085.86
	62,256.63 — 2,433.47	48,731.39	....	....	....	....	....
	.... 17,992.14	....	....	....	....	....	....
	$77,815.30	$146,646.27	$154,390.29	$175,881.83	$149,076.06	$175,535.72	$133,085.86
	....	21,227.67	....	21,344.38	19,774.37	18,587.00	16,560.18
	....	21,182.91	....	23,184.68	25,684.50	25,867.46	38,318.09
	....	44,437.33	....	48,833.27	56,195.55	58,228.49	53,726.49
	....	42,792.25	....	43,584.60	46,472.12	46,284.33	28,896.41
	....	7,544.98	....	8,688.72	9,111.19	10,324.92	10,456.53
	....	9,396.65	....	17,128.91	15,822.15	16,701.66	21,178.46
	....	5,330.21	....	6,236.25	6,198.71	6,206.19	5,992.35
	....	47,803.22	....	61,041.46	68,313.23	75,238.99	68,617.02
	$183,275.89	$199,715.22	$212,068.95	$230,042.27	$247,571.82	$257,439.04	$243,745.53
	$2,646.17	$2,782.57	$2,510.33	$1,911.36	$1,735.83	$1,568.66	$1,121.80
	$185,922.06	$202,497.79	$214,579.28	$231,953.63	$249,307.65	$259,007.70	$244,867.33
	680,825.75	739,874.59	800,179.76	837,872.70	905,310.23	882,550.23	769,940.04
	....	....	....	....	....	....	....
	$680,825.75	$739,874.59	$800,179.76	$837,872.70	$905,310.23	$882,550.23	$769,940.04
	.... 79,495.25	.... 5,716.98	20,000.00 * — 67,057.11	19,000.00 * 9,039.07	18,000.00 * 9,163.08	24,690.69	14,209.26 ....
	$79,495.25	$5,716.98	— $47,057.11	$28,039.07	$27,163.08	$24,690.69	$14,209.26
	154,092.60	229,916.95	142,991.77	17,692.53	10,404.25	2,775.92	12,861.60
	43,799.34	83,131.46	118,330.35	— 348.27	7,338.27	742.47	1,359.09
	....	1,132.59	1,057.56	55,072.83	22,126.45	25,816.93	23,642.66
	78,662,02	103,940.05	116,606.28	{ 134,837.41 { 13,587.74	85,582.72 25,748.33	85,111.43 37,758.42	77,473.39 34,630.74
	$276,553.96	$418,121.05	$378,985.96	$220,842.24	$151,200.02	$152,205.17	$149,967.48

	1921	1922	1923	1924	1925
Sewers					
Sewer Engineering †	....	....	....	....	....
Sewer Cleaning & Maintenance	31,220.78	25,197.65	21,259.63	26,594.54	32,280.72
Total Sewers	$31,220.78	$25,197.65	$21,259.63	$26,594.54	$32,280.72
Street Cleaning & Sprinkling ‡	....	....	....	....	....
Refuse Collection and Disposal					
Refuse Collection and Disposal	464,836.36	321,333.38	268,674.48	283,082.01	356,394.72
Garbage Collection and Disposal	202,500.00	202,500.00	202,500.00	202,500.00	202,620.00
Total Refuse Coll. & Disp.	$667,336.36	$523,833.38	$471,174.48	$485,582.01	$559,014.72
Street Lighting	$425,441.56	$483,421.53	$466,294.72	$459,900.61	$444,806.81
Public Comfort Stations	$15,371.04	$13,372.70	$6,825.20	$6,057.42	$6,940.37
Education					
University	415,469.06	370,284.60	452,425.66	406,573.68	489,815.87
Municipal Reference Bureau	....	....	....	....	....
Total Education	$415,469.06	$370,284.60	$452,425.66	$406,573.68	$489,815.87
Recreation Commission	....	....	....	....	....
Park Dept.	$188,774.13	$118,494.33	$79,266.67	$84,778.69	$99,861.74
Markets	$15,343.31	$13,935.74	$14,277.55	$13,998.23	$14,778.41
Municipal Airport	....	....	....	....	....
Public Utilities					
Public Utilities Dept.	18,996.50	18,181.44	17,804.68	17,661.01	18,601.21
Docks & Wharves	3,464.62	3,176.82	2,183.00	2,213.05	2,230.39
Taxicab Commission	....	939.94	2,499.03	2,419.20	2,446.75
Total Public Utilities	$22,461.12	$22,298.20	$22,486.71	$22,293.26	$23,278.35
Miscellaneous	$820.88	$333.65	....	$8,176.54	$7,313.94
Deduct: Reimbursements	14,028.28	20,465.32	....	....	....
: Refunds	556.07	101.43	....	....	....
Total Oper. Maint. & Outlay	$6,847,596.59	$6,171,704.82	$5,501,831.58	$6,180,629.19	$5,396,711.13
Motor Vehicle License Tax-expenditures	....	....	....	....	620,003.54
Gasoline Tax-expenditures	....	....	....	....	39,205.29
Waterworks Expenses	969,345.91	956,457.20	1,032,447.75	982,395.08	1,137,166.47
Total expenditures (except capital)	$7,816,942.50	$7,128,162.02	$6,534,279.33	$7,162,024.27	$7,192,086.43

* Indicates that division of expenditures between functions has been estimated.
† Included in Highway Engineering.
‡ Included in Refuse Collection & Disposal.

	1926	1927	1928	1929	1930	1931	1932
				74,565.97	75,291.99	80,198.66	68,587.51
	94,074.53	126,236.13	131,505.51	104,867.84	109,929.19	132,332.83	102,063.31
	$94,074.53	$126,236.13	$131,505.51	$179,433.81	$185,221.18	$212,531.49	$170,650.82
	....	....	....	$193,420.63	$163,969.43	$118,367.90	$31,171.63
	437,253.75	534,616.74	492,335.71	363,459.59	332,451.56	208,232.72	163,723.82
	202,500.00	202,500.00	219,375.00	202,864.38	203,374.59	401,455.04	376,025.91
	$639,753.75	$737,116.74	$711,710.71	$566,323.97	$535,826.15	$609,687.76	$539,749.73
	$572,545.32	$482,530.97	$563,598.04	587,387.80	546,433.19	544,335.53	548,201.64
	$7,382.83	$11,434.16	$11,978.66	$11,069.22	$12,301.28	$12,560.14	$15,129.96
	538,545.90	569,925.54	588,207.20	597,427.18	603,575.70	612,115.81	547,011.16
	....	....	3,222.58	2,682.94	3,314.69	3,370.08	3,178.76
	$538,545.90	$569,925.54	$591,429.78	$600,110.12	$606,890.39	$615,485.89	$550,189.92
	....	$97,149.77	$119,071.43	$160,093.11	$163,963.78	$154,426.34	$144,367.14
	$204,297.96	$213,289.42	$214,521.88	$232,494.66	$221,318.02	$220,719.20	$199,302.85
	$19,497.00	$25,511.04 *	$24,739.21 *	$21,314.41	$22,385.44	$21,242.58	$18,397.05
	....	....	....	$21,862.20	$37,738.69	$19,944.80	$17,370.15
	22,809.99	30,987.43	40,517.35	39,669.53	43,212.94	48,608.27	42,469.20
	2,453.15	2,520.79	2,315.95	2,609.45	2,678.26	2,467.27	1,466.14
	....	....	....	....	....	....	....
	$25,263.14	$33,508.22	$42,833.30	$42,278.98	$45,891.20	$51,075.54	$43,935.34
	$8,728.60	$7,509.19	$13,660.18	$12,464.31	$4,521.06	— $79.85	$5,076.80
	29,084.15	....	....	....	....	....	....
	296.77	....	....	....	....	....	....
	$7,336,624.12	$8,047,032.55	$8,430,150.68	$8,350,267.58	$8,492,726.43	$8,936,259.57	$8,190,006.23
	286,523.36	355,860.42	338,458.39	342,194.90	411,112.91	400,990.32	302,151.07
	275,392.22	319,265.83	278,865.95	344,970.74	446,328.56	516,796.17	636,610.60
	1,122,866.14	1,052,646.41	1,196,542.47	1,213,195.19	1,246,465.26	1,204,539.70	1,255,553.48
	$9,021,405.84	$9,774,805.21	$10,244,017.49	$10,250,628.41	$10,596,633.16	$11,058,585.76	$10,384,321.38

INDEX

Ach, Samuel, 151, 173, 200, 201, 215, 218
  candidate for commissioner, 196, 198
  candidate for treasurer, 123-125, 136-137
  record in office, 169-171, 216
Alexander, Edward F., 54-56, 65, 73 *note*
Allensworth, H. R., 191
American Commonwealth, Bryce, 10
American Telephone & Telegraph Company, 187
Anderson, A. E., 51 *note*, 137, 138, 140, 148, 163, 171
Armstrong, Bolton, 51 *note*
Ault, L. A., 157

Bader, Ferd., Jr., 138, 197
Baker, Newton D., 98, 100, 165, 173
Barrett Company, 172
Bauer, Dan, 128
Beckman, candidate, 200, 201, 215
Bell, Charles S., 166
Benham, Florence, 140-141
Bentley, Henry, 32, 134, 135, 142, 145, 146, 148
  address to women, 153-155
  Birdless Ballot League and, 52-54
  Branch Hospital row and, 46-49
  budget row, 84
  charter 1925 campaign, 56, 65, 68-69, 73 *note*, 77, 88, 91
  Charter program and, 74
  county 1926 campaign, 122, 123, 128, 137
  first Charter administration, 106-108
Bettman, Alfred, 15

Bettman, Gilbert, 164, 173, 199, 200
  charter campaign and, 68-69
  fusion ballot row, 198
  on city survey committee, 51 *note*, 63, 64
Bevis, Howard, 142
Bibliography, 249-250
Birdless Ballot League, 52-55
Blandford, John B., Jr., 120, 208, 222
Bode, Alfred, 18 *note*
Bookman, C. M., 30
Bossism in Cincinnati, Wright, 17 *note*
Bradford, L. J., 152, 158
Branch Hospital, 46-49
Brown, Clarence, 197-199
Brown, Clifford, 29, 138
Brown, Walter, 160, 161, 163, 164
Bryce, James, 10
Buchwalter, Alfred Z., 18 *note*
Bulkley, Robert J., 200
Burchenal, John J., 18 *note*, 51 *note*
Burman, Paul H., 203 *note*
Burns & McDonnell, 190, 193
Butterfield, candidate, 200, 201, 215

Caldwell, Judge, 166
Caldwell, William G., 9
Campbell, John V., 137, 138, 140-141, 162
Carrel, George, 23, 39, 44, 46-49, 189, 191
Central Labor Council, 79
Chamber of Commerce, 202
Charter, Upson Report and, 62
Charter administration, disgruntled favor seekers, 234
  finance statistics concerning, 224-230
  first municipal, 106-120

269

INDEX

Charter administration (Cont.)
  police improvements, 119, 208-209
Chicago, Ill., 1
Cincinnati, O., 1 *et passim*
Cincinnati Gas & Electric Company, 188
Cincinnati Gas Transportation Company, 188
Cincinnati Southern Railroad, 37 *note*
Cincinnati Street Railway Company, 112, 113
Cincinnati & Suburban Bell Telephone Company, 120, 187
Cincinnati Traction Company, 23, 112, 113
Cincinnatus Association, 122, 180, 189
  campaign of 1925, 80, 84, 85
  city charter 1924 campaign, 49-58
  extra 1923 levy and, 33-45
  organization and early activities, 31-33
Citizens League, Cleveland, 98
Citizens Committee, civil service row, 219-221
  county administration reviewed, 216-217, 230-233
  success in 1930, 199
  women in, 236
Citizens Republican Committee, 160, 196, 212
  county 1926 campaign, 125-142
  local 1928 campaign, 172-174
  new 1926 charter and, 142
  officeholders' records, 165-171
  women in, 138-141
Citizens School Committee, 16
City Bulletin, Cincinnati, 192
City Charter Committee, 55, 56
  administrative record, 175-179, 207
  city 1927 campaign, 145-159
  county 1926 campaign, 121-144
  future prospects, 235
  growth, 74-75
  internal structure and finances, 89-91
  literature, 89

City Charter Committee (Cont.)
  national and local 1928 campaigns, 161-174
  program and campaign of 1925, 66-70, 71-93
  women in, 153, 236
  (*see also* Charter administration)
City council, Upson Report concerning, 59-62
City Survey Committee, 74
Civil service, 109-110, 159
Civil Service Commission, 159, 217, 219
Cleveland, Grover, 10
Cleveland, O., 46, 71, 170, 191, 232, 233
  charter as model for Cincinnati, 54-55
  reform failure in, 235
Cleveland Civic League, 230
Columbia Gas & Electric Corporation, 24, 81, 187-188
Columbus, O., 191, 192, 197
Commercial Tribune, Cincinnati, 178
Community Chest, 29, 175, 180, 213
Conclusions, 234-237
Coney Island Race Track, 84, 129
Conference for Progressive Political Action, 54
Conkling, Roscoe, 2
Conrad, George W. B., 181, 183
Coolidge, Calvin, 39, 66, 71
Cooper, Myers, 173, 199
Cornick, Philip H., 202
Council of Social Agencies, 30
County Budget Commission, 84, 121
County Home Rule Amendment, 231-233
Cox, George B., 10-15, 26, 33
Crabbs, George D., 51 *note,* 155
Cronin, John M., 73 *note*
Crosley, Powell, Jr., 123
Curtis, Charles, 162
Cuyahoga County, 46, 170

Daly, candidate, 151, 158, 180, 183, 228
Davis, Chase, 152, 158

INDEX

Democratic party, 8-21, 77, 90, 148, 196, 236
Dempsey, Edward J., 12, 13
Dickerson, John H., 151
Dixon, Edward T., 77, 151, 180, 183
Downtown Property Owners, 205, 213
Drake Legislative Investigating Committee, 14
Druffel, John, 180, 183, 184, 211
Durr, Chester, 47, 134
Dwyer, William V., 84, 129, 132
Dykstra, C. A., 106, 120
  city manager, 186, 208, 221, 228, 230

Edwards, E. W., 18 note
Eisen, Charles, 108, 125 note, 151, 158, 180
Elections, results, 1925, 1927, 1929, 1931, Appendix D
Election frauds, 8, 69, 127, 128
Ellis, John D., 65, 73 note, 77, 88, 120, 208
  utility rate rows, 81, 190
England, 5
Ernst, Richard P., 161
Espy, Arthur, 211

Fagin, Viv, 26
Farewell to Reform, Chamberlain, 5
Fennell, Bessie, 55, 66, 73
Field, Tylor, 51 note, 77, 106, 146, 151, 152, 156
  retirement, 180
Foraker, Joseph B., 10
Fosdick & Hilmer, 193
Freeman, W. W., 81
Freiberg, Harry, 73 note
Friedlander, Edgar, 171, 173, 195, 196, 199, 201, 215
Friedman, Max, 180
Fusion, 22, 195-214

Galvin, John, 19, 20
Gamble, Cecil, 77
Garrison, Henry, 180
Gast, candidate, 218
Geier, Fred A., 30
Geoghegan, candidate, 218

Gilman, law department head, 208
Goldman, Robert, 69
Gorman, Frank, 14
Gorman, Robert N., 65, 142, 197, 200, 201, 216
Governmental Research, Bureau of, Cincinnati, 119, 156 note, 171, 177, 206, 221
  report titles and numbers, 246-248
  tax procedure report, 204
Governmental Research, Bureau of, Detroit, 52
Graft, 14, 27
Grand Rapids, Mich., 106
Grant, U. S., 3rd, 186
Great Game of Politics, The, Frank Kent, 3 note
Greenlund, Senator, 231
Gusweiler, E. W., 18 note

Hagenah, W. J., 191
Hall, Frank A. B., 158 note, 181, 183, 211
Hamilton, O., 209
Hamilton County, campaign of 1926, 121-144
  Upson Report and, 52
Hamilton County Republican, 132, 134
Hanna, Marcus A., 10
Harding, Warren G., 20, 135
Harmon, Judson, 33
Hatton, A. R., 54
Hauck, Henry G., 18 note
Hayes, Rutherford B., 2 note
Headley, Sanford A., 143, 148-151, 160, 162, 164, 219
  county 1926 campaign, 128, 134, 135, 138, 140
  fusion ballot row, 197
  race track row, 131
Heekin, James J., 18 note
Heintz, Victor, 135, 152, 196, 212
  Cincinnatus Association organizer, 31
  civil service row, 219-220
  county 1926 campaign, 123-125, 129, 134, 137, 140
  national 1928 campaign, 160, 161, 164, 165

INDEX

Hennegan, Edward K., 125 *note*
Hess, William E., 138, 200
Heuck, Robert, 142, 143, 145, 173, 195, 200, 215
  county 1926 campaign, 125 *note*, 136
  county 1930 campaign, 199
  real estate reappraisal, 201-207, 213
  record in office, 165-166
Hicks, Mary, 77
Higgins, William J., 77, 109
Hilton, Agnes, 56, 73 *note*
Hinsch, Charles A., 51 *note*
Hirsch, Max, 88, 134
Hock, candidate, 152
Hoehler, Fred K., 119, 171, 176, 213
Hoffman, Frederick L., 166
Hollister, John B., 212, 218
Holmes, John R., 16, 18-20, 230
Honest Elections Committee, 9
Holterhoff, Ralph, 73 *note*, 91
Hoover, Herbert C., 160-165, 218
Hornberger, Charles F., 59, 80, 112
Hunt, Henry T., 13-18, 177, 178
Hynicka, Rudolph K., 14-21, 24, 74, 124-125, 218
  Branch Hospital row and, 48
  charter campaign and, 68
  extra 1923 levy and, 39, 40
  gas rate row, 190
  instance of bossism, 28-29, 32
  race track row, 84

Illinois, 14 *note*
Imbus, Edward, 151, 158, 180, 183, 184
Independents, campaign of 1928, 161-164
Indianapolis, Ind., 17
Indian Hill Rangers, 201

Jelke, Ferdinand, Jr., 13
Johnson, Simeon, 65, 77

Kansas City, Mo., 235
Kearns, candidate, 200, 215
Kellogg, E. E., 41
Kentucky, 208, 209
Kessler, park expert, 13

Kirbert, August, 18 *note*, 24
Kiwanis Club, 47
Kneubuhl, Emily, 66, 73, 74
Knight, Walter, 69
Knights of Labor, 10
Kraft, Lou, 11, 79
Kroger, B. H., 123, 157
Krollman, candidate, 137
Krug, Frank S., 59
Kummer, Adolph, 51 *note*, 79, 80

Lackmann, candidate, 151, 158, 228
Lane & Bodley, 13
"Law Enforcement," T. W. Arnold, 3 *note*
Lawson, Fenton, 54
Lawson, Mrs. Fenton, 66
League of Women Voters, 231
LeBlond, R. K., 51 *note*
Legislative Investigations in Cincinnati, Espy, 14 *note*
Leverone, Charles J., 125 *note*, 134
Lewis, Frank, 41
Licht, William, 180
Lincoln, Abraham, 237
Little, A. S. B., 191
Livingood, Charles J., 51 *note*
Local Government in the United States, Seasongood, 199 *note*
Long, Huey P., 237
Longworth, Nicholas, 137, 161-163, 200, 214, 218
  death, 212
Lowenberg, Laurent, 81, 189
Luchsinger, Julius, 77, 108, 151, 158

McAllister, William, 9
McCarthy, Peter, 219, 220
McCulloch, Roscoe C., 200
Machine, persistence, 2
  support by good citizens, 4
  under proportional representation, 99
Mackentepe, Mrs. F. E., 51 *note*
McKinley, William, 10
McLean, John, 10
Mallon, Guy, 55, 56, 65, 73 *note*
Martin, Cliff, 24, 182
Matthews, Stanley, 77, 151, 180, 183, 211

INDEX

Mees, Anthony, 151
Merriam, C. E., 72, 74
Meyers, Charles A., Jr., 125 *note*, 136
Millard, Walter, 69
Milwaukee, Wis., 229
Mitchell, P. Lincoln, 51 *note*, 123, 137-140, 146-148, 152, 155, 158, 163
Morrill, Albert H., 18 *note*, 123, 134
Morris, Froome, 24, 39-41, 44, 68-69
Mullen, Mike, 9, 11, 13
Mumby, candidate, 134
Municipal finance, Cincinnati expenditures, *Appendix F*
   Cincinnati income, 1921-32, *Appendix E*
   problem in 1923, 35
   problems after defeat of extra 1923 levy, 46
   statistics, 224-230
   unemployment relief problem, 213-214
   unsound economies, 46
   Upson Report and, 63
   (*see also* Taxes)
Municipal government, "board system," 8, 142
   Bryce's conclusions, 10
   Cincinnati in 1921, 25
   proportional representation (*see* Proportional representation)
   ward basis, 11
Murray, Harold, 180

Nelson, Frank H., 30, 51 *note*
New Outlook, 94, 98
New York, N. Y., 2, 95, 235
Noctor, Thomas J., 65
Norwood, O., 127, 135

Ohio, constitutional provisions on city charters, 16
   general code, 46
   primary election laws, 160, 163
   tax laws, 33, 112
Ohio Public Utilities Commission, 120, 187-191
"Ohio Warwick, An," Herbert Koch, 17 *note*

Omwake, John, 51 *note*
Organization, advantage in primaries, 195
   anti-reform propaganda, 156 *note*
   blunders, 79-80, 127-132, 196-198
   charter campaign and, 66-70
   county 1926 campaign, 127-142
   county 1932 campaign, 218
   defeat in 1930, 199
   dominance until 1923, 22-30
   extra levy campaign of 1923, 39-44
   fund raising, 111
   knifing tactics, 107, 156, 158, 164-165, 199
   local 1928 success, 172-174
   misleading statistics issued, 224-230
   municipal finance under, 159
   muzzling, 151
   national 1928 campaign, 164-165
   obstruction, 73, 128, 129, 205-207, 210
   party emblems in elections, 52-54
   power in Hamilton County, 121
   race problem, 159 *note*, 212
   reform within, 230
   women, 139-141
Orr, James P., 51 *note*, 123, 157

Patterson, Alex, 180
Pendleton, E. H., 12, 13
Pittsburgh, Pa., 106
Pogue, Province, 51 *note*
Political Behaviour, Frank Kent, 3 *note*
Politicians, sources of power, 3
Politics, ballot difficulties, 199
   "economic municipalism," 221-223
   election frauds (*see* Election frauds)
   fusion (*see* Fusion)
   history in Cincinnati, 8-21, 22-30
   influence-and-service tactics, 26
   machine (*see* Machine)
   practical instance, 46-49

Politics (Cont.)
  practice of the science of government, 3
  primary fixing, 174
  publicity, 80
  reform in (*see* Reform)
  spoils system weakened, 16
  ticket building, 76-80, 196, 216
Poliak, Julian A., 73 *note*, 180, 183, 184
Poor, George T., 18 *note*
Post, Cincinnati, 24, 80
Pressler, Clara M., 73 *note*
Primary elections, patronage formula for control of, 26
Procter, William C., 18 *note,* 51
Proportional representation, 55, 78-80, 92, 94-106
  Cleveland failure, 100
  counting method, 101-105
  effect in Cincinnati, 98
  example of count and eliminations, 1925 and 1927 vote, *Appendix D*
  tally sheet, *Appendix D*
  true representation, 158 *note*
Public Service Commission of Kansas, 189 *note*
Public Utilities, 187-194
Puchta, politician, 18

Rapid Transit System, 23
Rauh, Julian, 51 *note*
Rauh, Louis L., 18 *note*
Real Estate Board, Cincinnati, 42, 202
Reed, C. Lawson, 28, 29
Reed, Thomas B., 59-62
Reform, apathy and fear as obstacles to, 27
  background of the problem, 2-7
  conditions for success, 235-237
  criticism and derision of, 1, 5
  practical success, 6
  publicity as a means to, 49
Regional Crime Committee, 208
Reichert, Joseph, 82-84
Remus, George, 168-169
Republican party, campaign literature, 22-24
  charter campaign and, 67-70

Republican party (Cont.)
  factions (*see* City Charter Committee, Independents, Organization)
  political tactics in Cincinnati, 8-21
  women, 236
Republican Executive and Advisory Committee, 18, 19, 51, 52, 62, 84
Republican Executive Committee, Hamilton County, 146, 160, 161
Roosevelt, Franklin D., 14 *note,* 156 *note,* 221
Root, J. C., 208, 222
Rose, Charles O., 138, 140, 146, 148, 151, 152, 156, 161, 180, 211, 228
  campaign of 1925 and, 78
  fusion ballot row, 197
  officeholding record, 184
  public utility litigation, 189-194
Rotary Club, 47
Rowe, Stanley M., 73 *note*

Saturday Evening Post, 105 *note*
Sargent, John G., 84
Schmidt, Walter, 73 *note*
Schneider, Herman, 51 *note,* 75, 202
Schneller, Fred, 146, 172, 180, 218, 228
  campaign of 1925, 79, 80
  city 1927 campaign, 151-153, 158
  county 1926 campaign, 137, 138, 140, 141, 143
  national 1928 campaign, 161, 163
Schools, politics in, 15, 44
Schorr, Ed. D., 134, 171, 172, 173
Schuessler, E. G., 182
Seabury, Samuel, 94
Seasongood, Murray, 172, 183, 198, 212; *notes on* 18, 51, 73
  charter campaign and, 56, 65, 69
  city 1925 campaign, 74, 77, 80, 86-88

INDEX

Seasongood, Murray (Cont.)
  city 1927 campaign, 146, 151-153, 155
  civil service row, 220
  county 1926 campaign, 124, 127, 130, 134, 140
  extra 1923 levy and, 35-43
  first Charter administration, 106-108, 118
  fusion ballot row, 197
  retirement, 180
  Upson Report and, 62-64
Sherrill, C. O., 121, 132, 146, 155, 179, 208
  made city manager, 106, 107, 109
  record in office, 113-120, 175, 176
  resignation, 185
Shinkle, Mrs. A. C., 51
Skinner, candidate, 218
Small, Len, 14 *note*
Smith, Alfred E., 94, 98, 100, 101
Smith, Leonard, Jr., 35
Smith, Leonard S., 18 *note*
Smith, Rufus B., 113
Southern Railway Co., 37 *note*
Spiegel, candidate, 18
Stephens, A. E. B., 18
Strohm, Edna, 74, 89
Swing, Frederick C., 142, 199, 218
  campaign of 1928, 171, 173
  city 1927 campaign, 151
  county 1926 campaign, 125 *note*, 134, 136

Tafel, Gustav, 11-13
Taft, Charles P., 2d., 51 *note*, 63, 69, 73 *note*, 136-137, 212, 231
  candidate for prosecutor, 123
  charter views, 55
  experiences as prosecutor, 142-144, 166-169
  president of the Cincinnatus Association, 80
Taft, Robert A., 44, 112-113, 142, 155, 212, 215
Taft, W. H., early political activity, 9, 123
Tammany, 237
Tawney, Guy, 56

Tawney, Mrs. Guy A., 73 *note*
Taxes, 33-45, 112, 169-171, 201-207
Tibbles, George W., 18 *note*
Times-Star, Cincinnati, 20, 24, 56, 128, 134, 180

Union Gas & Electric Company, 24, 81, 187-189, 193
United Labor party, 10
Upson, Lent D., 52, 62
Upson Report, 51-53, 73, 120, 127, 179, 202
  city council, section, 59-62
  recommendations and results, 238-245
Urban, Charles H., 171, 173, 199, 200, 216
Urner, Henry, 159

Vare, William S., 237
Voellmecke, Carl H., 73 *note*

Waite, Henry M., 178
Warrington, George, 28, 32, 51 *note*, 52, 62, 120
Washington, D. C., 106
Watson, James E., 162
Weinig, John, 66, 77, 156
Western Distributing Company, 189
White, Archibald, 188
Willis, Frank B., 161, 162, 163
Wilson, Russell, 56-59, 82, 83 *note*, 180, 183
  mayor, 184, 198, 210, 213
Withrow, John M., 16, 72, 73 *note*
Witt, sheriff, 85
Woeste, Joseph H., 180, 224-226
Women, 138-141, 153, 236
Wood, Leonard, 20
Work, Hubert, 160, 161
World's Work, 168 *note*
Wrassman, Fat, 167

Yale Daily News, 2, 5
Yale Law Journal, 3 *note*
Yeatman, candidate, 156, 158, 180

Ziegler, Philip, 73 *note*
Zielonka, city solicitor, 24